CHICANO EAR

CHICANO RAP

Gender and Violence in the Postindustrial Barrio

Pancho McFarland

University of Texas Press Austin

A slightly different version of Chapter Four (with co-author Beauty Bragg) was published as "The Erotic and the Pornographic in Chicana Rap: JV vs. Ms. Sancha" in *Meridians: Feminism, Race, Transnationalism*, Vol. 7, no. 2, pp. 1–21.

An earlier version of Chapter Six was published as "Here Is Something You Can't Understand: Chicano Rap and the Critique of Globalization" in *Decolonial Voices*, pp. 297–315, ed. Arturo J. Aldama and Naomi Quiñonez (Bloomington and Indianapolis: Indiana University Press, 2002).

The poetry by alejandra ibarra quoted in Chapter Seven is copyright © 2000 by Reina Alejandra Prado.

Requests for permission to reproduce material from this work should be sent to:
    Permissions
    University of Texas Press
    P.O. Box 7819
    Austin, TX 78713-7819
    www.utexas.edu/utpress/about/bpermission.html

♾The paper used in this book meets the minimum requirements of ANSI/NISO Z39.48-1992 (R1997) (Permanence of Paper).

Library of Congress Cataloging-in-Publication Data

McFarland, Pancho.
  Chicano rap : gender and violence in the postindustrial barrio / Pancho McFarland. — 1st ed.
    p. cm.
  Includes bibliographical references (p.   ) and index.
  ISBN 978-0-292-71802-9 (cloth : alk. paper) — ISBN 978-0-292-71803-6 (pbk. : alk. paper)
  1. Rap (Music)—History and criticism. 2. Mexican Americans—Music—History and criticism. 3. Sex in music. 4. Violence in music. I. Title.
  ML3531M34 2008
  782.421649—dc22

                                   2007044636

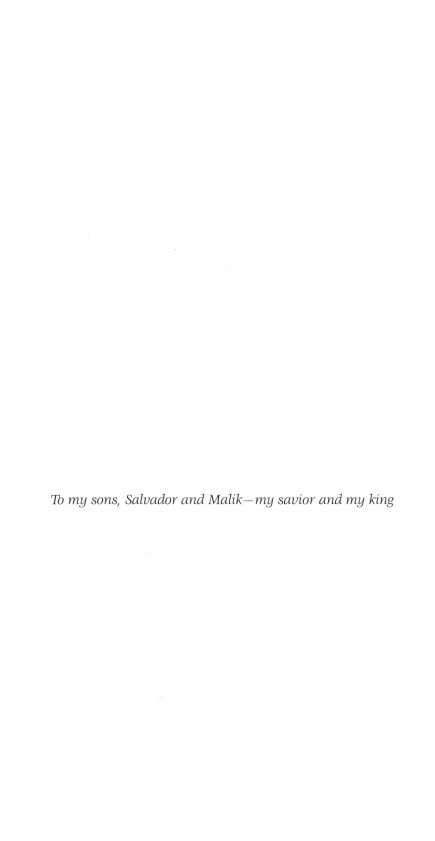

To my sons, Salvador and Malik—my savior and my king

CONTENTS

ACKNOWLEDGMENTS

While I take full responsibility for this book, many people contributed ideas, good wishes, friendship, and places to work. To all of you I give my heartfelt thanks. During the initial data-gathering phase, I worked with many excellent colleagues at The Colorado College, the University of Colorado at Colorado Springs, and Colorado State University. Thanks to all of those colleagues, including Victor Nelson Cisneros, Bill Grant, Margie Duncombe, Vera Fennell, Kee Warner, Abby Ferber, Irene Vernon, Roe Bubar, Joon Kim, and Norberto Valdez. After moving to Milledgeville, Georgia, I encountered colleagues who helped develop the ideas in this book. Many thanks to Sunita Manian, Richard Lou, Valerie Aranda, and Sandra Godwin. An extra-special thanks goes to Beauty Bragg, who more than anyone else helped me assemble this book. The Blackbird coffeehouse in Milledgeville and the Nazarene Bean coffeehouse in Macon provided the necessary caffeine boosts and comfortable work environments at important points during the writing phase of the project.

In 2005 I was fortunate to land a job teaching sociology at Chicago State University, where smart, dedicated colleagues have contributed ideas and otherwise helped. Among them are Victor Sorell, Yan Searcy, Dean Rachel Lindsey, Art Redman, Fernando Diaz, Aref Hervani, Roland Wulbert, and Kate Gillogly. Another special thanks goes to my co-researcher, Leslie Baker-Kimmons. T.A.C. Karate and Shihan Larry C. Tankson provided me with a place to release tension and center myself in the often hectic environment of Chicago.

Thanks also go to the reviewers and editors of journals that have published or considered my work, including *Race, Gender, and Class*, *Latino Studies*, *Callaloo*, *Bad Subjects*, and *Meridians*. Among those who have provided a forum for developing my work are Arturo Aldama, Naomi Quiñonez, the National Association of Chicana and Chicano Studies, the Black Music Section of the Popular Culture Association, and Maria De Leon of the National Association of Latina/o Arts and

Culture. I have traveled across the country and met people who have influenced me profoundly; these include Ruben Martinez, Devon Peña, Kyra Gaunt, and Luis Alvarez.

I must also acknowledge those who contributed to my early intellectual growth: those MEChistas of The Colorado College whom I ran with in my early days; and the members of Acción Zapatista, the Advanced Seminar, SubTex from Austin, and faculty members from the University of Texas who provided intellectual stimulation, mentorship, and friendship, including Harry Cleaver, José Limón, Les Kurtz, Gilbert Cardenas, David Montejano, and Craig Watkins. raulsalinas also provided mentoring and inspiration through his poetry and other work. For my knowledge of Chicano rap I thank the thousands of Chicano rap fans who have introduced me to artists and ideas. I thank all of the artists, without whom I would not have a book project or the joy that comes from listening to great music. Special thanks go to Mark Ramirez (Krazy Race), who continues to make excellent music and work hard for his community; Zero, Sista D, Victor E., Iron Sheik, Fernando Escobar, Felipe Cuauhtli, Jack Gonzalez, Sal Rojas, and Jehuniko, all of whom are making inspiring art.

The anonymous reviewers of this book manuscript and Theresa May, Lynne Chapman, Tana Silva, and Allison Faust of University of Texas Press deserve multiple thanks for their contributions. These acknowledgments would not be complete if I did not thank my family, especially my sister, mother, and brother-in-law, who fed and housed me at various times throughout my life and during the writing of this book. *Mil gracias* to the hundreds of students in high school, elementary school, and college who have inspired me to work hard to understand and positively impact youth culture. This includes, of course, my reasons for being, my two sons. I wish them a fulfilling life in hip hop or whatever they decide to do.

A HIP-HOP PROJECT

In 1980 my cousin Pete Cortez introduced me to the Sugar Hill Gang's "Rapper's Delight." It was unlike anything I had heard or seen. The cover to the fourteen-minute extended-play single was eye-catching, with a bright orange, yellow, and red psychedelic cylinder shape on a sky-blue background. The music of "Rapper's Delight" consisted of reinterpreted disco funk sounds including a sample of Chic's 1979 hit "Good Times." But it was the vocal delivery and lyrics that most intrigued me. The three MCs boast and tell funny stories in short, rapid, rhythmic, and rhyming phrases. Big Bank Hank uses part of his verse to court an imaginary woman by comparing himself to Superman and boasting that he is, in fact, far superior. Wonder Mike tells of an awful dinner at his friend's house. I thought the song was musical and lyrical genius. I enjoyed the word play, clever use of image and metaphor, the way the MCs gave new meaning to familiar words, and the use of disparaging humor that was similar to the dozens (a form of African American humor in which two people compete to deliver the most creative insult).

Growing up in mostly Mexican American/Chicana/o communities of the Southwest, I witnessed and learned to participate in verbal joking and humorous storytelling sessions with aunts, uncles, and peers. The lyrics to "Rapper's Delight" reminded me of family get-togethers, hanging out with friends at parks and in school, and the type of humor to which I had become accustomed. I later learned that the type of disparaging humor in Mexican/Chicana/o communities I witnessed was called *cábula*. The way the Sugar Hill Gang practiced *cábula* or the dozens was especially fun and entertaining. I, like millions of other Black, Brown, White, Asian, and other youths, was hooked.

I listened to my piano idol, Stevie Wonder, and other funk pioneers; Mexican (American) *rancheras*, *cumbias*, and other popular music my mother played; and the psychedelic rock and roll my father preferred. But after this initial exposure to rap in my cousin's basement in Colorado

Springs, Colorado, I began seeking out rap music. By the mid-1980s I had become a full-fledged hip-hop head. Through mass media outlets including movies such as *Breakin'* and *Wild Style* and tapes of "White Horse," "The Message," and Herbie Hancock's "Rock It," I learned about and participated in hip-hop culture. During my junior high school years in my hometowns of Raton, New Mexico, and Pueblo, Colorado, we developed a "scene" of b-boys and b-girls (male and female breakdancers) along with other rap enthusiasts. A few of us got together to practice the breakdance moves we saw on the big screen and in some early music videos. I, like all hip-hop enthusiasts, began to integrate and innovate. I invented new moves to complement the standard popping, locking, ticking, windmilling, and backspinning of the early days and fused aspects of the Chicana/o culture that surrounded me with aspects of Black expressive culture that captured my imagination.[1] The language of my Mexican American peers, the street slang, graffiti writing, the cool style of the Chicana/o stroll and attitude, and the intimate and intricate dance steps I learned at Chicana/o bars, weddings, and other celebrations merged with the dance steps I practiced in my living room watching Michael Jackson and Prince videos, the breaking moves I saw in the movies and in youth gatherings in Pueblo and Raton, and my faithful Saturday morning viewing of *Soul Train*.

My identity was dramatically impacted by all of these aspects of Black and Chicana/o culture and the rural *nuevo mexicano* culture of Raton. I walked the walk and talked the talk of the emerging Chicana/o hip-hop culture. My clothes, my attitude, my stare exhibited a unique cultural syncretism that would continue to influence my worldview, consciousness, and personal interactions. In many different ways, hundreds of thousands of Chicana/o youth since the 1980s have created a new culture and new cultural identities out of the multiple cultural, political, and social influences found in Mexican America. This new *mestizaje* (mixture) of Black, Mexican, Chicana/o, Native American, and corporate pop cultural elements shapes today's ethnic Mexican youth. How young people of Mexican descent understand themselves and their world in the postindustrial United States is a subject that few have addressed. In this study I examine hip-hop culture and rap music and Chicana/o participation in this new subculture in order to begin uncovering how the racial, cultural, economic, and political environments of the late twentieth century shaped the experiences of a large segment of Chicana/o youth.

Rap "blew up," becoming a mass, global phenomenon, in the mid- to late 1980s with the incredible commercial success of Run DMC and the Beastie Boys (my first rap concert). But by then I was in college, and the predominant culture of The Colorado College rejected rap for a stylized, neo-hippie environmentalism. Few there danced. Few appropriated, mixed, and reinvented (three central aspects of hip-hop culture) the street style that helped solidify and strengthen my identity. As a result, I felt myself in a cultural wasteland, and my dorm room and frequent visits home were my cultural oases. My associations with the campus MEChA (Movimiento Estudiantil Chicano de Aztlán) and the Black Student Union kept rap and hip-hop culture alive for me. Kid Frost, also known as Frost, released his anthem, "La Raza," in 1990, and our weekly parties featured several listenings. Even so, I no longer danced. I had no one with whom to dance, riff off, or appreciate the artistry of rap music and hip-hop culture. In hip-hop one needs a crew to do what we do.

I would not return to rap and hip-hop culture with the same kind of need until late in my graduate school career when I needed the Black and Brown stylings, attitude, and outlook of hip hop as a shield against the often oppressive, soul-crushing, and Eurocentric culture of academia. Rap became my model for resisting the academy (Bragg and McFarland 1998). Its creative use of language, its communal nature, its "reality," its subject matter, its pedagogy, and its expressed privileging of people of color and our cultures provided inspiration and served as a model for my intellectual life and career. Like many youth of color, I used rap to survive. It is a release, a way to keep my dignity, sanity, and identity. Without it I could not have finished the dissertation, gotten a job, published articles, or helped maintain a family. From my years of participating in hip-hop culture and researching it and other expressive cultural forms, I am certain that it helped millions of young people of color succeed in their later lives. These pages, my raps, analyze some of the issues central to Chicano rap over the years. Perspectives of young Chicanas/os on gender and violence in particular, as well as their views on identity, politics, economics, love and other topics, have been largely overlooked, underappreciated, or reviled in the larger, dominant social, political, and cultural spaces of the United States. But in hip-hop culture and rap music, their voices are provided a stage. It is upon this stage we should look for a Chicana/o youth perspective.

RESEARCHING RAP

I began writing about rap music in 1997 when my partner and I would wake up nearly every morning and press the Play button on our CD player. In an instant our house was filled with the beautiful and angry baritone instrument that was Tupac Shakur's voice. Tupac's unapologetic pro-Black, pro–people of color rants, at once comforting and disconcerting, allowed us to navigate the choking traffic that was the 8 A.M. commute in Austin, Texas. After our desperate search for parking, we would walk to our offices chanting familiar lines from Tupac's *Makaveli* CD. We were ready to meet the day and our choice: assimilate and earn our degrees or be ourselves, speak out, and, most likely, flunk out. So we rapped "It's a White man's world" and then sang the response "Who knows what tomorrow brings?"

One morning while listening to Tupac we agreed to an experiment in the decolonization of our minds. We stayed home and began to write about the importance of rap and hip-hop culture to people like us, students of color frustrated at the crushing assimilative effects of the academy. In a few short weeks we wrote an article, shared it with friends and colleagues, and had it accepted for publication. I was in the middle of my dissertation research concerning the Zapatista uprising in Chiapas, Mexico, and was eager to finish. As soon as I finished my Ph.D., I began to more rigorously research rap phenomena. I chose to focus on Chicana/o participation in rap because only a small handful of articles had documented it. It was natural for me to look at Chicanas/os in rap and hip-hop culture since I had been a Chicano hip-hop head, I had studied Chicana/o culture formally for nearly a dozen years, and in my new surroundings (I had moved to Colorado Springs, Colorado) a large number of Chicana/o youths were involved in the culture. I began to speak to Chicana/o youths about rap and began listening to the artists they talked about. By the end of 1999 I developed a strategy for taking a sample of Chicano rap songs and coding them by topic.

METHODS

Since the early 1990s Chicano rap entrepreneurs have distributed their product via the Internet, grassroots advertising, and small distribution companies and out of the trunks of their cars at festivals, car shows, and swap meets. With some exceptions, Chicano rap acts have received very little radio airplay or national recognition. Most Chicano rap acts are known and supported in their hometowns and regions and work in small concert venues within a limited circuit that primarily encompasses the southwestern United States, though many have taken their acts to other countries.

Few scholars have conducted research into this subculture. Del Barco (1996), Delgado (1998), Kelly (1993), Rodriguez (2003), and Saldívar (2002) provide useful analyses of some of the early and most popular Chicano rappers, such as Kid Frost, Chicano 2 Da Bone, A Lighter Shade of Brown, Latin Alliance, Aztlán Nation, and Cypress Hill. These initial discussions do not address the explosion in Chicano rap that occurred in the mid-1990s. While a focus on the nationalism of early Chicano rappers provides much-needed understanding of the politics and social critique of Chicano youth, such a small sample of the large and growing subculture fails to provide insight into the multiple and complex dialogues taking place in the Chicano hip-hop subculture. Thus, I have identified a need to expand upon the work of Del Barco, Delgado, Kelly, Rodriguez, and Saldívar by collecting and examining a large and diverse sample of Chicano rap songs.

Since previous scholarly work on Chicano rap focused primarily on Los Angeles musicians, I believe it is necessary to include rappers from all other major Chicano rap regions: San Diego, San Francisco and northern California, Texas, and Chicago and the Midwest. I also expand upon the narrow slice of Chicano rap presented by previous scholars by including work from different subgenres. Moreover, since the early 1990s, a new generation of Chicano rap consumers with different tastes and preferences has begun to participate in Chicana/o hip-hop culture.

I learned about youth preferences on websites and in focus groups with Chicanos ages twelve to twenty. Important websites such as the Chicana/o culture site Brown Pride (www.brownpride.com) and those of Chicano rap recording labels and artists provide a wealth of information on consumer preferences. The Brown Pride website had ten million visitors per month in 2004 (Krazy Race 2004d). It has chat rooms, bulletin boards, and forums where hundreds of Chicano rap aficionados discuss Chicana/o culture, society, and politics. Every day Chicano rap fans post hundreds of messages discussing their favorite artists, arguing over the importance of artists, conducting informal polls, and otherwise exchanging information about Chicana/o hip hop. Two other groups of youth enhanced my knowledge of Chicano rap. Various judges in Colorado Springs, Colorado, sentenced Chicanas/os of middle school and high school age to attend a youth program designed by a nonprofit Chicana/o family advocacy organization. These young people agreed to share their knowledge of Chicano rap with me. They introduced me to rappers who claimed "gangsta" or "thug" identities and who rapped about the often violent environments of working-class urban Chicanas/os. They emphasized the importance of groups such as Brownside, Darkroom Familia, Proper Dos, and Low Profile artists.

The other group of youths came from a very different place. They were middle-class, privileged Chicana/o students who loved hip hop but tended to avoid the gangsta styles and narratives enjoyed by working-class youth. They rejected these rappers as taking advantage of White America's stereotype of Chicanas/os as violent and ill-mannered. They saw gangsta narratives as counterproductive. Instead, they talked about "old school" artists and those with an overtly progressive political stance. They focused on the ways in which certain artists spoke of love and kindness and presented "positive" plans for social change. Artists such as Delinquent Habits and Kid Frost often came up in conversations as well as many progressive and/or underground Black rap artists such as Oakland's The Coup, Los Angeles' Jurassic 5, and dead prez.

Between 1999 and 2002 I carefully monitored Chicana/o rap Internet sites and participated in dozens of stimulating discussions and debates about Chicano rap. I gained a wealth of information concerning important artists. This research, combined with years of Chicano rap consumption, provided me with valuable background on which artists Chicana/o youth preferred. Based on this research I chose a sample of Chicano rap artists and 470 songs for analysis. I coded the songs for themes of women, drug use, police-community relations, identity, violence, and social conditions in the communities. I have chosen to examine what Chicano rappers' discussions of violence and gender can tell us about their experiences in the postindustrial United States, their gender and ethnic identities, and their understanding of political and economic processes.

Over the past five years I have discovered other artists and have been in conversations with many of them. Through email correspondence and phone conversations with Krazy Race, Zero, Slush the Villain, Transcend, Pony Boy, Shysti, Fernando Escobar, Jacken, and Jehuniko, my knowledge of Chicano rap artists has grown. This book presents what I have learned through conversations with youths and leading underground artists, four years of Internet monitoring, and seventeen years of listening to Chicana/o rap.

CHAPTER SUMMARIES

This project is concerned with several issues I have identified as central to understanding Chicano rap and Chicanas/os participating in hip-hop culture. The first broad set of issues involves how to read Chicano rap. Chapters One and Two are dedicated to understanding the cultural, political, historical, and economic contexts in which this culture has evolved. In Chapter One, "Reading Chicano Rap: The Patriarchal Dominance Paradigm in the Postindustrial Barrio," I develop a theoretical framework from which to examine Chicano rap discussions of violence and gender. I use the idea of "articulation" as a "theory of contexts" in which we examine the political, cultural, economic, and social fields of a given moment in order to understand the development and significance of cultural products. To understand Chicano rap violence and misogyny we must keep in mind the violent and misogynist contexts out of which it develops. I argue that we must examine the dominant, corporate-controlled culture industries, Mexican American oral culture, the popularity of gangsta rap, the political economy of the past three decades, and political violence. Through such an examination of the contexts of the late twentieth century we find that the dominant paradigm for understanding human relations in the United States is "the patriarchal dominance paradigm." This paradigm favors dominance and misogyny as opposed to cooperation and love and uses violence as a means of solving disputes. The paradigm encourages personal interactions based on competition and conquest, dichotomous understandings of others, xenophobia, and racism. This paradigm dominates the worldview of many U.S. denizens and contributes importantly to the worldview developed in some Chicano rap.

Chapter Two, "Chicano Rap Primer: A Guide to Artists and Genres," provides a brief overview of Chicano rap regions and styles. Chicano rap is incredibly diverse and has more than a twenty-year history. From the early innovators like Kid Frost, Cypress Hill, and Lighter Shade of Brown to today's underground groups, Chicanas/os in rap prove to be as diverse as the Chicana/o/Mexican population in the United States. Chicanas/os differ regionally, linguistically, generationally, racially, politically, and economically. Chicano rappers come from a variety of cities, have widely varying musical, political, and cultural influences, have myriad complex worldviews, and dress and speak differently depending upon locale and experience. This chapter details some of these distinctions. Importantly, I further examine the influence of urban African American youth culture on Chicana/o rap. Intercultural exchange between Blacks and Chicanas/os living in close proximity in urban settings such as Los Angeles and the popularity of urban Black culture have helped shape Chicana/o hip-hop culture, youth attitudes and worldview, and rap rhetoric of violence and misogyny.

The second set of issues I examine in this study involves images of gender and what these representations tell us about Chicano gender socialization and attitudes toward gender identity, gender relations, and gender roles. Chapter Three, "*Machos y Malas Mujeres*: The Gendered Image," examines how the dominant U.S. culture and our Chicano patriarchal traditions contribute to a rigid understanding of gender for most Chicana/o youth. In Chicano rap, men are hypermasculine, dominant creatures, and women are hyperfeminine, sexualized Others. Through a discussion of Chicana/o and Mexicano expressive culture and the representation of women in popular culture, we see how closely representations of gender in Chicano rap resemble long-held dichotomous notions of gender. Moreover, these representations are powerful in that they tend to normalize gender inequality and violence and to socialize youth into narrow beliefs about gender roles and identities—beliefs that more often than not are detrimental to women and lead to dangerous male behaviors.

In Chapter Four, "Sexual Agency in Chicana Rap: JV Versus Ms. Sancha," I examine the work of these two Chicana rappers. They create their music on a thin line between the misogyny of the dominant and youth cultures and their own experiences as strong young women. While they must participate in a youth subculture that privileges males and their worldviews, they recognize that as young Chicanas their experiences, worldviews, and attitudes differ from and often challenge those of their male peers. Their balancing act consists of mastering a male-dominated art form, language, and style that rap audiences prefer without repeating and strengthening the misogyny and violence of much of Chicano rap lyrics. This chapter presents two very different perspectives on female identity and sexuality. Ms. Sancha represents an uncritical, sexually objectified woman under patriarchal control. JV, on the other hand, presents herself and womanhood as complex and contradictory. She presents women as sexual subjects and agents of their lives. She is out of male control but is not always a Xicanista (Chicana feminist).

The third set of issues concerns the violent lyrical content of much Chicano rap music. Chapter Five, "Violence and Chicano Rap: Mirror of a Belligerent Society," examines the ways in which an aesthetics of violence, interpersonal violence, and a politics of violence are central parts of the cultural field from which young Chicanos draw to develop their discussions and analyses of violence. I examine the ubiquity of violence in U.S. popular entertainment and how close readings of Chicano rap reveal the influence of movies, video games, and gangsta rap music on hip-hop culture. The rise in interpersonal violence, especially the sanctioning of violence against women and the epidemic of gang violence during the 1980s, also contributes to young Chicanos' understandings of violence. Misogynist violence in Chicano rap reveals a devaluing of women similar to that found in our dominant media and in our culture, which naturalizes violence against women and fails to protect them from assault and other abuses by men.

Misogynist and entertainment violence are part of a larger culture of violence upon which U.S. identity, polity, economy, and territory are based. The history of state violence to capture territory and resources and to subdue resistance to U.S. colonialism, slavery, and ongoing violent racism is celebrated in our schoolbooks, national holidays, and media. Recent and current military exercises and wars and their depictions in the corporate media socialize our youth into a belief that U.S. government violence is always right and moral and that solving problems by violence is legitimate and necessary. Many Chicano rappers reflect these attitudes in their lyrics. Chicano rappers whom I label "gangsta rappers" are quick to use violence to solve rivalries or to gain resources. Other rappers connect our long history of state violence to elite greed, racism, and colonial desires for the expansion of territory and control of others' resources. They critique state violence and argue for resistance to it.

Chicano rap has developed in a period of capitalist globalization, economic restructuring in the United States, and a push to the extreme right in national politics. Working-class Chicana/o youth of the 1980s and 1990s have suffered some of the worst consequences of these trends. We have seen our job prospects become more limited, our schools deteriorate, our incarceration rates increase dramatically, and an all-out war against us in the name of the war on drugs and "tough on crime" legislation. Many of us have seen our very existence criminalized as anti-immigrant legislation and rhetoric have spawned a new nativism among the U.S. citizenry, and the gang threat has led to egregious civil rights abuses that include not allowing many young people to gather in large groups, drive their cars, or listen to certain types of music. Chapter Six, "The Chicano Rap on Globalization," is intended to assist those who have misinformation or no information about working-class Chicano youth and the consequences of globalization understand the effects on our communities that the past thirty years of oppressive legislation have had. I examine the work of a small group of Chicano rappers who address the consequences of globalization in their lyrics. Through an engagement with this extremely marginalized sector of the

U.S. population we can begin to see globalization from the perspective of those victimized by it. Moreover, as I suggest throughout the book, Chicana/o youth are not simply victims of a "crazed world," but they speak back to power and have created a subculture that is often beyond the control of the market, the political parties, and the cops.

The final broad issue I examine is developing a rap pedagogy. In Chapter Seven, "Confronting Dominance and Constructing Relationships with Young People," I examine the challenges to the patriarchal dominance paradigm posed by Xicana feminist scholarship, some Chicano rappers, and cultural work that explores the radical, life-affirming possibilities of community and love. Xicana feminists expand the possibilities of understanding gender, peace, and human relationships. They explode oppressive categories like male, female, Chicano, and democracy while creating examples of egalitarian, anti-authoritarian cultural and social practices that might serve as models for working-class Chicana/o and other youth. Groups like El Vuh, Victor E, 2Mex, and 5th Battalion speak for unity, peace, justice, and the transcendent power of love. They gain an ever-greater following each year they spread their messages. As we approach a new historical epoch, what the Maya called "the Sixth Sun," these artists disperse a call of revolution rooted in indigenous traditions and spirituality, love, understanding, and hospitality. Luis Rodriguez, veteran of inner-city street wars, racism, and economic inequality, has emerged as a leading critic of U.S. domestic policy concerning youth, criminal justice, drugs, class, and race. He has advocated for Chicana/o, Black, and other youth for more than two decades. He speaks about the revolutionary potential of community building for changing problems facing our youth and our society. He challenges elders and all community members to take our youth as our number one priority, not give up on them, and realize our responsibility toward them (L. Rodriguez 2001).

In accepting the advice and wisdom of these groups of Chicana/o intellectuals, I argue for a pedagogy of hip hop that addresses youth in their places while constantly challenging them to venture toward new ideas and possibilities. Rap music and hip-hop culture continue to impact the lives of young people. My experiences in the classroom discussing rap music have taught me that with our guidance, youth cultures can have powerful positive effects. Hip-hop and rap have the potential to transcend the patriarchal dominance paradigm, but they also have the potential to further drive our youth and our world into violence, authoritarianism, and misogyny. The actions of elders, professors, teachers, police personnel, family members, and other community members can tip the balance in favor of positive change.

A NOTE ON LABELS AND LANGUAGE

I prefer the term "Chicano" as opposed to other ethnic identifiers for several reasons. First, often the rappers of Mexican and Mexican American descent in the United States on whom I focus here use "Chicano" as their central racial/ethnic identifier. Second, any in-depth examination of the genre will be able to draw a clear line between the music, lyrics, attitudes, language, and politics of these rappers and Mexican American, Mexican, and Chicana/o history and culture. Chicano rap as I define it in these pages is clearly a part of a tradition that begins in the Valley of Mexico several hundred years ago, continues through the Spanish and U.S. conquests of the colonial period (1519 to the early 1900s), and culminates in the Chicano movement of the 1960s and 1970s. These rappers are part of the historical legacy of the fateful period in Mexican and U.S. history when the United States of America took possession of Mexico's northern frontier through warfare. Chicano rappers are the sons and grandsons of Mexicans who were dispossessed of their lands after the Mexican-U.S. War (1846–1848) or who because of the United States' dominance of Mexico since the war have chosen to (or been forced to, depending on one's perspective) migrate to what was once northern Mexico. Third, "Chicano" is as much a political identifier as an ethnic one. These young men (and some women) challenge the postcolonial, postindustrial politics of the United States of America. Their rebellious attitudes, independent spirits, and often radical rhetoric are implicit, if not always explicit, critiques of contemporary U.S. society. In the 1960s "Chicano" became the identity of choice for young people who similarly challenged U.S. society. For these reasons I choose the term "Chicano" as opposed to "Mexican," "Mexican American," "Mexican-American," "Mexicano," "Latino," or "Hispanic."

I often refer to Chicanos—that is, males. I do this purposefully, leaving out females because this is a male-dominated cultural scene, and I am mostly referring to young men. Rappers are overwhelmingly young men. While females participate, I am primarily speaking about a male expressive practice. This does not mean that young women are absent or that they have had no impact on the culture. It simply suggests that the dominant discourses, attitudes, styles, language, and themes result from the cultures and concerns of young men. This, of course, is changing, and I describe the work of important Chicana rappers in Chapter Four. When I speak of young women and men together I use the term "Chicanas/os." Otherwise, I use the gender-specific terms "Chicano" and sometimes "Chicana."

Throughout the book I also use the terms "Latino," "Latina/o," and "Hispanic," reluctantly, when quoting others or citing data that use these pan-ethnic terms. "Hispanic" is problematic because many see it as an ethnic identifier forced upon U.S. communities of Latin American descent; it is not a label freely chosen by these communities. Second, "Hispanic," like "Latino," as a pan-ethnic term is misleading in that it condenses vastly different peoples and cultures under one label. The various groups that constitute "Hispanic" have different histories, settlement patterns, economic situations, racial makeups, and relations to other races. "Latino" is problematic because it is not specific to the community I am examining. Many find it more acceptable since the term is, at least, in Spanish.

"Latino" and "Hispanic" also privilege the European aspects of the cultures of people of Latin American descent, many of whom have begun to recover and take pride in their indigenous heritage. Many suggest that this erasing of the indigenous in our biological and cultural makeup furthers European colonization and is, at its root, racist. However, there are times when I feel it is appropriate to speak of U.S. communities of Latin American descent. In these cases, I prefer the terms "Latino" or "Latina/o." I occasionally use the term "Mexicano," which suggests Mexican culture in both Mexico and the United States.

I use the terms "rappers," "MCs," and "artists" consciously and for specific purposes. Since this book is concerned primarily with the lyrics as rapped and written by Chicanos, I most commonly use the term "rapper" to describe them. "Rapper" emphasizes oral ability and the use of written language and poetics. "MC" is a term that many old hip-hop heads use to distinguish good rappers from bad ones and that I use interchangeably with "rapper." However, "MC" is common only within certain sectors of the hip-hop community and is not used or even known by those outside of this community. Thus I generally use the term "rapper," as it is a more common identifier. I use "artist" throughout the book to emphasize more than the oral or lyrical abilities of the rappers and to suggest that these young men and women are more than poets or wordsmiths. They are artists who use music, other sounds, language, style, facial expression, clothes, and dance to express themselves and communicate to their audience and peers. I intend to deliberately challenge those who reserve the term "artist" for what is often referred to as "high art." The elitist notion of high art versus popular culture or low art has been used to suggest the inferiority of popular or folk artistic expression. It has often been used in racist ways to distinguish European classical art and music from the "folk" art of ethnic Others. The music and lyrics of the best Chicano rappers and music producers are every bit as complicated, nuanced, and sophisticated as European classical music, for example. While most Chicano rappers and music producers are not formally trained in music, they have a complex understanding of rhythm, vocal delivery, the biological and psychological impacts of sound on their audiences, and other aspects of music. They may not be able to articulate their knowledge in ways that music professors or classical musicians might understand and respect, but it is important knowledge nonetheless. And their knowledge may be more important and pertinent to the contemporary society and culture in which we live.

The Patriarchal Dominance Paradigm
in the Postindustrial Barrio

Chicano rap discussions of violence and gender can be understood only within the larger context of U.S. culture and history, contemporary popular culture, globalization and de-industrialization, the neoconservative political system dominated by White males, and Mexican American culture and history. Fantastic stories of murder and criminality told by Chicano rappers must be read against a backdrop of the Hollywood action movies and the increasing sales of lifelike video games. Similarly, Chicano rap depictions of women as objects of pleasure for male bodies and egos cannot be understood without reference to the male-centered lineage in Mexican American culture as well as the devaluation of women in the broader U.S. culture.

Beginning from this position, then, I use articulation theory as the starting point for my analysis of Chicano rap lyrics. I will examine the historical context and discuss the cultural, economic, and social fields affecting the experiences of young urban, working-class Chicanas/os at the turn of the millennium. This context includes cultural and economic globalization, racism, sexism, and misogyny in U.S. and Mexican American cultures. Importantly, cultural exchange with African Americans, particularly Black youth, is also an important aspect of the young Chicano's experience. In this chapter I describe the theoretical frameworks of my analysis: articulation theory, Marxist political economy, feminist archetypal analysis and Xicanista cultural critique, and new men's studies. Examinations of dominant cultural trends in U.S. and Mexican American cultures reveal that our media, expressive cultures, and popular culture help socialize young men, and to a lesser extent young women, into developing attitudes and a general worldview that I describe as the patriarchal dominance paradigm. As its name suggests, this orientation stems from a patriarchal worldview that restricts gender roles and values, sees others as not only different but inferior, and posits human relations as antagonistic. Through instilling notions of masculinity as hypermasculinity and femininity as weakness, young men learn to see difference as something to be shunned, defeated, or dominated. To understand how such a world-view is established we must examine the political, cultural, economic, and social contexts of Chicana/o experience and identity in the postin-dustrial United States of America.

SETTING THE CONTEXT: ARTICULATION

Stuart Hall and other scholars of culture argue that any attempt to un-derstand the significance of a cultural product must take into account its embeddedness within a larger societal discourse (Morley and Chen 1996). Articulation theory suggests that an understanding of the dis-course of violence, power, and gender in Chicano rap requires a rigor-ous examination of the society of which it is a part. Articulation as a method of inquiry and a "theory of contexts" helps us understand the importance of cultural phenomena by allowing us to see how the vari-ous components of a social formation at a given historical moment co-here to allow for a new discourse to take shape (Slack 1996). The politi-cal, ideological, cultural, and economic sectors constitute the backdrop against which a discourse takes on meaning (Grossberg 1995).

The discourse of violence in Chicano rap does not develop in a vacuum. The violent scenarios depicted in the music result from the intersection of personal experience with contemporary social violence, popular culture, and their representations and celebration in the com-munications media. Violence in Chicano rap arises and takes on mean-ing because it is articulated in the larger societal discourse of the 1980s and 1990s that foregrounded violence as entertaining, masculine, and a pragmatic solution to a variety of problems. To set the stage for under-standing violence in Chicano rap, I examine violence in our dominant U.S. culture, Mexican (American) culture and history, and certain com-modified aspects of African American male culture.

VIOLENCE IN THE DOMINANT CULTURE

Since at least the early 1980s in the United States, we have been fed a steady diet of media violence. Even before cable took it to new levels, Gerbner found that during prime time, network television program-ming averaged five acts of violence per hour (1993). Giroux estimated that by the time she or he was eighteen, the average American in the early 1990s had viewed approximately 18,000 murders on television (1996, 60). In recent years movies have grown more violent, with heroes "packing more heat." The news media endlessly recount the most heinous crimes, and popular TV series pick up where the news leaves off by depicting outrageous acts of violence (Fishman and Cavender 1998). Giroux has called this the "spread of the culture of violence" in the United States (1996, 28).

This spread is assisted by a growing emphasis on violence as a key trait of manhood. Scholarship within the field of new men's studies argues that over the past three decades the definition of masculinity has become ever more rigid in the face of the women's and gay and lesbian movements. Since the late 1960s men have witnessed an erosion of their unfettered gender dominance. Where once it seemed that gender roles were set firmly in place with women being the passive partners to men, now women have gone into the workplace, established alternatives to the patriarchal nuclear family, and challenged men's cultural and social dominance. The result is a feminist backlash and a recovery of traditional (read: patriarchal) "American" values (Faludi 1992). Men's outdoor clubs, Christian organizations such as the Promisekeepers, and other men-only groups have established a "safe" place for men to relearn how to be "real" men.[1]

Elite men have used their power and influence in the culture industry to socialize boys into a hypermasculine notion of manhood. Action figures have become bigger and carry more weapons; heroes and superheroes kill and maim and in the end win the love of beautiful women; cartoons reinforce strict gender roles and make violence look fun; video-game violence has increased, and its visual images have become more lifelike; music videos link power, sex, violence, and masculinity.[2] School shootings, road rage, date rape, school bullying, and other dangerous and violent behaviors have increased; 90 percent of this violence is perpetrated by men and boys. In the film *Tough Guise* (Jhally 1999), psychologist Jackson Katz says that violent masculinity has become a cultural norm. A young boy learns to equate violence with normal male gender roles and nonviolence with abnormality and femininity (Jhally 1999).

Violence on small and big screens has increased, and studies point out that this violence has been racialized. Maciel and Racho write (2000) that television and Hollywood overwhelmingly depict the Chicana/o experience as one of crime and drugs. Citing Gerbner's studies of television programming, Escalante notes that 63 percent of Latino male characters were perpetrators or victims of violence (2000, 138).

For most middle-class White Americans, crime is synonymous with young urban males of color (Giroux 1996).[3]

Violence seems to increase the marketability of many popular-culture products. Chicano rappers have witnessed the images of Chicano violence disseminated via the television and the movies and the skyrocketing record sales of African American gangsta rap from the mid-1980s through the 1990s.[4] These astute young men recognize that violence sells, and many reason that if anyone is going to sell images of Black and Brown urban youth violence, it might as well be them. The highly valued (in dollars) images of Chicanos killing each other and selling drugs undoubtedly calls to young poor Chicanas/os who have few chances for attaining the American Dream through accepted channels. And in this age when big- and little-screen violence has become hyper-real,[5] with ever more blood, bullets, guns, and drama, Chicano rap entrepreneurs have followed suit by sometimes vying with each other to be "more gangsta than thou."[6]

THE MASCULINE IN MEXICAN AND
CHICANO MALE ORAL CULTURE

Dominant, corporate-controlled U.S. culture is not the only place where young Chicanos learn to become violent men. Mexican patriarchal culture has a long history of touting the violent exploits of male heroes and, in the process, teaching boys to be hypermasculine. In relating colorful tales of our relatives who rode with Villa and Zapata, boxing-club exploits, and bar legends of physical conquest, older men teach younger men that being a man, a Mexican or Chicano man, requires strength, toughness, and violence.[7]

The *corrido* is an important and influential example of how hyper-masculinity is transmitted in Mexican patriarchal culture.[8] The *corrido* must be read in the context of Mexican/Chicana/o resistance to the violent Anglo-European, or gringo, conquest of the borderlands and the U.S. Southwest as a resistant, even revolutionary, art form; however, we also must recognize that this resistance is almost always enacted by a dominant, violent, and virile male hero. Rarely do *corridos* document the myriad other types of resistance that did not involve gun violence. This encompasses but is not limited to "weapons of the weak" that undermined and defeated aspects of the Anglo conquest.[9]

Importantly, *corridos* neglect women's central roles—as individuals, workers, mothers, wives, artists, activists, and intellectuals—in the historical and ongoing struggle to maintain and defend Chicana/o cultural

and economic structures. Mothers and wives in service to men constitute part of the idea of *la mujer buena*. Certainly, Chicanas/Mexicanas
have played these roles along with many others that have contributed
to Chicano survival. Recognizing women as only mothers and wives
is problematic. Recognizing them as wives and mothers within a
complex of important roles is more in line with Xicanista and other
female-centered perspectives. *Corridos* help maintain patriarchal
gender distinctions that define women as passive, erase their agency and accomplishments, and emphasize hypermasculine models of
Mexican/Chicano manhood.

The work of José Limón in *Mexican Ballads, Chicano Poems* (1992)
provides a framework for understanding violence in Mexican/Chicano
male expressive culture that links Mexican patriarchy, relations between Mexicans and dominant Anglo society, and changing economic conditions. Limón argues that the "*corrido* is a master poem" that
strongly influences later Chicana/o expressive culture (1992, 2). An
understanding of the *corrido* and how it transmits archetypal gender
roles including male violence provides a historical grounding for analyzing violence in contemporary Chicana/o rap.

The *corrido* became an important form of expressive culture in
greater Mexican society as a result of a number of important conditions:
(1) a ballad tradition handed down from the Spanish; (2) an adversarial
relationship with the dominant Anglo society; (3) life in relative isolation from world events; (4) a strong oral tradition; (5) a patriarchal
culture; and (6) a form of community-based "vernacular democracy"
(Limón 1992, 19–20). Anglo domination of the Mexico-Texas border and
the decades of ethnic conflict after the U.S.-Mexican War led to an assault on the native Mexican way of life. Anglo-European culture, political and legal systems, and capitalist transformation eroded Mexican
and later Chicana/o culture. In this context the *corrido* glorified and
celebrated Mexican rebellion. The *corrido* narrated and mythologized
acts of rebellion that symbolized Mexican heroism, and Mexicans in
South Texas found heroes in the social bandits of the *corridos*.[10] Paredes
writes that the peaceful man pushed to violence by Anglo or other oppression was the dominant theme of *corridos* on the border (1959).[11]

The capitalist transformation of the West in the late nineteenth
and early twentieth centuries caused intense cultural conflict between
Mexicans and Anglos. This conflict played a key role in the emergence
of Mexican/Chicana/o folklore that depicts the wise and savvy Mexican pitted against the naïve and greedy Anglo (Paredes 1959).[12] Racial violence against Mexicans at the hands of the Texas Rangers, other

police apparatuses, and private citizens (with the support of the Anglo-dominated government) was parallel to that being suffered by African Americans in the South during the same period.[13] Mexicans and Chicanas/os resisted the violence, domination, and cultural erosion. The folklore often only documented the male response. In *corridos*, the proper masculine response was to fight back, "pistol in hand." The honorable Mexican/Chicano defended his family and his community.

Corrido composers neglected female exploits and devalued women.[14] In the patriarchal tradition informing the dominant *corrido* narrative, men were important because they were the defenders of the family, community, and nation. The *corrido* as popular cultural expression became an important mode of reinforcing patriarchal values throughout the community and transmitting them to future generations. The peaceful man turned violent, the hero of the *corrido*, reflects on one level an ethos of male resistance simply as violence but also works to challenge social/power relations in South Texas. The man "with his pistol in his hand" becomes an outlaw, a social bandit. His lawbreaking serves to illustrate the illegitimacy of Anglo law while affirming the traditional Mexican value system of the borderlands and greater Mexico.

The ethos of the violent male social bandit found in *corridos* dominated notions of masculinity in Mexican/Chicana/o communities during the twentieth century. By the 1960s the Chicano Movement further emphasized the ideal of the Chicano male fighting against oppression, especially racial oppression. The gender distinctions of past Mexican/Chicano tradition and folklore remained. The rebellious and often violent behaviors and attitudes of Chicano street youth were lauded as models of Chicano male behavior. Male heroes of the Mexican/Chicana/o past such as Pancho Villa, Emiliano Zapata, and Cuatehmoc were recast with an emphasis on their violent characteristics.

The problem with this interpretation of past heroes is that while they engaged in violent revolution, that clearly is not all they did. They fought oppression using a wide variety of tactics. The values expressed in the idealization of Chicano warriors repressed the voice and struggle of Mexican women and men who chose different strategies and tactics. Women were not often the protagonists in *corridos* or later movement expressive culture, and when women occasionally entered the *corrido* narrative, it was almost exclusively as the saintly mother figure. The contributions women made to resisting Anglo domination were rarely the subject of Chicano movement art, *corridos*, or lowrider art. This orientation toward masculinity and violent resistance can be found throughout Chicano expressive culture, which plays an important role in Chicano youth socialization.

GANGSTA RAP

Rap primarily serves young men of color. It is a way to voice their anger at U.S. society, communicate with one another (Chuck D 1997), and "create a sense of order out of . . . contemporary urban life" (Allen 1996, 160). Allen explains that

> in place of organizational structures such as the Student Non-Violent Coordinating Committee, the Black Panther Party, or the Spirit House Movers, for example, the principal generative form of a reawakened black consciousness of the eighties and nineties has arrived, rather incredibly, via a poetic/musical form known as "rap." (159)

Rap is a resistant oral expressive cultural form of the emergent subculture of hip hop.[15] Young inner-city residents created hip hop out of the destruction attending the 1970s and 1980s backlash against the gains of the civil rights and Black Power movements. Rap, like *corridos*, grew out of changing political economic conditions; primarily, deindustrialization, economic restructuring, and militarization of the inner city. Young inner-city residents were being victimized by deindustrialization, capital flight from the cities, fiscal malfeasance on the part of municipal governments, job loss, the drug epidemic, and AIDS.[16] The political economy of the city was being completely reorganized. The few good industrial, unionized jobs gained by African Americans and other people of color as a result of the civil rights movement and the war on poverty were quickly being taken away as the U.S. economy globalized and moved toward the service and communications sectors.[17]

The result is a generation of angry young women and men of color. They often express this anger through their music. During the 1980s young men of color felt unashamed to tell stories of violence and the heroic exploits of new urban (anti-) heroes with machine gun in hand. The genre known as "gangsta rap" has its origins in Los Angeles, though gangsterism has been part of rap since its origins and extends in the Black diasporic oral tradition, at least, to the "badman blues" tradition.[18] Tales of Stagger Lee and other "bad niggas" reflect an ethos among many that celebrates the strong Black man who defies all authority and makes his own way in life. The badman tales recited in the blues, novels, and folklore inspired even more detailed descriptions of violence in pimp and prison narratives, "blaxploitation" films, and "toasts"—part of Black oral tradition in which the exploits of a hero or honored individual are told; according to Hebdige (1987) and Kelley (1994), pimp toasts and Jamaican dancehall toasts influence rap. In turn, during the mid-1980s performers such as Ice-T and N.W.A. began narrating stories of violence, power, and domination in Los Angeles over the heavy bass lines and rhythms of funk music.[19] These stories had a strong impact on young Chicanos in Los Angeles who found themselves in similar economic and social situations as young Black men and who, primed by the machismo and sexism of Mexican/Chicano patriarchal culture and the dominant U.S. culture industries, incorporated some of the vocabulary, style, and attitude of their fellow inner-city denizens.

GLOBALIZATION: THE POLITICAL ECONOMIC CONTEXT

The recent change in the form of capitalism from a nationalist-based, protectionist variety to a transnational capitalism (or capitalist globalization) affects everyone on earth. Chicanas/os and Mexican immigrants are some of the hardest hit here in the United States. Prior to the 1970s, capitalist accumulation was primarily structured along nation-state lines, with the bourgeoisie of each nation competing for ever-greater shares of labor, resources, means of production, and, of course, capital. Thus, conflict was centered between nations based on the national bourgeoisies' needs and desires for increasing accumulation. Today more than ever in history, national bourgeoisies are aligning themselves not against each other but against the rest of the world, disregarding nationalist ideals and practices that ultimately constrain their godlike attempts to remake the world in capitalism's image. Barriers to free trade such as taxes, tariffs, import restrictions, and environmental regulations have—along with the Berlin Wall—been toppled and dissolved.[20] This neoliberal cooperation between elites (known as transnationalism) has further subjugated the world's poor, leading to exponential increases in the numbers of people living in poverty or extreme poverty.[21]

An important aspect of the globalization process that warrants comment here is the continued subordination of the South to the North. While national bourgeoisies in Southern countries have embraced the free trade logic of globalization, they have done so as junior partners. They have been coerced and cajoled by international financial institutions such as the World Bank (WB) and the International Monetary

Fund (IMF) to accept an economic strategy that includes austere public spending, lower trade barriers, privatization of industry, and changes to property laws and other codes that would allow for multinational control over increasing proportions of their country's land and human resources. The loss of indigenous land to multinational corporations and subsequent proletarianization of indigenous and other peasantry, the dismantling of the social safety net (decreased welfare and other public spending), and increased unemployment in Southern cities have led to the dislocation, disenfranchisement, and ultimately immigration to the North for millions of the world's poor.[22]

Particularly important for this discussion is the situation for Mexican peasants and laborers since the early 1980s. Since the 1981 Mexican debt crisis, austerity measures have crippled the Mexican economy. The social safety net that provided benefits such as tortilla subsidies and medical insurance for workers has been dismantled as the government has been forced to cut its spending on social services. Land use practices that protected Mexico's small farmers and farming communities changed in 1991 with the reforms to Article 27 of the Mexican Constitution. Now communal landholdings may be sold or forfeited due to debt.

With the advent of the North American Free Trade Agreement (NAFTA) in January 1994 and additional laws that allowed U.S. corporations to own Mexican businesses, corporate land speculators swooped down upon small landowners in Mexico and gobbled up newly available land. Cheaper corn grown by subsidized agribusiness in the United States has flooded Mexican markets, adding to the burden placed upon Mexican peasants. Mexican peasants have been forced off their lands and have immigrated to the United States in droves since NAFTA took effect in 1994. J. Faux reports on data suggesting that "two and a half million farmers and their families have been driven out of their local markets and off their land" as a result of competition from heavily subsidized agribusiness from the United States and Canada (2004, 11). Most end up in the United States working on the same agribusiness plantations that forced them off their land or in other dangerous, low-wage jobs. In these ways and countless others the fate of the poor, especially people of color, in both the North and South are linked through globalization.

Since globalization accelerated in the 1970s and due to U.S. social and economic policies in the Reagan era, Mexican and Chicana/o communities have become postindustrial barrios characterized by increasing levels of poverty, incarceration, desperation, violence, drugs, and gangs and decreasing numbers of industrial manufacturing jobs, good schools, and social service programs.[23]

In Moore and Pinderhughes' important introduction to their edited volume *In the Barrios: Latinos and the Underclass Debate*, they define economic restructuring as "changes in the global economy that led to deindustrialization, loss and relocation of jobs and a decline in the number of middle-level jobs" (1993, xiii).[24] These changes have adversely affected Chicanas/os and Latinas/os in the United States. Accompanying the downward economic pressure on minority communities, policing of them has become more repressive. Policing agencies in urban areas and along the Mexico-U.S. border have become militarized, and their role as enforcer of elite economic policy has been solidified while their stated goal, "to serve and protect," has devolved into a darkly ironic cliché.[25]

Most indicators reveal that the economic situation of Latinas/os has been steadily declining since the beginning of the globalization process in the 1970s.[26] During the period in which Chicano rap began to emerge (1989–1996) and young Chicanos began commenting on *barrio* environments from their perspectives, the median household income for U.S. Chicanas/os fell by nearly $3,000 (M. Davis 2000, 116). And while Chicanos and Chicanas have high labor-force participation rates (LFPRs), their "high levels of work effort . . . [do] not translate into high occupational or income achievement relative to other groups" (González-Baker 1996, 13).[27] An important cause of low income for Chicanas/os is underemployment, which for men of Mexican origin was twice that of non-Hispanic White men in 1987 (De Anda 1996, 44). Similarly, rates of unemployment have historically been much higher among Chicanas/os than among non-Hispanic Whites.[28] Chicana/o earnings remain well below those of their non-Hispanic White counterparts.[29] Median household income, a further illustration of this trend, was $33,574 in 2002 for Chicanas/os and $48,900 for non-Hispanic White families. Statistics concerning wealth, which is a much more accurate indicator of a group's or individual's economic situation than income, reveal that Chicanas/os and Latinas/os were struggling in the economy of the 1990s. Davis reports (2000, 121) that in 1995, White median wealth ($45,700) was ten times that of Latinas/os ($4,700). Due to this poor economic situation, "the 1990 U.S. census identified one in four Chicano families as poor, versus 9.5 percent of non-Hispanic white families," while one in three Chicana/o children and one in eight non-Hispanic White children lived in poverty in 1990 (González-Baker 1996, 15).

In California, where the Chicano rap phenomenon began and has the largest number of artists and fans, the economic situation of Latinas/os and Chicanas/os is even worse than the 1990 Census indicated for Latinas/os and Chicanas/os as a whole. Davis reports (2000, 115) that the median income for Latinas/os in California in 1998 was $14,560, well below the average incomes of Whites ($27,000), Asians ($24,000), and Blacks ($23,000). In Southern California, Chicano male median income slipped relative to non-Hispanic White men between 1959 and 1990. In 1959 (that is, before the civil rights era and affirmative action), Chicano males made 81 cents for every dollar earned by a non-Hispanic White male. By 1990 that figure had plummeted to 61 cents (118).[30] Paul Ong and Rebecca Morales found that earnings gaps in Los Angeles increased as education increased; they noted that "the earnings gap between a highly educated Chicano and highly educated Anglo is greater than that between a minimally educated Chicano and minimally educated Anglo" (in M. Davis 2000, 119).

Especially troubling for the Chicana/o and greater Latina/o population in the United States is our relationship to the criminal justice system, which is closely related to our economic situation. Rates of incarceration, percentage of new admissions, percentage of new admissions for drug offenses, length of sentences, recidivism rates, juvenile detention rates, and many other indicators of criminal activity and contact with law enforcement agencies reveal that Latinas/os interact with the criminal justice system at levels disproportionate to their percentage of the U.S. population. In 2002 in California, for example, Latinas/os constituted 35.2 percent of the prison population, African Americans 30 percent, and Whites only 29.2 percent (A. Davis 2003, 13). The National Criminal Justice Commission (NCJC 1996) reported for the nation as a whole that while the African American prison population far outnumbered that of non-Hispanic Whites and Latinas/os, the latter comprised the "fastest growing minority group in prison from 1980 to 1993."[31] A study conducted by the Sentencing Project in 1995 found that 32.2 percent of Black males and "more than one in ten Latino males" ages twenty to twenty-nine were in prison or on parole or probation (in A. Davis 2003, 19). If these trends continue unabated, 25 percent of "Hispanic" men between the ages of eighteen and thirty-four will be imprisoned by 2020, creating an overall "Hispanic" male prison population of 2.4 million (Donziger 1996, 106). The prison-industrial complex has grown rapidly since the early 1980s through new legislation, tougher sentencing, charging juveniles as adults, mandatory minimums, "three-strikes" laws, drug policies, and the aforementioned economic trends. We can expect that without a revolutionary revision-ing of criminal justice, the NCJC projections for Latina/o incarceration in the coming decades will be met or even surpassed.[32]

FEMINIST ARCHETYPAL ANALYSIS:
EXAMINING THE GENDERED CONTEXT

Herrera-Sobek's feminist archetypal criticism can be employed to help us understand how a limited number of sexist images of women persist in Chicano rap music and how others have developed. She defines it "as a type of analysis that views archetypes as recurrent patterns in art, literature, film, songs, and other artistic endeavors depending on his-torical, political and social forces for their formation" (Herrera-Sobek 1990, xiii).

Feminist authors have expanded upon and complicated Jung's original conception of the archetype as a quasi-biological phenomenon that structures our psyches. They have replaced Jung's explanation with a feminist historical materialist analysis. Herrera-Sobek explains that

> human beings inherit the capacity to form images as they
> inherit the capacity to speak a language. And just as the
> language an individual speaks depends on the social con-
> text in which he or she is raised, the archetypal images
> an individual structures depend on his or her historical
> circumstances. (xiv)

Feminist historical materialism allows us to analyze how the Mexican-origin community has come to privilege certain images of women and how contemporary art forms help to perpetuate and modify them. Most Mexican/Chicano male music and other expres-sive cultural products have represented women in only a few ways that Herrera-Sobek calls archetypes. Images such as La Malinche, La Llorona, *la madre dolorosa* (the sorrowful mother), La Virgen, and the seductress have, within Mexican patriarchal culture, confined many Mexican-origin women to roles of either *la mujer mala* (the bad woman) or *la mujer buena* (the good woman). In examining female images in *corridos*, Herrera-Sobek argues that we must examine four socio-historical determinants: "patriarchal ideology, social class of the *corridista* [performer or composer of *corridos*] and the *corrido* audience, Mexican history, and Western literary tradition" (xiv). In analyzing the images of women in Chicano rap I use Herrera-Sobek's framework. Below I examine the Chicano rap audience, patriarchal ideology through masculine socialization, images of women in Mexican and Mexican American expressive culture, and representations of women in the dominant, corporate, Anglo-male-controlled media.

The Chicano Hip-Hop Nation

The Chicano hip-hop nation consists primarily of young working-class Chicanas/os from our nation's inner cities. As such, most have grown up in the hostile environments of the de-industrialized city (Moore and Pinderhughes 1993). The advent of economic restructuring in the 1970s brought profound changes that doomed Chicana/o youth to situations of unemployment, poor health, violence, and drugs.[33] Life chances in our barrios diminished as jobs that paid living wages or better fled the cities, leaving an employment and income vacuum that has been filled either by low-wage service work or the informal and illicit markets (Moore and Pinderhughes 1993). Educational opportunities stagnated during the same period (Pérez and Salazar 1997). The little ground gained from the efforts of educational reformers during the 1970s was lost in the 1980s and 1990s as affirmative action, bilingual education, and other programs that benefited Chicanas/os were undermined. Moreover, we have seen a resegregation of schools and college counselors replaced by military recruiters.[34] As poverty and illicit economic activity have increased, so too has police activity in the barrios, leading to a war on gangs and drugs that has caused Latinos to become the fastest-growing ethnic group in prison.

In my experience I have found that most of the young people who participate in hip-hop culture are drawn to it because of its uplifting and empowering qualities. Hip hop provides an expressive outlet for kids and young adults who otherwise do not have many such outlets. They use their affiliation to form identities and community bonds. Rappers, DJs, and producers are musicians. Taggers—who, explains Phillips (1999, 312), "limit their work to simple 'tags' (often nametags)"— and graffiti writers are artists. And the audience is made up of youth who share a language, customs, and a value system. Chicanas/os in the hip-hop nation are creating a dynamic culture out of the traditions of Mexican America and African America at least partly in response to the dominant culture of the United States and the attacks on their communities accompanying globalization.

Patriarchal Masculine Socialization

Adolescent boys attempting to become masculine, heterosexual men use misogynist representations as a means of policing gender boundaries and creating an Other by which they can define their identities. The production and consumption of sexualized, feminized, and dominated images of women serve as a ritual that helps boys become hypermasculine men.[35] In male expressive culture, the feminized, sexualized, dominated female Other is contrasted with the idealized, hypermasculine male: dominant, aggressive, violent, uncaring, and unemotional. This dichotomous view of gender helps remove any ambiguity about gender and creates an opportunity for adolescent boys to feel secure about their gender identity.[36]

bell hooks calls the dominant notion of manhood in the United States "patriarchal masculinity," in which being a man requires wealth and power that can be gained by any and all means. In this social-Darwinist approach to manhood, "survival of the fittest" reigns. Eldridge Cleaver wrote that "the logical culmination of this ethic, on a person-to-person basis, is that the weak are seen as the natural and just prey of the strong" (in hooks 2003, 27). Mass media work as propaganda, convincing youth that manhood means domination. Television, movies, music, and other forms of media privilege images of patriarchal masculinity and hypermasculinity.

Many Chicano youths internalize patriarchal masculinity and reinterpret it in male-dominant Chicano rap.[37] For numerous complicated reasons, women have been marginalized in hip-hop culture and the rap industry (Raimist 1999).[38] This marginalization of female voices allows for depictions of women in Chicano rap lyrics that erase the complex subjectivities of women and the importance of women to Chicana/o culture. Chicano rappers fill their lyrics with disparaging, dehumanizing images of women derived from Chicano/Mexican, European, and African American patriarchal cultures.[39]

Moreover, Chicano rap is homosocial. Young men mostly interact with other young men. As Ice-T explains in *Rhyme and Reason* (1997), "When you rap you are basically rapping to another rapper." Rap is a stage upon which to perform masculinity.[40] Because male culture thrives on competition, rappers attempt to outdo each other. Kimmel argues that "masculinity must be proved, and no sooner is it proved than it is again questioned and must be proved again" (1994, 122). Men must continually perform masculinity for male peers. And men must perform a particular kind of manhood. Kimmel explains that

this hegemonic masculinity involves unrealistic and damaging understandings of power and control to which all men must measure up.
Hegemonic masculinity includes the following characteristics: "repudiation of the feminine" or anti-femininity; wealth, success, power;
"holding emotions in check"; and daring and aggression (125–126).[41]

In rap, Chicano MCs perform their masculinity by demonstrating
verbal prowess on the "mic" (microphone). They often tell lurid, juvenile tales of sexual prowess and the domination of young women.
Women appear as objects whose bodies young Chicano rappers use to
wage verbal battle. Images of breasts and buttocks of young women are
valued as a form of capital that young men exchange in verbal bouts
of one-upmanship. Chicano MCs rap about the numbers of women
they have bedded and the women's physical sexiness (especially their
voluptuousness) and "freakiness" (the different sexual acts and tricks
they are willing to perform for the men).

Chicano rap lyrics imitate and expand upon the images of women
found in previous Chicano/Mexican music genres. In the *corrido*, *conjunto*, and other Mexican music forms, women are marginalized and/or
presented as *mala* or *buena*. Rarely do Mexican or Chicano musicians
or songwriters depict women as complex, multifaceted subjects. Chicano rap also has origins in Black expressive cultural forms.[42] Thus, in
Chicano rap, demeaning images of women from Black American male
culture and the dominant U.S. sexist culture have combined with those
from Mexican patriarchal tradition. Many Chicano rappers combine
the pimp discourse and iconography highly valued in some forms of
Black rap with old Mexican images of women.[43] At the same time, and
perhaps more importantly, Chicanos are bombarded by the controlling
images of women presented in the Anglo-dominated mass media and
culture industry and the larger cultural ethos that ties masculinity to
domination and violence, especially against women (Jhally 1999).[44]

Women in Mexican Expressive Cultures

Chicano rap owes much to previous Mexican and Mexican American
music and other expressive cultural forms. The archetypal images of
women they employ develop from those expressed in Mexican music
and from images of women in Chicano paintings, in murals, on lowriders,[45] in tattoos, and in literature. Feminist cultural critics have identified some predominant archetypal images of Mexican-origin women
within Mexican and Chicano expressive culture. Herrera-Sobek focuses on the good and bad mother, the mother goddess, the Lover and

the Soldier in *corridos*; all of these images focus on the woman's relationship to a man or men (1990, xix). Rosa Linda Fregoso's studies of Chicana/o film culture identify virgins and whores, supportive wives and mothers, and *Malinches* (traitors) as the main images of women found in Chicano-produced films (1993a,b). Fregoso argues that even more important than the actual images of women in these films is that filmmakers depict Chicanas as objects of the male gaze. In Chicano films, Chicanas lack agency, subjectivity, and authority (1993a, 94). Fregoso calls this practice "the male-centered lineage" in Mexican and Chicano expressive culture (1993a, 3).[46]

Male violence, defiance against Anglo and other domination, cultural nationalism, and sexism are the mainstays of the Chicano/ Mexican oral tradition.[47] Throughout our history these themes and the patriarchal worldview from which they stem have been challenged. Women singers and musicians have interpreted songs from a female point of view. Lydia Mendoza's version of "Mal Hombre" portrays a complex Mexican/Mexican American womanhood. Broyles-González writes that this song along with the often misunderstood "Mujer Paseada" (Experienced Woman) "defy academic and popular stereotypes of Latina chastity and virginity" (2001, 189). They along with many other songs "cemented a strong popular platform for the launching of later womanist (*mujerista*, feminist) values." The songs and their interpretation by Mendoza and others help develop a popular feminism among Mexicana women that prefigures Chicana feminism that begins during the 1960s. Among others, Mexican singers Chavela Vargas and Chelo Silva and Mexican American singers Linda Ronstadt and Selena perform music that present Mexican women in diverse and complex ways.

However, we have yet to see a significant challenge to the patriarchal worldview in Chicano rap, though some rappers have attempted to develop narratives of women that convey more complexity and respect. Few Chicanas have emerged in the rap world. With the exception of some of JV's work, no feminist or proto-feminist analysis has developed in Chicana rap.

José Limón argues that in the case of *corridos*, the central gender problem is the invisibility of women and not their representation: "Of far greater importance than these limited negative and positive female images is the *corrido*'s larger gender politics and poetics of exclusion and repression" (1992, 37). The findings of a content analysis of two major collections of Mexican American music confirm both Limón's and Herrera-Sobek's conclusions about representations of women in

Mexican (American) musics. The collection *La Música de los Viejitos* (Loeffler 1999) records a total of ninety-five songs, of which fifty-three have lyrics; among these twenty-six make references to women, most of them passing references and not discussions of women, gender difference, sexism, or womanhood in any depth. Of the sixty-six songs in *A Texas-Mexican Cancionero* (Paredes 1976), twenty-eight have even passing references to women. In both sources, more than half the references to women involve a woman in relation to a man. Few women have agency in these songs, and when women are central protagonists in songs it is often as victims.

None of the songs in either collection depict women in roles outside of the archetypes found by Herrera-Sobek.[48] *Corridos* and other songs from the Mexican tradition have been understood as oral histories of the struggles, successes, resistances, and worldviews of Mexican-origin people. However, in none of the songs recorded in either collection is the rich history of Mexicana/Chicana resistance, culture, and values praised. Instead, women are most commonly depicted as mothers, lovers, and wives and/or in religious-themed songs.[49] As might be expected, women are seen as objects of the male gaze in five of the songs that reference women in *Viejitos* and eight of the songs with women in *Cancionero*.[50] So, it seems that both Limón and Herrera-Sobek are correct in their assessments of the gender politics of *corridos*. Women are commonly absent from *corridos* and other Mexican (American) musics. And when they do appear, they are represented archetypically as good or bad in relation to men.

More recent music forms such as *conjunto* and *tejano* similarly represent women in archetypal ways. To take one prominent example, throughout the album *San Antonio Soul* the world-renowned Flaco Jimenez plays his virtuoso accordion to lyrics straight out of the sexist Mexican/Chicano tradition. On this album no single song that discusses women depicts them as whole, complex beings. For example, the song "La Mojadita" warns of treacherous immigrant women who deceive men out of their love and money.[51] Similarly, "Vengo a Ver Unos Ojos," "El Bingo," "El Perdido" and "La Dueña de la Llave" describe women as treacherous and having uncontrollable sexual desires. In these songs and "Que Lo Sepa el Mundo," women are the cause of the downfall of the male protagonist, and female actions are responsible for male bitterness and resentment toward women. Potentially dangerous women in this misogynist worldview cannot be trusted.[52]

This worldview has the effects of controlling young women's behaviors and bolstering their status as the Other to men. In this worldview women's sexuality should be controlled. Jimenez' recording and songs such as "Don Simon de Mi Vida" emphasize the importance of young women behaving modestly (Loeffler 1999, 87). Of course, a double standard exists. Male sexuality should be allowed as much freedom as possible. So it is on Jimenez' album.[53]

The relationship between controlling women, especially their sexualities, and violence is commonly depicted and justified in the male-centered lineage in Mexicano culture. Upon discovering that his wife has been unfaithful in "El Perdido," the male protagonist takes up a knife to kill her. Instead he drowns his sorrow in alcohol at a cantina where historically only women whose sexuality was readily available to the men, i.e., prostitutes, were allowed entrance. In the end the song sympathizes with the male protagonist, who because of a woman returns home shamed, and it naturalizes his violent disposition toward women and alcohol abuse.[54]

Certainly these are not the only depictions of women in Mexicano music. However, my research has shown that these are the most prevalent images of women in Mexican male oral and expressive cultures. The long tradition of sexist images in Mexican culture does not by itself explain the misogyny of contemporary Chicano youth culture, especially as depicted in rap lyrics. Many other factors must be considered before drawing conclusions about the persistence of misogyny in this new cultural movement.

Women of Color in the Dominant Corporate Media

A central argument in bell hooks' "Gangsta Culture—Sexism, Misogyny: Who Will Take the Rap?" (1994) is that the misogyny of Black male culture emulates that of the dominant culture. African American misogyny is not deviant in our society. It is part and parcel of a continuum of misogyny that includes disparaging images of women, violence against women, and economic subordination of women. Professor hooks points out that the rap industry is controlled by corporations headed by White men who ultimately make the decisions about the content of today's rap music. Thus, it is part of the dominant or corporate-controlled media. The increasing consolidation of the entertainment and communication media in the hands of fewer corporations whose interests do not lie with entertainment or journalism has narrowed the gender, racial, and other content on television and radio.[55] Historical and contemporary practices of the dominant corporate media influence how women are understood and then re-presented by young Chicanos.

Patricia Hill Collins argues that throughout history the dominant White media have used images of Black women to control them. The concept "controlling images" of Black women involves a practice of "portraying African-American women as stereotypical mammies, matriarchs, welfare recipients, and hot mommas [and it] has been essential to the political economy of domination fostering Black women's oppression" (1990, 67). Hill Collins argues further that these stereotypes or archetypes become normal and natural to many non-Blacks. She quotes Hazel Carby, who "suggests that the objective of stereotypes is 'not to reflect or represent a reality but to function as a disguise, or mystification, of objective social relations.' These controlling images are designed to make racism, sexism, and poverty appear to be natural, normal, and an inevitable part of everyday life" (68). Stereotypes become reified markers of identity that hide social relations of racial and gender domination/subordination. Stereotypes serve the additional function of objectifying women, especially women of color, as the Other, an object to be manipulated and controlled.[56]

Historically, the dominant media have portrayed Latinas in similar ways.[57] Gary Keller found that in the first few decades of the Hollywood film industry, "there [were] few other avenues of behavior [for Mexican females] other than the sexually charged ones . . . nonsexually foregrounded female characters rarely appear in film during the first decades" (1994, 39). Latinas are almost exclusively portrayed as the "Latin Spitfire," the seductress who more often than not causes the downfall of the story's protagonist. This is the Anglo-dominated corporate media's twist on *malinchismo*.[58]

These archetypes continue to thrive in more recent films such as the gang fantasy *Colors* (1988), in which Maria Conchita Alonso's character, the only woman with a significant role in the movie, betrays Sean Penn's rogue cop character by sleeping with the gang enemy. In his films *El Mariachi* (1992) and *From Dusk Till Dawn* (1996), Robert Rodriguez has used Hollywood's lurid depictions of the Mexico-U.S. border region and the Latina seductress image. He has used Salma Hayek's body to cash in on White desires and stereotypes of Mexican women.[59]

In the final analysis, many factors contribute to the persistence of misogynist images in Chicano male expressive culture. Throughout dominant, White-controlled, corporate media and in the expressive cultures of Black and Brown men, women have been consistently represented as the objects of the male gaze and sexual gratification, as sexually immoral and therefore whose sexuality must be controlled, and as dangerous and traitorous. The result of this saturation of images of the "bad woman" is a socialization process that causes young boys to see women in unbecoming and dehumanizing ways and to see themselves in a relationship of domination with them. If rap as popular culture contributes to the creation of shared maps of meaning for groups of young men that help solidify their identities and worldviews, then we can expect that the misogynist attitudes toward women expressed in rap have an effect on men's behaviors toward women.[60] While not excusing them, we should expect that young Chicanos who cannot escape the misogynist messages that fill their visual and aural landscapes will reproduce these images in their art.

THE PATRIARCHAL DOMINANCE PARADIGM

U.S. society is rife with the patriarchal dominance paradigm. A violent and misogynist "us versus them" worldview is common throughout our cultural, economic, social, and political systems. This way of believing and acting similarly influences young Chicanas/os including rap artists. The patriarchal dominance paradigm is Manichean in its makeup. It views the world in either/or dichotomous terms that categorize Others as strange, threatening, and inferior, to be opposed and dominated. This paradigm calls for understanding human and social relations in antagonistic ways. Inasmuch as women are seen as fundamentally different under patriarchy, the paradigm relegates them to the status of inferior Others. This fosters a climate of misogyny, male privilege, and violence.[61] The patriarchal dominance paradigm is disseminated to young people via popular culture and the media. The music videos, Hollywood films, magazine advertisements, and television commercials of the dominant U.S. popular culture are all laden with vivid images of this paradigm (Jhally 1997b, 1999). The rhetoric of masculine Chicanismo found throughout Chicano/Mexican patriarchal culture further influences young Chicana/o notions of power and gender. Chicanos were valued inasmuch as they adhered to a rebellious, hypermasculine model, while ideal women's roles involved passivity and family and household labor. Many men believed that "good" Chicanas should occupy nurturing and sexually submissive roles and that they should be treated as inferiors (A. García 1997).

Chicano rappers use similar constructions of masculinity, femininity, and violence in their stories. Figures such as the male social

bandit and the female sexual object reflect a Chicano/Mexican patriarchal worldview as well as patriarchal dominance attitudes of the larger
U.S. society and popular culture. This paradigm as expressed in Chicano rap lyrics and hip hop culture takes shape within increasingly
violent, globalized, deindustrialized, incarcerated, and impoverished
postindustrial barrios. To fully comprehend the violent and misogynist rhetoric of most Chicano rappers, we must recognize the artists'
embeddedness in a violent and misogynist society as well as the gendered discourse in much of Mexican American and African American
culture. Next we will look at the work of several important Chicana/o
rap artists and the contribution to their music and rhetoric by African
American youth culture.

CHAPTER TWO

CHICANO RAP PRIMER

A *Guide to Artists and Genres*

hicanos have been rapping for more than two decades. Over these twenty-odd years, Chicanos have sampled a wide range of music; rapped about everything from gangbanging to peace and love in the barrio; developed numerous lyrical and musical styles; rapped in English, Spanish, variations of code-switching, slang, and *caló* (working-class Chicana/o street slang);[1] and used various methods of distributing their music. Since Chicano rappers are an extremely varied and complex group, I believe a brief primer is required. In this chapter I examine a cross-section of some of the most significant Chicana/o rappers and their various styles and themes. We begin with the "Godfather of Chicano Rap," discuss new rappers including women such as JV and Sista D, and travel from the birthplace of Chicano rap—Los Angeles—to the Midwest, all the while paying attention to the various cultural, regional, and other influences, especially intercultural exchange with African Americans.

THE GODFATHER OF CHICANO RAP

I first heard Kid Frost in 1990. His first single off of his first LP, *Hispanic Causing Panic* (1990), was "La Raza." In the late 1980s, many of the members of The Colorado College's Chicana/o student group, MEChA, listened to rap music, but no one we heard was rapping about the Chicana/o experience. So, at our parties when we wanted to stir up Chicana/o pride, we played Santana or Los Lobos. Then "La Raza" became our theme song, and upon hearing the instrumental opening of the song, a sample of "El Tirado" by one of our favorite groups, El Chicano, everyone at MEChA parties would run to the dance floor.[2] "La Raza" inevitably kicked our parties into higher levels of fun, pride, and sexuality. Soon afterward, I purchased Chicano rap CDs by A Lighter Shade of Brown (*Brown and Proud*, 1990), Proper Dos (*Mexican Power*,

1992), and Latin Alliance (*Latin Alliance*, 1991, which went to number 83 on the Top R&B/Hip-Hop Albums chart).[3]

The MEChistas were dancing to the polyrhythmic syncopated beats characteristic of the African diaspora. The rhythmic structures of Frost's music, as well as that of Santana and the blues of Los Lobos, result from our very long history of living in close proximity to and exchanging worldviews and culture with African Americans. Gaye Johnson writes that "for as long as they have occupied common living and working spaces, African American and Chicano working-class communities have had continuous interactions around civil rights struggles, union activism, and demographic changes" (2002, 316). Steven Loza argues that in Los Angeles this intercultural exchange began in the 1930s and 1940s when Black migrants moved to Los Angeles: "The availability of low-rent housing in the Mexican neighborhoods of east and south-central Los Angeles prompted many blacks to settle there" (1993, 80). Loza quotes Ruben Guevara, who points to the importance of radio stations that broadcasted swing music to multiracial audiences: "Blacks and Chicanos, isolated together, began to interact and, in large numbers, they listened to the same radio stations" (81).

Matt García also points out that during the 1930s and 1940s, Los Angeles dancehall promoters recognized that a new generation of Mexican Americans not only enjoyed Latin music styles but also were drawn to the popular swing music of the time. Swing was the music of choice for the young Mexican, Black, Filipino, and White working-class practitioners of zoot culture. Dance promoters seized upon the popularity of swing and zoot culture and showcased popular swing bands at multiracial dances. In the 1950s the popularity of rock 'n' roll music continued to draw a multiracial youth audience to dances.[4] García argues further that "the racial/ethnic intermixing facilitated a blending of cultural influences . . . [that created a music that] possessed a broad-based, cross-cultural appeal, which facilitated understanding among a racially diverse audience" (163).

Such multiracial youth interaction in the middle part of the twentieth century resulted in a process of cultural exchange and borrowing that birthed lowrider culture, rock and roll music, and contemporary gang and street culture.[5] Both García and Johnson contend that the resultant youth subcultures challenged racial prejudices and stereotypes. García found that intercultural dancehalls along with interracial socializing at school and participation in multiracial political organizations led to improved relations between Blacks and Chicanas/os. García's informants stated that they even began to date interracially. One interviewee remembered the El Monte dancehall as "a melting pot" where interracial dating was not uncommon (164).

Over the decades, Chicanas/os and Blacks continued to interact in Los Angeles and other cities of the Southwest. With the continued popularity of African diasporic-based music including R&B, soul, and funk, Chicanas/os became even more familiar with Black musical and cultural sensibilities, and many produced "Black" music of their own. Certainly, relations between the two groups have not always been ideal. As a result of the competition for scarce resources and the uncritical acceptance of racist stereotypes of both groups imposed upon us by the racist, capitalist U.S. society, an uneasy tension and high levels of animosity also have characterized Chicana/o-Black relations (Vaca 2004). Times of economic instability in the United States tend to increase racial animosity because Chicanas/os and Blacks are positioned among the lowest in the labor and social hierarchies, increasing each group's socioeconomic difficulties and thus competition between them. The deindustrialization process of the late twentieth century, oppressive social conditions, drugs, AIDS, police violence, and draconian legislation aimed at controlling people of color created such an atmosphere in the 1980s.[6] Gaye Johnson writes that as a result of these problems, "Latinos and African Americans have sometimes identified each other as impediments to their own community's progress" (2002, 321).

Incredibly, against these odds in the middle of the 1980s Brown and Black inner-city cultural exchange led to the development of Chicano rap and hip-hop scenes throughout the Southwest. Kid Frost, a product of the deindustrialization process and the growing hip-hop movement of the 1970s, exemplifies the intercultural exchange at the root of Chicano hip hop.

Kid Frost was the first Chicano to have a successful widely released rap album. The "Godfather of Latin Rap" was the first to bring the beats, attitude, and lyricism of rap to many Chicana/o audiences. His unapologetic *raza* pride and barrio tales rapped over hard beats and familiar samples from oldies and Chicano groups such as El Chicano and Malo opened the door for many Chicana/o youths to participate in rap and hip-hop culture. Since his first release, Kid Frost (now Frost) has released more than a dozen albums, greatest hits collections, and mix tapes. His music and career exemplify African American–Chicana/o cultural exchange. His first hit, the song that MEChistas danced to during the early 1990s, "La Raza," uses the El Chicano interpolation of African American composer Gerald Wilson's "El Tirado." Frost also acknowledges R&B pioneers such as Teddy Pendergrass, Al Green, and Earth, Wind, and Fire as some of his early influences. In an interview with Brian Cross for the book *It's Not About a Salary* (1993, 95), Frost cites Mary Wells and Bill Withers as important figures in his early development. Following *Hispanic Causing Panic*, Kid Frost released *Eastside Story* (1992). His second album follows the first with stories that he argues "must be told." Notable tracks "No Sunshine" and "Smiling Faces" are homages to songs by the great soul singer Bill Withers that have become classics in Chicana/o neighborhoods.

Frost's third album, *Smile Now, Die Later* (1995), exhibits the importance of Black music to Chicana/o hip hop. The vocal arrangements and styles throughout this album recall 1970s soul singing. Diane Gordon's vocals on tracks such as "East Side Rendezvous" and "Look at What I See" and sample backing vocals on "Mari" and "La Familia" exemplify this influence. Uses of samples and reinterpretations of funk and soul music on many tracks further demonstrate the Chicana/o fondness for Black oldies. For example, producers Tony G. and Julio G. use several elements from Sly and the Family Stone's "Family Affair" and Rick James' "Mary Jane" on "La Familia" and "Mari," respectively.

The song "You Ain't Right" exemplifies the complex nature of cultural exchange and transformation that has occurred between Chicanas/os and Blacks. The backing track for this song is the Clint Ballard Jr. composition "You're No Good." The song was initially recorded by African American soul singer Betty Everett of "Shoop Shoop Song (It's in His Kiss)" fame. "You're No Good" gained national popularity with a mid-1970s version by popular Mexican American artist, Linda Rondstadt. In 1995 Frost and his producers added heavy bass drum sounds and other West Coast rap musical elements to create an entirely new song laden with African diasporic sounds but uniquely Mexican American in the song's narrative and worldview.

Frost's producers also rely on typical West Coast rap sounds such as the heavy use of funk guitars and bass lines on "Mari" and "Nothing but Love." On "Mari," funk legend Rick James performs a cameo, and Frost samples James' hit "Mary Jane." The song, like James' original, renders the pleasures that many find in smoking marijuana. Another important aspect of the musical production on this album includes the use of high, "whiny" synthesizer sounds and piano chords held over several measures ("Family Affair," "You Ain't Right," "Look at What I See," and "Youseemurda") that DJ Muggs of Cypress Hill describes as typical of the West Coast sound. Instead of snare drums, the producers of "How Many Ways Can You Lose A Body" and "Bamseeya" rely on hand claps, a typical feature of West Coast rap music, according to Muggs.[7] The musicians on this CD also borrow from ethnic Mexican cultures. The uses of Southwestern sounds such as Spanish guitars and references to Pancho Villa in "Bamseeya" locate the music in the Mexico-U.S. borderlands. Other examples of the ways the music borrows from and locates its production in ethnic Mexican cultures of the Southwest include the use of samples of the popular group El Chicano's "Chachita" and "Look of Love" on "La Familia" and "La Raza Part II," respectively.

The uses of Black diasporic sounds and the music's development in the multiracial Los Angeles hip-hop scene demonstrate the interracial cultural exchange between Chicana/o and Black youth that begins as early as the 1930s in L.A. dancehalls and school yards. While heavily influenced by Black diasporic musics and Black Angelenos, the many references to Chicano life and uses of popular Mexican American sounds also point to Frost's rootedness in ethnic Mexican culture and society.

In 1995 Kid Frost changed his name to Frost, suggesting his maturing. He has recorded solo albums such as *When HelL.A. Freezes Over* (1997), *That Was Then, This Is Now*, volume 1 (1999) and volume 2 (2000). Frost's many accomplishments were compiled in 2001 and released under the name *Frost's Greatest Joints*. He has also been involved in compilations and collaborations including the important early album *Latin Alliance* (1991) with A.L.T., Mellow Man Ace, and Tony G. that included the homage to a Chicana/o favorite, "Lowrider" by War, the multiracial group from Los Angeles that used "Latin" rhythms and some Chicana/o themes in its music. The song "Lowrider" and the group War further illustrate the cross-fertilization of Chicana/o and Black cultures. Lowriding, according to Yamaoka (1998), developed from important contributions by both Chicanos and African Americans in the late 1950s and early 1960s.

G-SPOT STUDIOS

Frost's success and alliances with L.A. Chicana/o hip hoppers resulted in part from his work at G-Spot Studios. The G-Spot—a triple-entendre referring to gangstas, sexuality, and Gonzalez, after founder and producer Tony G (Gonzalez)—has sparked the careers of many Chicano rappers. Tony G worked on pioneering Lighter Shade of Brown's first album, *Brown and Proud*. This album hit record stores the same year as Kid Frost's *Hispanic Causing Panic* (1990) and is considered a classic in Chicano rap circles. Tony G reappeared on Lighter Shade of Brown's *If You Could See Inside Me* (1999).[8]

Frost's Latin Alliance bandmate A.L.T. started his career making demos with Tony G. After his work on the Latin Alliance project, he released two solo albums. *Another Latin Timebomb* (1992) featured the hit "Tequila," which made it onto *Billboard*'s Top 40 Pop Chart and was even more popular in other countries, including Australia, where it went to number 1. In 1993 he released *Stone Cold World* and has continued to work on compilation and soundtrack albums and collaborations with Chicano and non-Chicano artists.[9]

Slow Pain, who began his career beatboxing with the group Street Mentality in 1992, also has a long history of collaboration with Tony G and G-Spot Productions. All of his solo albums include production from Tony G. In 1993 Slow Pain hooked up with A.L.T. and Kid Frost to form a short-lived group, Three Deep. He eventually signed with Thump Records, and in 1995 he released his solo debut, *Baby OG*. Slow Pain followed with *Hit List* (2000), *Lil' Don Juan* (2001), and *Presents Old Town Gangsters* (2001). Slow Pain has been part of many collaborations, including appearing with the group G-Fellas. His most recent work is with a supergroup called M.I.A., which features Nino Brown and Sick Jacken from Psycho Realm.

G-Spot also recorded the gangstas-turned-rappers Brownside. Their music, filled with detailed descriptions of street violence, was enthusiastically recommended to me by a group of Chicano juvenile offenders during my first focus group session concerning violence in Chicano rap. Brownside's was the favorite music of these Chicano street youths, who liked the music because it was "real," "hard," and "gangsta" like themselves. Brownside's albums include *Brownside* (1992), *Eastside Drama* (1997), and *Payback* (2000).

Tony G continues to produce Chicano rap artists such as G-Fellas—*Crime Stories* (1999) and *Gangsta 4 Life* (2001)—and has worked on several CD compilations of Chicano rappers including South Park Mexican's *The Purity Album* (2000). The G-Spot sound is all over Chicano rap and the broader rap scene. Tony G has worked with dozens of Chicano, Latino, Black, and other rappers. Besides launching the careers of Chicano rappers, Tony G has lent his talents to many well-known artists, including Above the Law, Eazy-E, DJ Pooh, Boo-Yaa T.R.I.B.E., Mellow Man Ace, Rappin' 4-Tay, and 2 Live Crew.

CHICANO RAP PRIMER 41

SMOKIN' STRAIGHT OUTTA SOUTHGATE:
THE CYPRESS HILL FAMILIA

Cypress Hill is probably the best-known Latino rap group on the planet. This multiracial group includes an Italian from New York, DJ Muggs; a Cuban, Sen Dog; and a Chicano Cuban, B-Real. I include them in this history of Chicano rap because they are from and rap about the Chicana/o city of Southgate in the Los Angeles area, they use Chicana/o slang and imagery, and their fan base includes many Chicana/os. Their multiracial makeup and use of Chicano and Black street slang (including the word "nigga") appeal to multiracial audiences, and their music illustrates the centrality of intercultural exchange to Chicano hip hop. Cypress Hill has not only created a new genre of slow, beat-heavy, marijuana-influenced rap music but also has made it a point to extend the hip-hop community by reaching out to White rock fans (on the alternative-rock Lollapalooza tour) and Spanish-speaking Latina/o communities (on a Spanish-language version of their greatest hits in 1999). They have always been conscious of rap and hip hop culture as a multi-ethnic, multiracial youth cultural form and have refused to limit the possibilities of rap's global influence.[10] In an interview with Dumisani Ndlovu (2000), B-Real argues that "music is for everybody" and defends his group against critics who fault Cypress Hill for reaching out to youth of all races. Sen Dog and Muggs explain their cultural politics of interracial alliance in a 1991 interview conducted by Brian Cross (1993, 238):

> **SD [Sen Dog]:** We feel you can all be down with your own, but not when it comes to the music; you all got to be together.
> **Muggs:** We feel the niggas, the Mexicans, the Chinese, white kids, it don't matter.

Cypress Hill promotes hip-hop culture and rap music as venues for multiracial youth dialogues, places where young people of different races can "feel" each other, can enjoy each other's company and share culturally, politically, and emotionally.

Cypress Hill's cultural politics and body of work are indicative of the close proximity of people of color in the postindustrial inner city. They have worked with White rappers House of Pain and a long list of Black rappers from all regions of the country; they speak fondly of their relationship to the Samoan rappers of Boo-Yaa T.R.I.B.E. and have mentored the Chicano rappers Psycho Realm and Delinquent

Habits. Their attitudes, style, language, and music reflect a ghetto-centric or barrio-centric experience. They revel and take pride in their underclass, urban roots. Their use of the word "nigga" exemplifies Kelley's argument concerning the development of a ghetto-centric identity and culture in gangsta rap:

> [T]o be a real nigga is to be a product of the ghetto. By linking their identity to the 'hood instead of simply skin color, gangsta rappers implicitly acknowledge the limitations of racial politics, including black middle-class reformism as well as black nationalism. (1994a, 210)

"Nigga," for some in Black communities, is a sign of a shared identity. Black people reclaimed an epithet that had been used for centuries by Whites as a means of humiliation. Just as they did with the term "Black" in the 1960s, Americans of African descent took a linguistic tool of oppression away from racists, changed it to meet their cultural and linguistic needs (note the dropping of "er" and its replacement with "a"), and gave it new cultural significance. Of course, many in Black communities feel that the term "nigga" is derogatory and furthers degrading stereotypes of Black people. Furthermore, many in Chicana/o and Latina/o communities use the term in all its racist and derogatory meanings. While the term is controversial, its use by Cypress Hill suggests the importance of working-class, Black, urban culture and people to Chicana/o rap's growth. A brief examination of Cypress Hill's discography illustrates the uniqueness of this group as well as the importance of Black culture to their work.

Their self-titled debut appeared in 1991. It includes their well-known songs "How I Could Just Kill a Man" and "Pigs" and their celebration of Spanglish, "Latin Lingo." Their second release, *Black Sunday* (1993), includes their best-known song, "Insane in the Brain," and numerous cuts devoted to analyzing marijuana use and its effects. Many other songs discuss gang and police violence, a theme that continues on their third album, *III Temples of Boom* (1995); B-Real describes the song "Throw Your Set in the Air" as a critique of gang life. The group released *IV* in 1998 and in 1999 extended its reach southward across the U.S.-Mexico border with the Spanish-language album *Los Grandes Éxitos en Español*. Their later albums include *Live at the Fillmore* (2000), the rap-rock fusion *Skull and Bones* (2000), and *Till Death Do Us Part* (2004). With the double album *Skull and Bones*, Cypress Hill continued to break new ground, dedicating half of the album to exploring hip-hop beats and lyrics and the other half to a rock-punk fusion. Their most notable song from *Skull and Bones* is the critique of the rap lifestyle and superstar image, "(Rap) Superstar." *Till Death Do Us Part* continues to explore the fusion of musical styles and includes reggae tracks.

DJ Muggs' production style has created a unique sound that relies on West Coast G-funk pioneered by Dr. Dre (of N.W.A. fame), Latin rhythms and instrumentation, and samples of many classic R&B songs. This unique sound has led Cypress Hill to have an enormous influence on Chicana/o and other rappers. On many songs from their later albums they feature important Black rappers, including members of Wu Tang Clan. DJ Muggs produced the compilation albums *Soul Assassins* chapters I (1997) and II (2000), which feature many well-known rappers: KRS-One, RZA, GZA, Mobb Deep, MC Eiht, Xzibit, Goodie Mob, and Kurupt. B-Real has collaborated with diverse artists ranging from Atlanta's OutKast to Puerto Rican rapper Big Pun and Irish rappers House of Pain. The Mexican group Control Machete borrowed from Cypress Hill and rapped in Spanish about street life in Mexico over DJ Muggs-like production. On their first album, *Mucho Barato* (1997), Control Machete thanks Cypress Hill for their inspiration.[11]

The members of Cypress Hill also have been teachers and mentors for important Chicano rap groups such as Delinquent Habits and Psycho Realm. Sen Dog began working with Delinquent Habits on their self-titled debut album in 1996. They have since released three more albums: *Here Come the Horns* (1998), *Merry Go Round* (2000), and *Freedom Band* (2003). Delinquent Habits distinguishes itself in the Chicano rap world by creative use of *mariachi* and Tijuana brass samples and Latin American rhythms and instruments. Producer-DJ O.G. Styles uses horns, Latin piano riffs, oldies and funk samples, and scratches to create sonic masterpieces. Kemo and Ives of Delinquent Habits have been rapping for more than a dozen years and have matured into important storytellers who denounce violence and celebrate parties, fun, music, and peace. Kemo released his solo debut, *Simple Plan*, in 2004, and in *Not So Rich and Famous* (2007), Kemo continues the mentoring tradition with his relationship to Jehuniko and Almas Intocables. Jehuniko from Los Angeles released his solo debut, *La Pura Vida*, in 2006. Kemo produces six songs and adds strong rap performances to the songs "Last Day in Paradise," and "While in Handcuffs." Jehuniko has joined with two other MCs, Lady Binx (of Houston) and Ikuestion (of Mexico City), to form Almas Intocables.

Another branch of the Cypress Hill family tree includes Psycho Realm. B-Real and brothers Jacken "Sick Jack" and Duke Gonzalez formed Psycho Realm. The group began its recording career with the four-song *Unreleased* EP and in 1997 released a self-titled debut on a major label. *Psycho Realm* reached number 68 on the Top R&B/Hip Hop Albums chart and shocked the rap world with articulate and lucid critiques of U.S. society. B-Real exited the group after its 1997 major-label debut. While Jacken and Duke enjoyed the amenities that come with being attached to a major label, they felt artistically restrained and decided to work independently thereafter.[12] *A War Story, Book I* was released in 2000 under Psycho Realm's own independent label, Sick Symphonies. The lyrics on this album analyzed in more depth and detail the power structures in the United States and local struggles including police violence, drugs, gang violence, and the 1992 Los Angeles rebellion that followed the not-guilty verdict in the trial of the police officers who beat Rodney King. They consider themselves revolutionaries who use the power of the mic and African and American rhythms to extol their vision of an alternative society. They have appeared on many compilations and collaborations with artists such as 2Mex, Son Doobie of Funkdoobiest, Delinquent Habits, Slow Pain, and Mexican rock-rap artists Cartel de Santa.

Psycho Realm released *A War Story, Book II* in 2003, continuing the formula of hard beats, street sounds, and revolutionary lyrics. The Sick Symphonies label also released *Steel Storm* by the group Street Platoon and the CD *Sick Symphonies: Sickside Stories* (2005), a collaboration between Psycho Realm and Street Platoon.

On January 28, 1999, Psycho Realm's greatest fears and the concerns that they had been rapping about for years hit home. Duke Gonzalez became a victim of gun violence when he was shot outside of a restaurant after attending a Delinquent Habits concert. The shooting left Duke paralyzed and changed Psycho Realm immeasurably.[13] This incident, the lives of Jack and Duke, and Psycho Realm lyrics can teach something to all of us about conditions in postindustrial barrios.

THE BROADER L.A. CHICANO RAP SCENE

Today, the Chicano rap scene in Los Angeles is as varied as the city's geography and population. People of Mexican descent including recent immigrants, those whose families have lived there since the nineteenth century, working- and under-class members, the middle class, professionals, activists, gang members, and college students live throughout the diverse neighborhoods and towns that constitute the Los Angeles metropolitan area. They live in complex relationships with fellow Angelenos from equally diverse backgrounds, classes, and races/ethnicities. Chicano rap mirrors the diversity in L.A.'s ethnic Mexican population.

The group Proper Dos was an early Los Angeles Chicano rap trailblazer. Ernie Gonzalez and Frank V. (Villareal) formed the group in 1990 and by 1992 had released their first album, *Mexican Power*, under Rhino Records. Notable cuts from the album include the Chicano hip-hop anthem "Mexican Power," the gangsta-styled "Uno Ochenta Siete (187)" and "Life of a Gangster," and the biting critique of the public education system, "First Day of School." Proper Dos followed their classic first album with *We're at It Again* (1995), *Heat* (1998), and *Overdose* (1999). Proper Dos' successes opened doors for other Chicanos who would later rap about themes of racial pride, gang lifestyles, and political and social phenomena.

Since I picked up the Latin Bomb Squad's CD *Neighborhood Creepas* in 1999, I have cherished it as an exemplar of Chicano rap. The group raps about urban street life in the 1990s with emotional urgency. They speak of the pain caused by violence in our communities and argue against Brown-on-Brown violence. The production is top-notch, and the music is well made. Unfortunately, I have not been able to find more of Latin Bomb Squad's music. In November 2003 a fan informed me that rapper Lefty had become a Christian and given up on rap.

A Chicana student from Denver urged me to see a rap concert featuring several artists. In early 2003 I walked into a small club in Fort Collins, Colorado, and was blown away by the fire and passion coming out of the mics of Los Angeles rappers 2Mex, Xololanxinxo, and Busdriver. 2Mex exemplifies the complex hip-hop scene in Los Angeles. He is part of the multiracial rap crew the Visionaries, who are underground favorites for their lyricism, political and social critique, and unique, old-school-flavored hip-hop beats and sounds. He has worked with the group Shape Shifters and Anglo American producer Mum's the Word in the group MindClouders. In 2000, 2Mex recorded his first solo CD, *Words Knot Music*. His debut relies heavily on spoken-word styles and does not include music. He followed this with the lyrically and musically innovative CD *B Boys in Occupied Mexico* (2001). On "L.A. (Like . . .)" he provides a "roll call" of important underground Los Angeles rap groups. He collaborates with Xololanxinxo (*People Kill the Person*, 2003) and Fermin of the Mexican rap group Control Machete on the Mexican pride song "Control Mexica." He teams with Xololanxinxo and Sick Jack of Psycho Realm on "Doctors, Drums, and Danger" and provides uplift with "The Truth," "Wonderful Memories," and "Offering." 2Mex is one of a rare few Chicano rappers who reveal vulnerability, as he does in "I Didn't Mean to Touch Your Hand." His other remarkable and unique CDs include *Sweat Lodge Infinite* (2003), *2Mex* (2004), and *Over the Counter Culture* (2005, which he recorded under the moniker SonGodSuns).

Recently the 5th Battalion has been making noise in the Chicano rap underground scene in Los Angeles. Group member Fernando Escobar wrote in a 2003 email to me that "the 5th is testimony to the power music has to redirect our anger into a positive celebration of what the people united are capable of when they put down their colors, guns and fears and open their ears to a message of change." The 5th Battalion began in 1998 as a production crew consisting of Fernando, DJ Quad, and a circle of artists. In the email Fernando discussed the significance of their name: "5th stands for the five fingers in a hand, when clinched it forms a fist for the show of strength. Battalion represents the masses in the struggle." For the 5th Battalion, "struggle" is not just an idea and revolution not simply a theory. They actively work with organizations dedicated to social change and provide their services to benefit concerts and compilation CDs.

The 5th Battalion has worked with a number of up-and-coming Los Angeles rap artists including O.T.W., Brown Town Looters, Los Tumbados, Groundkeepers, El Vuh, La Paz, Global City, and Stricte 9. Each of these artists appears on the groundbreaking double CD *The Never Ending Battle* (2003). This CD served as a fundraiser to assist the family of Steve Rivera, who, like Duke of Psycho Realm, was shot outside of a performance. Many of the songs on the CD discuss the shooting, Steve's life, and the consequences of gun violence. Steve's family was not as fortunate as Duke's. The gunshot was fatal, leaving Steve's family without a breadwinner and plunging them back into poverty and dangerous neighborhood environs.

An important 5th Battalion collaborator is East L.A.'s Krazy Race, a.k.a. Mark "Markie" Ramirez. He has been in the hip-hop scene since the early 1980s and toward the latter part of the 1990s began to turn heads with his poignant political critiques. I first heard Markie on *The Ollin Project*, a collaboration between 5th Battalion, Digital Aztlán, and several underground artists. His popular song "Dedicated" teaches history over an infectious beat that keeps your head bobbin'. The song has been featured on other collaborations and the documentary film *Pass the Mic*. After hearing "Dedicated," I had to find out what else he had to offer. I found the Krazy Race website (www.krazyrace.com) and purchased his EP *New World Games*. Markie teams with several rappers and producers to create a fresh, politically astute, and important EP. His songs "Illuminati" on *The Never Ending Battle* (2003) and *New World Games* LP (2004) and "Fact or Fiction" on *New World Games* LP (2004) focus our attention on the national political scene and critique the elite power politics, secret societies, and "politricks" that have caused the income gap between rich and poor to grow. His 2006 work, *The Movement: Strength in Numbers*, has received airplay on Internet radio stations and websites and is proving popular with Chicano rap fans on Brown Pride online. Markie's work on behalf of youth and peace makes him one of the most important voices coming out of Los Angeles. As a dedicated activist, he speaks back to empire and in "Illuminati" says, "I'm an activist/I'm not takin' these words back." Krazy Race shows his dedication to the music, to youth, and to radical social change through his mentoring relationship with teenage rapper Mic MC, who in 2003 at age fourteen already had built a loyal fan base.

The Chicano rap scene in Los Angeles is too large to include a discussion of all the artists from the area. Among those not already mentioned are Conejo, El Nuevo Xol, Frontline Officials, Juvenile Style, female rapper JV, "positive" rapper MC Blvd, Tha Mexakinz, Street Sweepaz, and Wicked Minds. The scene continues to grow as new groups cut CDs every month.

THE 619

Los Angeles is not the only place with a vibrant Chicano rap scene. Other California regions such as San Diego ("The 619," its area code) and the Bay Area have spawned successful Chicano rap acts. Led by Low Profile Records and its roster of Chicano rappers, San Diego boasts the second-largest Chicano rap music scene. Low Profile Records owner Royal T (*Coast to Coast*, 1998), Sancho, Proper Dos and O.G. Spanish Fly (*Back From the Dead*, 2001, and *Higher than Highland*, 2002) are among the rappers affiliated with Low Profile. Lil' Rob (*Crazy Life*, 1997; *Still Smokin'*, 2000; and *The Last Laff*, 2002) had a short-lived affiliation with Low Profile that ended in animosity when Rob felt he was cheated out of royalties from sales of his CDs.[14] Rob, who was voted best Chicano rapper of 2000 in an online poll, has continued to record songs about barrio living over laid-back oldies beats. With his 2005 single "Summertime," Rob finally received airplay outside of Southern California in places like Pueblo, Colorado, and the San Francisco Bay area. Other Chicano rappers from San Diego include Knightowl (*The Knightowl*, 1995; *Wicked West*, 1998; *Bald Headed Kingpin*, 2001; and *Ghetto Bird*, 2003) and Aztec Tribe. Mr. Shadow (*Till I Die*, 1998, and *Pit Bossing*, 2001) has also become a favorite in San Diego and throughout Southern California.

Shysti offers a different sound from San Diego. Shysti describes himself as a producer/poet/community activist and is co-founder of River Bottom Entertainment. With Lil' One he formed the group Califas and released the CD *rap en español*. River Bottom also produced two compilations, *Latin Kings* and *Lil' One Presents Sickosylum*, that feature Frost, Mr. Shadow, Don Cisco, and Aztec Tribe. Shysti has produced tracks for Frost, Baby Beesh (a.k.a. Bash), Don Cisco, and Tupac Shakur protegées The Outlaws. He describes the music of his debut album, *Border Music*, as "a unique blend of history, tragedy, crime, punishment, cultural awareness, and political activism." Shysti takes the troubles of the Mexico-U.S. border seriously. His music is part of a long activist-artist tradition in San Diego that includes Los Alacranes, the Border Arts Workshop, and Calaca Press.

Brown Pride music critic Gerardo Garcia (2004) describes Shysti's album by comparing him to important revolutionaries:

> Pancho Villa. Emiliano Zapata. Che Guevara. Malcolm X. Leonard Peltier. Cesar Chavez. Zapatistas. Those names evoke the true meaning of revolutionary. And when talking about the Chicano rap game, rapper/producer/poet Shysti definitely befits the definition of revolutionary. . . . From the outset, Shysti lets you know what his music is about and who it's for. With sharp lyrics in both English and Spanish that can match any of today's mainstream or underground rap stars, Shysti slaps you upside the head with the knowledge that will enable you to understand the Chicano culture like you never thought you could have before. With uplifting messages for our people to tales about the drug game and a little bit of street poetry, Shysti breaks down all frontiers with *Border Music*.

In addition, Shysti is a tireless promoter of Latino rap. His River Bottom Entertainment hosted the first Latin Rap Conference in July 2004 and continues as its central organizer each year. With partner Lil' One (a.k.a. Lil' Uno), he hosts the weekly Internet radio show *River Bottom Radio*.

NORTEÑOS

Many groups hailing from Northern California have cut albums. The multimillion-selling group N2Deep was one of the first "Northern Cali" Chicano-Anglo groups to make noise. N2Deep is Jay Tee (James Trujillo) and TL (Timothy Lyons) from Vallejo. They released their hugely popular debut, *Back to the Hotel*, in 1992. The album reached number 55 on Billboard's Hot 100 Album chart and number 29 on Billboard's R&B/Hip Hop Albums chart and went on to sell 900,000 copies.[15] Since their successful debut they have released five full-length CDs (*24-7-365*, *Golden State*, *Rumble*, *Slightly Pimpish/Mostly Doggish*, and *Unreleased Game 1993*) and two greatest-hits compilations. Jay Tee has collaborated with many Chicano artists including the supergroup Latino Velvet, which consists of Frost, Jay Tee, Don Ciscone, and Baby Beesh. In 1998 Latino Velvet released its debut, *Clique*, and in 2000 followed with *Velvet City*.

Another early and important *norteño* rap group is Funky Aztecs. Their 1995 CD *Day of the Dead/Día de los Muertos* includes "Salsa con Soul Food," an interpolation of the 1970 War classic "Slipping into Darkness" with updated lyrical themes. The song also features a guest verse from West Coast rap legend Tupac Shakur. Tupac provides a lucid critique of the police's hostile stance toward Chicano and Black youth interaction through hip hop and a show of positive Black-Chicano interracial relationships. Members Merciless, Indio, and Sapo-Loco rely on a range of samples from 1970s and 1980s Black funk bands to tell many stories and jokes and make pointed comments about the postindustrial environment for people of color. Their collaborations, friendships, and solidarity with Black youth are exemplary of the way in which Brown-Black alliances have changed urban culture, politics, and music. In their songs the Aztecs often refer to their friends and homeboys as "niggas" and "spics" and "a bunch of Black and Mexican blends." They, like Cypress Hill, use the terms "niggas" and "spics" in ways meant to signify their solidarity with Blacks and Mexicans. Funky Aztecs' album credits include numerous guest appearances and two additional studio albums, *Addicted* (1999) and *Chicano Blues* (1992).

From my examination of Chicano rap discussion lists, I found that the most important Northern California circle of artists of the late 1990s and early 2000s has been the Darkroom Familia. The Darkroom Family is an organization of several rap acts that work out of Darkroom Studios. Co-founder Sir Dyno is the best-known and most prolific of the Darkroom Family.[16] Other Darkroom Family members include Oso, K.I.D. (short for "Killer in Disguise"), Young D., Crooked, Dub, Duke, Los

Traficantes (who rap in Spanish), and N.K.A.[17] They also make gangsta movies such as *Smile Now, Cry Later*. Darkroom Familia has fallen on hard times due to financial and criminal justice troubles. In 2003 Sir Dyno was part of a massive indictment of people associated with the Mexican mafia. Members and suspected members of the Mexican mafia were indicted on hundreds of organized crime charges included drug trafficking, murder, fraud, and extortion. Time will tell whether Sir Dyno and his organization will recover from the indictments and financial troubles to become a force again in the northern California rap scene.

Chicano rappers from Northern California, like those throughout the United States, are a diverse group. Styles range from N2Deep's smooth, popular music to the funk styles of Funky Aztecs to the gangstas of Darkroom Familia. As our journey through Chicano rap regions moves east out of California, the diversity of Chicano rap continues and increases.

TEXAS

South Park Mexican (SPM) and Dope House Records from Houston have made a big splash in the Chicano rap game. South Park Mexican (Carlos Coy) released his first project in 1999. The CD was a huge hit throughout Texas and allowed him to expand Dope House Records and release two dozen solo and collaboration albums. Dope House has also produced two documentary films, *Latin Throne* and *Latin Throne II*. Dope House releases have been discussed widely on Chicano rap lists with Grimm's *Brown Recluse* (2003) receiving a lot of praise from Chicano rap fans in 2003–2004. Dope House artists include Powda, Juan Gotti, Rasheed, and Twin Beredaz. The career of SPM and the future of Dope House Records are under a great deal of pressure to survive as SPM remains in jail for a conviction related to sexual activity with a minor.

The Vallejo, California, native turned Houston denizen Baby Bash (sometimes Beesh) connected with SPM and has been making popular music ever since. Bash signed with Universal, which has given him considerable promotion and advertisement. One result was his third album, *The Smokin' Nephew* (2003), which was listed in *Billboard*'s Top 100 Albums chart in late 2003. The first single from the Happy Perez–produced album, "Suga, Suga," charted at number 1 in places like Denver, New Mexico, and Seattle, and *Billboard* listed the song in the top 20 nationally. Bash got his start working with Frost and Jay Tee in the group Latino Velvet. His influences are broad, including Bay Area rappers such as E-40, Mac Dre, and Too Short, along with funk pioneers Con Funk Shun and Sly and the Family Stone.[18]

Chingo Bling is another Houston rapper who has come onto the Chicano rap scene since the late 1990s. I first heard Chingo Bling on the *Pocos Pero Locos* radio show compilation *The Show*. Chingo Bling distinguishes himself in Chicano rap with his humorous, often plain silly songs. He is a rapper who likes to have fun. For many he is a refreshing face on the rap scene. An article in the *Houston Chronicle* (Lomax 2003) describes Chingo's style as a "satire of the underground rap scene." He takes a light-hearted view of the trends he sees in rap and uses stereotypes of northern Mexican accents and styles to humanize Chicanos/Mexicanos in the South Texas region. His first CDs were *Duro en la Pintura* and *El Mero Chingon*. In 2003 he released *Air Chingo: The Mex-Tape* and teamed up with Baby Bash for the Money and Masa tour (www.chingobling.com). He has a broad appeal and has played for audiences throughout the United States, including headlining a small show of Denver underground artists in 2004. Chingo Bling's entrepreneurial activities include soft-pornographic video distributing through his website (www.mañosas.net).

Capone released his first CD, *Chicano World*, in 1999 and reportedly has sold more than 100,000 CDs without major distribution. He has built a fan base through touring and aggressive independent marketing of his records and label, Latino Jam Records. He has performed on stage as the headliner for the 1999 Lowrider Magazine Tour and as an opening act for Amanda Perez, Ice Cube, and the Kumbia Kings. His albums include *Second to None* (2000), *Mis Carnales* (2000), *Barrio Dope* (2001), and the compilation *Raza Related* (2002), which includes Chingo Bling, Kinto Sol, Conejo, and Tattoo Ink. He has also worked with DJ Clue, Marley Marl, and Nas. More recent activities for Capone include La Pinta, a prison pen-pal program, and the much-discussed CD *Chicano World 3* (2005). Significantly, Latino Jam Records is the first to focus on New York City by opening an affiliate office there.

MIDWEST

Mexicans have lived in Chicago, Milwaukee, Detroit, and other Midwestern urban centers for more than 100 years, with a large migration and settlement beginning in the 1920s. Vibrant Mexican American communities such as Chicago's Little Village and Pilsen dot the Midwest. Today, more than 1.6 million people of Mexican descent live in Chicago alone (Ready and Brown-Gort 2005). Naturally, these dynamic communities have produced a diverse and complex musical culture. The Chicago rap and hip-hop scene produced Wicked Entertainment. The label's roster features Los Marijuanos, a group whose tales often allude to the consumption of marijuana (*yesca, hierba, mota*). In 1999 they released *Puro Pleito* and followed with *The Smoke Out* in 2001.

DJ Payback Garcia has produced many of Chicano rap's most notable artists. Payback projects include the compilation *Aztec Souls: The Best in Latin Hip Hop* (2002) and *Hecho en Aztlán* (2003). On these CDs Payback remixes songs from more than a dozen Chicano rap artists, among them Crooked Stilo, Psycho Realm, Los Marijuanos, Street Platoon, Knightowl, El Chivo, Mr. Shadow, Tattoo Ink, Delinquent Habits, and Conejo. The musically and lyrically complex *Hecho en Mexico* (2003) by Kinto Sol stands out in Payback's career. Payback uses a wide array of sounds to complement the tales of urban Midwestern Chicano youth rapped in Spanish. Kinto Sol members El Chivo, Skribe, and Payback are brothers born in Mexico and raised in Milwaukee, along with a fourth member, El Gordo. Songs of *raza* pride and unity ("Hecho en Mexico" and "Raza Es Raza") and descriptions of urban, working-class Mexican life are deftly woven throughout this powerful work. Kinto Sol released its debut album, *Del Norte al Sur*, in 2000 and *Hijos del Maiz* in 2007.

Los Nativos (formerly Native Ones) out of St. Paul–Minneapolis combine straight hip-hop beats and rhymes with social commentary and pro-indigenous lyrics. Their album *Dia de los Muertos* (2003) and live concert footage demonstrate that members Felipe Cuauhtli and Chilam Balam offer something new for Chicanas/os in hip hop. Los Nativos work with RhymeSayers Entertainment, home of Eyedea and Abilities, Atmosphere, and Brother Ali, among other well-known and respected underground MCs. Los Nativos have been with RhymeSayers from its inception in 1995, and their association with a multiracial, multigenre, rap/hip-hop organization undoubtedly contributes to their unique and compelling sound.[19] In 2005 they released the EP *Red Star Fist*.

Latino Saint (Tye Ramos) raps, writes, and produces music and has his own fashion line, LAFA Gear. He is part of a multiracial rap organization, La Familia del Sol, which hails from Battle Creek, Michigan.[20] The music of Latino Saint and La Familia del Sol has a pop flavor that recalls Fabolos, Lil' Bow Wow, Puffy Combs, and Bad Boy Entertainment artists. Latino Saint recently relocated to Tennessee, where he is better able to make a living in the music industry.

CHICANA RAPPERS

In hip-hop culture the role of women is often overlooked. Young women have been rapping, break dancing, graffiti writing, and singing since the 1970s.[21] However, few Chicanas have recorded songs. I have had the good fortune to encounter a few Chicana rappers, including Baby Wicked (Wicked Minds), Synful (Wicked Entertainment), Ms. Sancha, JV, Ms. Krazie, Sista D, and Powda. JV was the first Chicana to release a rap album. In 1994 she hooked up with Kid Frost and others from Thump Records to record *Nayba'hood Queen*. She followed with *It Gets No Reala* (1996) and *Ladybug* (2002). JV has appeared on numerous Chicano rap compilation albums. She takes on the men in songs such as "Women's Lib," "Naybahood Queen," and "Bow 2 No Man."

Ms. Sancha is Low Profile Records' first female rapper. In 2003 she released her solo debut, *Taking It Doggystyle*. Her provocative album cover shows her leaning over music production equipment wearing a G-string that prominently displays her bare buttocks. Her album is part violent gangsta tales and part porn over G-funk beats. She identifies herself as a feminine, ultra-sexy Latina with a violent gangsta side. Fans on brownpride.com liken her lyrics to international superstar rapper Lil' Kim.

Ms. Krazie from Santa Ana, California, released her first solo project, *Brown Is Beautiful*, in 2006 and followed it with *Firme Homegirl Oldies* in 2007. She appears on the new Ese Silent CD *Varrio Sound* (2004). She has worked with 505 Underground Records out of New Mexico.[22] Her webpage (www.mskrazie.com) discusses her life and provides photos, video clips, and music downloads. Baby Wicked is part of the Wicked Minds crew, an "organization of Latino rappers" created in 1994. Baby Wicked has one album to her credit, *Girls It Ain't Easy*, and appears on many of the organization's compilation albums.

Powda was a Dope House Records artist. Her lyrical style can be heard on compilations *Latin Throne* (1999) and *House Party Hits* (2001) and in guest appearances. Powda, from Galveston, Texas, has worked with Lifestyl (*Screwed, Leaned, and Chopped*, 2001), Lil' Black (*On the Road Again*, 2001), Twin Beredaz (*Twin Beredaz*, 2002), Mun-E (*Mun-E Makes the World Go Round*, 2001), Grimm (*Brown Recluse*, 2003), and Baby Beesh (*On tha Cool*, 2002). She was set to release her first solo CD, *Angel Dust*, in March 2004, but difficulties at Dope House slowed production. As of this writing she had not released her much-anticipated album.

Sista D from Denver, Colorado, has released four albums—*In the Mile High City* (2000), the critically acclaimed *RapStarr* (2003), *El*

Dorado (2006), and *The Chosen One* (2007). Her virtuoso style, which she describes as "unique" and "my own," reveals the influence of the early work of the great New Orleans–based rapper Mia X of Master P's No Limit Records.[23] Besides rapping to Midwest-type musical production and beats, Sista D sings, runs her company—D-Style Productions—cares for her children, breeds pit bulls, and began the Women's Rapp Alliance to bring young women rappers, producers, and hip-hop heads together. Sista D told me, "I created the Alliance because I felt women weren't being represented right in this industry. Yes there are a few now, which is great but we are always limited in our opportunities. The sad thing is most females on a local level never leave the local status, meaning they usually put out one CD in their careers. Hopefully, an organization like The Alliance can kinda influence more to get involved" (2004a).

CHICANO RAP STYLES

To speak of Chicano rap styles is to speak of both musical style (the beats, melodies, instrumentation, arrangements, and interpolations or samples) and the style of the performers (walk, dress, hairstyles, lyrical themes, slang). The most prevalent Chicano rap styles are lowrider, gangsta, political, oldies, smooth, indigenist, old-school hip hop, and funk.

The lowrider style has the longest history. The first successful artists with G-Spot Studios, Kid Frost, A.L.T., and A Lighter Shade of Brown fall under this category. References to and images of lowriders and cruising are abundant in this style. Rappers in this category often dress in *cholo* garb—e.g., jeans, Dickies, bandanas, T-shirts or Pendletons, and tennis shoes, work boots, or walking shoes; classic *cholo* attire entails sunglasses and attitude. Many including Lil' Rob have toured with Lowrider Magazine car shows. The art and symbolism accompanying the advertisement and shows resembles that found in lowrider culture: religious images (La Virgen, crucifixes, saints), idealized and stylized indigenous figures such as Ixta and Popo, and colorful landscapes. Much of the language you hear from such artists is *caló*, Spanglish (a mixture of Spanish, English, anglicized Spanish words, and Hispanicized English words), hip-hop slang, and new words to fit the environment and moods of urban working-class Chicanos.

Groups like Brownside and Low Profile Records and Darkroom Familia artists speak about, often glorify, often critique gangsta lifestyles. Their lyrics place them in the Latino gang genre of literature that Monica Brown describes in *Gang Nation: Delinquent Citizens in*

Puerto Rican, Chicano, and Chicana Narratives (2002). In this genre Brown finds hypermasculinity characterized by misogynist gender relations and gun violence as exemplified in Luis Rodriguez' *Always Running* (1993) and Miguel Durán's *Don't Spit on My Corner* (1992). Similarly, gun violence and violent gender relations figure prominently in Chicano gangsta rap iconography. Darkroom Familia is particularly "in your face" with gory, violent imagery—album covers feature slit throats, shotgun barrels, bandana-masked gang members, and other sadistic fantasy scenes. Brownside presents a hypermasculine, intimidating posture toward the world with menacing looks and guns displayed prominently in its photos and artwork as well as the frequent use of violent imagery in its lyrics. Low Profile Records artists revel in their identities as thugs, gangstas, and felons,[24] as do Slow Pain, Wicked Minds, and artists from 505 Underground Records.

Chicano rap of all sorts is political. Young Brown men act politically when they speak their minds about their experiences and worldviews and the state of their communities under a cultural, political, social, and economic order that does not value their thoughts and actively undermines their quality of life. They engage in the struggle for power and resources when they rap. They address stereotypes of young, urban, working-class Chicanos. Often they confirm stereotypes and contribute to the reactionary politics that have historically suppressed people of Mexican descent in the United States. Most of the time, however, they complicate our understanding of their lives and their communities.

While all Chicano rap is political, not all Chicano rappers are conscious of it, nor do they make power and politics central themes of their music. Rappers such as Psycho Realm, Street Platoon, Krazy Race, 2Mex, Xololanxinxo, and Shysti are conscious of the ideological roles they play. As such, they critique the dominant economic, political, and social institutions. They rap about, radically critique, and theorize on the education system, political system, globalization, capitalism, police and criminal justice system, militarism, race relations, racial inequality, and organized religion, among many other topics.

Indigenist and/or Mexica (as Aztecs called themselves) rappers discuss political and spiritual themes. The Mexica movement consists of Chicana and Chicano artist-activists, activists, rappers, and other cultural warriors. Their political lives and art are heavily influenced by an indigenist worldview in which the Chicanas/os' indigenous roots are emphasized and exalted. Their identities, language, style, clothes, music, poetry, rap, and art reflect an indigenist political philosophy. They strive toward a politics and lifestyle in which, as professor Ward

Churchill explains, one "takes the rights of indigenous peoples as the highest priority of [one's] political life, but who draws on the traditions — the bodies of knowledge and corresponding codes of value — evolved over many thousands of years by native peoples the world over" (1996, 509).

Rap artists El Vuh, Groundkeepers, Los Nativos, and Aztlán Underground reflect such an identity and orientation toward the world. The Groundkeepers' website (www.groundkeepers.com) explains the movement this way:

> The Mexica Movement aims at trying to get the institutions of this society and the people to learn the history of Anahuac (the true indigenous name of these lands). Their aim is to bring a sense of pride and justice to people of Mexican descent by giving them knowledge of self and the great accomplishments their forefathers have achieved.

The Groundkeepers as Mexica artists take seriously their political commitment. Their website is full of knowledge about pre-Columbian thought and society and discussions of the current environment for indigenous peoples and people of Mexican descent. They have a page of links with descriptions of the websites of important political organizations such as the Zapatistas, Mexica Movement, American Indian Movement, and Los Angeles Indigenous People's Alliance. Even their name suggests an indigenist orientation, as they explain:

> The group's name also reflects their view toward music and life in general — the ground, where roots grow, be it physical, spiritual, or mental, is the foundation for your way of life — the riches of knowing yourself. It is those views, ideas, and beliefs that is the Groundkeepers essence, and it is their goal to always keep them strong, as well as continually build them further.

Their CD *Burning Bridges* features a diverse mix of musical styles with lyrics that reflect their urban Mexica outlook.

El Vuh is also part of the growing Mexica movement. Victor E, E-Rise, and Zero cut their first album, *Jaguar Prophecies*, in 2003. As part of their Mexica philosophy and practice, members of El Vuh reject the labels "Hispanic" and "Latino" to describe themselves. Reflecting their indigenous ancestry, in particular Aztec, they identify as Mexica. Members of El Vuh trace their ancestors to the Mexica and follow native spirituality and worldview, learn the Nahuatl language, and examine current conditions through the lens of native Mexican knowledge and wisdom. The lyrics and symbolism of El Vuh reflect their Mexica outlook. For example, the cover art for their album *Jaguar Prophecies* is a unique blend of Aztec symbolism and hip-hop culture. The front cover depicts three indigenous men; one raps into a mic, the second is writing rhymes, and the third is working turntables. The three Mexica hip hoppers are surrounded by a border of Aztec symbols and writing.

Another well-known Mexica rap group is Aztlán Underground. They are an underground rock/rap group formed in 1990 by Bean, Yaotl, Bulldog, Bobby, Joe, and Rudy. Their CDs include *Decolonize* and *Subverses*. They are favorites with Chicano college students and often play at student gatherings and Chicana/o studies meetings, where I first encountered them in 2000. Aztlán Underground also runs the Chicana/o arts group Xicano Records and Film, through which they produce films and distribute information and music of other Xicano artists. Their song "Lyrical Drive-By" on *The Ollin Project* CD is noteworthy for its clever use of gun and violence metaphors to describe artist and activist goals of struggling against a violent, racist society.

The music of Chicana and Chicano rappers varies widely, showing multiple and varied influences: "Latin" music, 1970s and 1980s funk, soul and R&B, rock, and heavy metal. Many early Chicano rappers like A Lighter Shade of Brown and Proper Dos used melodies, beats, and interpolations and samples of oldies music. Lil' Rob, Knightowl, Angel Loco, and Hispanic MCs also feature these sounds. Delinquent Habits and Frost occasionally borrow oldies sounds to help tell their stories. Oldies artists sample or otherwise borrow music, vocals, and lyrics from artists like Mary Wells and Bill Withers. Knightowl distinguishes himself among oldies rap artists, as he delivers rapid gangsta lyrics over mellow oldies tracks in an expert fashion unduplicated by other Chicano rap artists.

Nasty Boy Klick (now NB Ridaz) out of Phoenix and Afaze out of Las Vegas exhibit flashy personas. I call rappers of this type "smooth." They might be described as players and/or ladies' men who live the good life with beautiful women and expensive clothes, alcohol, and cars. Their music uses soft, harmonious melodies and laid-back beats. They attempt to impress women with their style, romantic overtures, and musical and lyrical abilities. Nasty Boy Klick released four CDs: *Tha First Chapter* (1997), *Tha Second Coming* (1998), *I Know You Want*

Me (2001), and *NB Ridaz.com* (2003). They had early success with the single "Down for Yours," which reached number 10 on the hot rap charts. Afaze consists of Las Vegas–based cousins Krome and Jesse James. Their first single, "It's Just Afaze," has brought them local airplay and a consistent touring schedule. Krome's single "Panty Pullers" (2004) received local airplay in Las Vegas.

Early Chicano rap pioneers Kid Frost, Julio G., and LSOB were part of the G-funk West Coast rap sound defined by Dr. Dre and N.W.A. The use of funk rhythms, melodies, and bass lines structured much of the West Coast G-funk sound. Today, Mr. Shadow is perhaps the funkiest of Chicano MCs. His style recalls Snoop Doggy Dogg, Kurupt, and Tha Dogg Pound. South Park Mexican, who uses a wide range of sounds and styles to tell his street stories, often relies on funk. Low Profile artists use 1980s funk styles to tell many of their gangsta stories. The production on Ms. Sancha's CD is laced with funk sounds, and the talkbox of Fingazz is reminiscent of the funk innovations of Roger Troutman and his group, Zapp.

Raquel Rivera describes Puerto Rican rappers in "Hip Hop and New York Puerto Ricans" (2002) and *New York Ricans from the Hip Hop Zone* (2003). In describing two different types of Puerto Rican rappers she uses the terms "Boricua/Latino-centric" and "core." Rappers in the first category are "closely affiliated with the rap and reggae music being produced in Puerto Rico" (2003, 16). "Core" is Rivera's term to describe the multi-ethnic New York rap scene that is at the heart of hip hop locally and internationally.

Chicano rappers occupy similar zones. Many work wholly from a Chicano perspective and exclusively with other Chicano rappers. Their music is made for and by Chicanas/os. Royal T makes this point about Low Profile Records in the documentary *Money, Power, Respect* (Hall 2003). They distinguish themselves from African American rappers, for example. Their fashion and iconography reflect older Chicano symbolism and newer gang culture symbols, style, and attitude. The lyrics of artists from Low Profile, Darkroom Familia, and Wicked Minds, along with Conejo, Capone, Slush the Villain, Knightowl, Proper Dos, and Slow Pain, among many others, speak primarily to young Chicana/os, especially working-class and underclass street youths. They use language unique to working-class Chicana/os, including concepts such as *carnalismo* and Aztlán and address their stories and messages to inner-city Chicana/o youth. They perform for primarily Chicana/o audiences and market themselves to Chicanas/os.

Others like 2Mex, Krazy Race, and 5th Battalion participate in a multiracial core hip-hop scene in Los Angeles that encompasses African American artists such as Busdriver, Black Eyed Peas, and Jurassic 5. Chicano rappers from the L.A. core differ from their gangsta or Chicano-centric brethren in that they make little distinction between themselves and rappers from other ethnic/racial groups. They refer to their music as rap or hip hop and not Latin rap or Chicano rap. In response to my question about the term "Chicano rap," Krazy Race responded that he does not really like the label. He does hip hop. He said "Chicano rap" is used to describe rappers of Chicano descent who are very different stylistically. These are often gangsta and/ or lowrider rappers.[25] While rappers like Krazy Race and 2Mex also use Chicana/o language, style, concepts, and symbols in their music, lyrics, and personas and discuss their experiences as Chicanos in the postindustrial U.S. city, they recognize and participate in a multiracial, multi-ethnic youth subculture. Theirs is a postmodern, postindustrial culture and experience in which racial and ethnic boundaries are more fluid, flexible, and porous.

Cypress Hill defined a genre of music. B-Real's nasal delivery, complex rhymes, and vivid descriptions of the trials of being young and Latino in Los Angeles as well as the pleasures of smoking marijuana were unique in hip hop and have influenced countless others. Sen Dog delivers in a rough, often shouting voice that makes you feel the impact of his words. He has brought the art of chanting and shouting to another level of creativity. As well, the production style of DJ Muggs in collaboration with his two partners became a style of its own that has influenced the music of newer Chicano and Mexican rap artists. His patented beats, unique instrumentation and arrangements, knowledge of music, and careful, surprising, and well-placed samples make him arguably one of the most creative producers in rap music history.

Kinto Sol and Akwid use Cypress Hill–like production. Payback Garcia does not simply rely on Muggs' beats to formulate his important rhythm tracks. However, Muggs' instrumentation and beats clearly influence Garcia's work. Many of El Gordo's, El Chivo's, and Skribe's lyrics reflect B-Real's style. Akwid—brothers Sergio and Francisco Gomez, originally from Michoacán, Mexico—incorporates Muggs-like production into their complex sound of regional Mexican musics, *banda*, mariachi, and ballads. Their rap also is influenced by N.W.A., Snoop, DJ Quik, and Hi-C. Akwid began to gain wide attention in the music world in 2006 with the song "Anda y Ve," which received airplay on Hispanic urban (hurban) radio stations. They, like Kinto Sol and Delinquent Habits, incorporate Mexican and other Latino music and vocal styles into their work. Control Machete, Gente Loca, Psycho Realm, and Los Marijuanos also owe a debt to Cypress Hill.

THE MULTI-ETHNIC MAKEUP OF CHICANO RAP

Hip hop arises out of African musical traditions such as call and response, communal musical composition, polyrhythms, and resistance.[26] Analysis of Chicano rap shows that it borrows and transforms African diasporic traditions. Chicano rappers and music producers' use of funk, soul, R&B, blues, jazz, and Afro-Latino rhythms and the musical vocabulary of Black rappers demonstrates a history of Black-Chicana/o interaction and mutual creation of a powerful youth subculture. This interracial cultural creation is witnessed in the music and lyrics as well as a shared worldview, collaboration on musical projects, linguistic innovations, and shared identities as "thugs," gangstas, and hip-hop heads.

African and Mexican diasporic peoples continually renew the U.S. urban landscape and re-create culture. One of the results is the youth subculture known as hip hop. The new culture relies on African and Mexican cultural traditions while utilizing technologies, ideas, and behaviors adopted from the dominant U.S. culture. Hip-hop heads transform aspects of the dominant culture to serve their cultural, economic, social, and political needs and desires using their cultures of origin and the dynamic processes of multiracial youth interaction. What results is not African or Mexican, Black or Chicana/o. In this way the culture challenges commodified notions of "Blackness," "Mexicanness," "youth," "authenticity," and "hip-hop culture." The news media, gang exploitation films, and the corporate, dollar-driven rap industry have distorted hip-hop culture and its multiracial practitioners, causing those of us distanced from youth, inner cities, and/or people of color to misunderstand, devalue, and denigrate youth and hip-hop heads. The resultant stereotypes characterize Black and Brown youth as criminal, irresponsible, and irrationally violent.

The culture industry has manufactured caricatures of hip hop and other youth cultures and their practitioners that are belied by analysis of the music and lyrics. The hip-hop subculture and the identities that stem from it often transcend cultural and racial barriers established by the dominant racial paradigm that have often been uncritically accepted by people of color. The draw of music, especially the polyrhythms of the Black diaspora, has brought youth of color into mutually respectful and gratifying relations and has fostered what Gaye Johnson calls "alternative communities of allegiance." (2002, 327). These alternative communities reject the strict cultural nationalism of their parents' generation and the ascribed identities of youths and people of color and open up the possibility for sustained interracial cooperation.[27] Much of what occurs in hip-hop culture is a multiracial exchange of joy, emotion, and knowledge. The corporate mass media reflect little of this behavior, preferring instead to demonize hip hop and deflect our attention from the real causes of violence, misogyny, drug abuse, and poverty.

From the multiracial interaction apparent in hip-hop culture, new understandings of race, politics, gender, and morality continue to develop. These new understandings have the potential to chart a new course in racial understanding between Black and Brown people. The interracial cooperation at the root of Chicano rap has allowed for the hopeful destruction of debilitating racial barriers in this era when Black and Brown people are forced to compete for valued resources such as jobs, housing, and education. The music of Chicano rappers bears witness to the intercultural exchange and breaking down of racial barriers developing in inner cities of the Southwest and to the choices of affiliation made by youths of color that challenge racial categorization.

While rap music and hip-hop culture have brought people of different races and ethnicities together and have the potential to develop an anti-racist, anti-sexist, democratic, and anti-authoritarian politics among large sectors of the U.S. population, without attention to the sexism and violence in Chicana/o and other rap lyrics and the broader societal forces of misogyny, aggression, and dominance that inform our young boys' and girls' sensibilities and outlooks, rap and hip hop can exacerbate gender inequalities and lead to an even more violent world. In the chapters that follow I analyze Chicana/o rap discussions of gender and violence by contextualizing them and teasing out the influences on young people's worldviews of various institutions and cultural, political, and social phenomena.

CHAPTER THREE

MACHOS Y MALAS MUJERES

The Gendered Image

In the spring of 2000 I began a series of focus groups and workshops with Chicana/o youth from Colorado Springs, Colorado. My first group included approximately a dozen youths ordered by local judges to attend classes and workshops organized by Ways Out Academy Inc. as part of their sentences for various criminal convictions. I had the good fortune to speak with these young people about rap music. Our discussions were illuminating. We began by playing rap songs and discussing the lyrics. Together we examined violent and sexist lyrics. Since many of these youths identified as gang members, they preferred the style and lyrics of Chicano gangsta rappers such as Brownside and Proper Dos. They found nothing wrong with the violence discussed in the lyrics. In fact, the opposite was true. The more graphically violent the lyrics, the more most tended to like the music.

The same could be said about the sexist messages in the songs. They saw no problem with the way women were depicted in the music. "That's life," they said. The words and sentiments were nothing new to these thirteen- to seventeen-year-olds. When I asked them about the names that were often used to label women—names like "ho," "hoodrat," "hoochie," and "bitch"—I received several interesting responses. One particularly articulate young man began his input by apologizing to my research assistant, Leonor, saying that he hoped he would not offend her with what he was about to say. He explained that the word "bitch" was just another word for woman! He and his friends meant no harm by the term. According to him, the word did not mean anything derogatory, nor did it cause him to see women as inferior. Most of the other young men in the group nodded or verbalized their agreement. They saw this as an unimportant issue and wanted to move on to talk about other issues including police brutality, the education system, and gangbanging.

This anecdote suggests the importance and insidious nature of sexism in today's society. Sexist representations of women abound in U.S. popular culture and everyday discourse. These young men made it clear that the images of women in the Chicano rap that we listened to were nothing new and nothing to be concerned about. "Bitch," referring to women, was a normal part of their everyday speech. They had heard it all before. The question is, Where had they heard this language and picked up these images? How did words like "ho" and "hoochie" and images of women as sex objects become naturalized, normalized, and internalized in the minds of these adolescents?

GENDER SOCIALIZATION

Scholars of diverse backgrounds and interests have focused on under-standing gender socialization as a key component of the development of youth identity and worldview. Of concern to many feminist scholars and their allies is the way in which early childhood and adolescent gender socialization has created in both boys and girls a narrow understanding of gender roles and gender relations. Many powerful agents—mass media, families, schools, and churches among them—teach adolescents to abide by patriarchal notions of what it means to be a man or woman and how women and men should relate to each other.[1] I examine Chicano rap music to develop a picture of the ways Chicanos understand masculinity, femininity, and gender relations. Cultural studies scholars have demonstrated that expressive culture can tell us a great deal about a group's worldview. Both quantitative and qualitative analyses of rap music allow for a bottom-up, grassroots investigation by which we gain direct data from the youths themselves about their feelings, attitudes, and behaviors concerning gender roles and relations.

Previous research on related subject matter suggests that if gender socialization for Chicanos results from a combination of factors such as misogyny and hypermasculinity in the dominant culture and patriarchal Mexican male culture, then we should expect to find in the musical production of young Chicanos representations of women that reflect misogyny and hypermasculinity. Specifically, we should find representations of women as sexual objects, as "good women" (*mujeres buenas*), as "bad women" (*mujeres malas*), and in relation to men and not as autonomous subjects. Men will be represented as dominant, violent, and otherwise hypermasculine.

CONTEXTUALIZING GENDER IN CHICANO RAP

A study of misogyny in Chicano rap music must take into account the representations of women and gender in the broader U.S. society. In this case, we must ask: What is the relationship between representations of women in the dominant, corporate-controlled communications and entertainment media, youth culture, and Mexican American culture and the misogynist discourse developed in Chicano rap? How have sexualized representations of women in advertising, movies, music videos, and the booming pornography industry contributed to young Chicanos' desire for and attitudes about women? How has the backlash against women's rights as represented in our popular culture contributed to the devaluation of women in the minds of young Chicanos? How has the normalization of hypermasculinity as the ideal trait of manhood affected young Chicanos' notions of themselves as men-in-training?

The work of new men's studies scholars such as Jackson Katz and Michael Kimmel and feminist archetypal criticism forms the theoretical foundation upon which I analyze gender representation in Chicano rap music.[2] Kimmel would likely argue (1987, 1994) that the hypermasculinity found in the violent lyrics of Chicano rap results in part from the "crisis in masculinity" found throughout U.S. society. Kimmel argues (1987) that in several epochs in U.S. history men have perceived their status as the dominant gender coming under attack and have reinforced their masculine dominance through creating an attack on "corrupt" values and strongly reiterating "traditional" patriarchal values: man as the head of the heterosexual, nuclear family; macho protector; primary breadwinner; and stoic, unemotional bedrock of society. The social movements of the 1960s and 1970s, especially the women's and gay and lesbian movements, were threats to men's unfettered dominance and to patriarchal notions of masculinity. The result was a crisis in masculinity. Faludi has charted the response as a backlash against women and homosexuality and the normalization of a hypermasculine understanding of manhood (1992).

In films by director Sut Jhally (1997a and 1999, respectively), social critic bell hooks and psychologist Jackson Katz argue that this hypermasculine response can be seen most clearly in our popular culture. Katz points out that the strict gender divisions that have boxed both boys and girls into limited understandings of who and what they can be and how they can behave are ferociously guarded in our popular culture. Likewise, Giroux contends (1996) that the corporate communications and entertainment media rarely present alternatives to the dominant, aggressive model of manhood or the passive, submissive model of womanhood. Instead, since the 1980s, popular culture has increased the policing of gender boundaries and presented boys and girls with static, oppressive models of gender. Katz notes that the most common images of women in popular culture depict the ideal, beautiful, good woman as small, weak, passive, irrational, and emotional, while the ideal man has become unbelievably large and muscular, violent, and emotionally cold (in Jhally 1999). His comparison of the changing body sizes of male and female dolls during the last half of the twentieth century is one of many examples. Female dolls such as Barbie have grown smaller with larger breasts while male dolls such as G.I. Joe have grown larger with more and larger weapons. Examinations of female and male film stars show similar results. A National Institute of Drug Abuse report (NIDA 2000) highlighted the harmful physical and mental health effects of the dangerous phenomenon of anabolic steroid use by teenage boys emerging in the 1980s and the newer generation of growth stimulants, demonstrating how idealized representations of the hypermasculine man may affect youth.[3]

Hypermasculinity is a defining trait of manhood in today's society. Acts of violence and daring are part of male gender performance that prove to young men that the risk-taking adolescent boy is not weak, feminine, or gay and is instead tough, hard, and violent.[4] The result for boys is often deadly. Drunken driving, suicide, male violence, schoolyard bullying, road rage, binge drinking, and the like have dramatically increased since the 1970s.[5] These efforts to prove and perform one's manhood also harm women, as incidents of rape, murder, and other acts of violence against women remain commonplace. The National Crime Victimization Survey (NCVS) found that between 1992 and 2000, attempted rapes, completed rapes, and sexual assaults against women averaged 366,460 per year in the United States (USDJ 2002). Hypermasculinity as the marker of manhood has led to stricter notions of gender and created a much more dangerous environment for teenage boys and girls and adult women and men.

Hypermasculinity has become the norm by which other male behaviors are evaluated.[6] Katz points out that for young men of color the pressures to be hypermasculine are even more intense. The dominant, corporate-controlled popular-culture industry has presented Black men in few roles other than as hypermasculine perpetrators of violence.[7] Old racist notions of the Black Buck (Riggs 1987), the Black rapist (A. Davis 1981), the criminal, and the gangster have been recycled in contemporary popular culture through the gang exploitation genre of film and corporate rap music.[8] Moreover, many young Black men see themselves depicted in these ways and imitate them, recognizing that in our society power is intimately linked to violence and domination. They are thus influenced to model hypermasculine behaviors in order to establish themselves as men and to approximate the power and influence of big-screen heroes and real corporate and government power brokers.[9]

Much the same can be said of how popular media influence young Chicanos' gender socialization. In our popular imaginary, males of Mexican descent are extremely violent and deviant. Hollywood movies have depicted Mexican men as savages, dumb children, or criminals (Keller 1994; Wool 1980). On television, Mexican American men are most commonly presented as perpetrators or victims of violence (Escalante 2000). Scholars of Mexican American culture have found that our history of Catholicism, rugged individualism, and patriarchal notions of Mexicanness has presented Chicano boys with few models of manhood—mostly defined by hypermasculinity. But in sports and popular culture, such a man is strong and protective and uses violence when necessary to solve problems. The ubiquity of boxing clubs in our barrios is a case in point. The boxing ring serves as an arena where young men of Mexican descent can prove their masculinity as well as their ethnicity. Boxing, for many, is deeply intertwined with nationalism and manhood.[10]

The same cultural forces have defined womanhood in similarly narrow ways. María Herrera-Sobek has used feminist archetypal criticism to examine and codify the ways in which the Mexican American *corrido* genre of music has represented women (1990). In examining Chicano film culture, Rosa Linda Fregoso shows that depictions of gender have a long history of male-centeredness (1993a). This male-centered lineage forms an ideological foundation in Mexican/ Chicano culture that informs contemporary notions of masculinity, femininity, and gender relations. The patriarchal values and behaviors of Mexican American men (and some women) are reinforced and transmitted through the generations, in part via our popular culture, where idealized representations often serve as morality tales for proper gendered behavior.

Importantly, contemporary ideas about gender roles and relations in Chicano youth culture have another influence that we must consider when examining Chicano rap music. The degree of cultural exchange and influence between inner-city Chicanos and Blacks has led to lowriding,[11] Chicano rock music,[12] fashion,[13] rap music style,[14] attitude, and language, and other aspects of their expressive cultures.[15] Through Black gangsta rap, badman and pimp folk characters have influenced young Chicanos' ideas about masculinity and gender relations.[16] These hypermasculine figures have served as models of Black social banditry that appeal to young men of color who are denied success through conventional channels in the United States. Many young men of color see hypermasculinity in the form of the pimp or gangster as their only possible road to success.

The corporate music industry has championed music that presents this model of Black masculinity. The old racist stereotypes of the dangerous Black man find new fertile ground in gangsta rap. Alternative models of Black masculinity are rarely marketed by record companies eager to cash in on this new twist on an old stereotype. The record-buying public, including Chicanas/os, is much more willing to consume these images of Black hypermasculinity than more representative and diverse models of Black manhood. Many young Black men have realized this and express virulent misogyny and hypermasculinity in their records in order to gain fame and wealth (hooks 1994). The combination of a hypermasculine and misogynist street mentality (Vigil 2003) and commodified Black manhood influences young inner-city Chicanos who consume the violent and sexist images of corporate rap music. In turn, we find narratives of the pimp and player and the irreverence of the Black badman in Chicano rap.

Using articulation theory as a guide to investigating Chicano rap suggests that three types of cultural products or phenomena contribute to the misogyny and hypermasculinity of Chicano rap: dominant, corporate-controlled mass media; patriarchal Mexican/Chicano culture; and commodified aspects of Black manhood. Theories of masculinity and feminist archetypal analysis help us understand the most common representations of women and men in Chicano rap music. My examination of Chicano rap lyrics reveals that rappers link manhood to violence and to domination over women, and they represent women primarily as sex objects and secondarily as "good" women.

IMAGES OF MASCULINITY AND MISOGYNY

In my sample of 470 songs, 56 percent (263 songs) have some discussion of women; of these, 37 percent (98 songs) represent women as objects of the male gaze and talk about women's bodies, beauty, sexiness, and clothing. In these songs women are represented simply as objects of male desire and pleasure. Of the songs that mention women, likewise 37 percent (98 songs) discuss sexual intercourse. In none of these songs are women represented as having sexual agency or having the right to define their own sexuality. Instead, Chicano rappers place women in submissive positions and demonstrate pride in deceiving women into having sex with them. Women who have sex with Chicano rappers and the fictional characters in their rap stories are most often depicted as "sluts," "whores," and "freaks." In fact, 36 percent (170) of all 470 songs I examined refer to women by such epithets. Other "bad" women are fortune-seekers ("gold-diggers"), unfaithful, or the cause of men's downfall. Lyrics that represent "good" women are usually presented in the context of discussing familial relations—wives, mothers, grand-mothers, daughters, or other family members.

Of the entire sample, 71 percent (336 songs) discuss violence, which along with domination are overwhelmingly the most common themes I found in my sample. Violence—whether as social commentary, street reportage, metaphor, or a way to increase record sales—is closely linked to power, money, and fame. But misogynist violence is relatively rare in Chicano rap. Chicano rappers endorse or celebrate misogynist violence in only 4 percent (19) of the songs I examined. Armstrong found that in one of Chicano rap's precursors, gangsta rap, 22 percent of the songs he analyzed involve misogynist violence (2001, 96). While Chicano rappers discuss misogynist violence much less than their African American gangsta counterparts, the fact that some young Chicanos endorse and make fun of violence against women is alarming and telling.

MASCULINITY AS DOMINATION: VIOLENCE

New men's studies scholars argue that violence and domination are the central characteristics of contemporary notions of masculinity. Kimmel (1994), borrowing from Butler's (1990) ideas about gender as performance, writes that masculinity is a very unstable trait. One must continually prove his masculinity by distancing himself from femininity and homosexuality and by engaging in acts of daring and aggression; boys and men must continually "perform" masculinity. Expressive culture is an important place for the performance of aggressive masculinity. Locker-room braggadocio, sports fields, alcohol and drug use, and music are places where ambiguous sexuality and gender identities can become solidified into an unambiguous hypermasculinity. Chicano rap as an arena for performing masculinity reveals a strong tendency to define male gender as hypermasculine. While I found that 71 percent of the songs in my sample discuss violence, certainly 71 percent of the activities in Chicano barrios are not related to violence. Why, then, do

Chicano rappers spend so much of their time rapping about violence? What is it that they are saying about violence?

Dominant popular culture representations of hypermasculinity influence Chicano rap. Superhuman violence of the sort depicted in Hollywood action movies is reflected in Chicano rap lyrics. I have labeled this type of violence "commodified." It is extremely graphic, offering the viewer or listener detailed descriptions of violent acts and their results. Katz (in Jhally 1999), Giroux (1996), and others have noted that violence and the detail of its graphic depictions have steadily increased in Hollywood movies. The Hollywood action genre is characterized by muscular White male heroes with an unending assortment of weapons engaging in superhuman feats of violence. The action hero protects his values, country, and/or family with incredible levels of violence. Moreover, the violence is not simply implied as in early Hollywood movies but is shown in graphic detail with massive explosions and blood, guts, and limbs flying through the air. Violence is rarely insinuated in today's action movies. Instead, it is foregrounded while the storyline takes a secondary role.[17]

In many songs, violence was not used as a vehicle to tell a cautionary tale but rather becomes the protagonist of the narrative. Violence is sold Hollywood-style. The Funky Aztecs' "Is This Real?" (on *Day of the Dead*, 1995) exemplifies the influence of the action film. The narrator of this story wakes up to gunshots and runs from violent situation to violent situation throughout his day. The protagonist uses several high-powered weapons, including two machine guns at once à la Sylvester Stallone's Rambo character. He eventually gets shot in the leg but escapes by jumping five stories into a hotel swimming pool. In true Hollywood style, the hero of the song surrounds himself with women. At one point he has two women in bed. One of his "bad" women looks out the window and is shot in the head. The callousness with which the Funky Aztecs depict her death characterizes the way women's lives are devalued in hegemonic masculine culture. The imagery and pace of the song, its urgency and graphic detail call to mind any number of action movies over the past two decades. To further draw our attention to the fantasy nature of the song, between verses the rapper asks, "Is this shit real/or am I just trippin'?" Clearly, the story is fictional, as such superhuman feats rarely occur and instead are reserved for big-screen fantasies. This type of violence abounds in Chicano rap. Rappers such as Brownside, Knightowl, and Darkroom Familia and Low Profile artists scarcely let a song go by without graphic depictions of how, where, and when they commit violent acts.[18] For example, the Brownside CD *Payback* (1999) has a total of eleven songs; ten detail violent actions, and the other is a lament about a dead friend.

While it is hard to quantify the amount of gratuitous violence in Chicano rap, it is safe to say that many discussions of violence take their lead from Hollywood movies. Further evidence of this is found in the use of names of notoriously violent characters from movies, references to rappers' similarity to action superstars Schwarzenegger, Stallone, and others, and samples of dialogue from war movies and gangster movies like *Scarface, Serpico, American Me,* and *The Godfather* trilogy. Moreover, a great deal of the rappers' iconography represents violent exploits. Album covers, posters, symbols, and webpages of many Chicano rap artists and recording labels display images of guns, blood, homeboys in menacing poses, and the like.

Violent metaphors are also common in Chicano rap. Because they are intended as metaphor and not as actual violence, this type of song has the potential to reveal the ubiquity of violence in our culture. Chicano rappers use metaphors to communicate their superiority to other young men. As the focus is verbal ability and cleverness, any type of metaphor would serve the purpose of demonstrating one's microphone skills. Curiously, though, rappers choose to talk about "blastin'"—leaving opponents bloody on the ground—and knocking people out rather than using metaphors devoid of violence and domination. This demonstrates an understanding of masculine power as "domination over" rather than alternative notions of power as uplifting, enlightening, and enabling.

Analysis of violent content in Chicano rap songs confirms the link to hypermasculinity as the norm for male behavior in broader popular media and culture. The large number of songs with hyperviolent content and those that use violence as metaphors for domination indicate that notions of masculinity, power, and violence are intimately linked. To further understand the ways in which a normalized hypermasculinity contributes to the imbrication of violence with masculinity in Chicano rap we should examine how and when Chicano rappers discuss domination over women.

MASCULINITY AS DOMINATION OVER WOMEN

Chicano rappers distinguish themselves from the sexual Other, woman, who is the passive sexual partner. Men are the active agents who have sex with many women without getting emotionally involved. This attitude mirrors Kimmel's argument that two key traits of contemporary masculinity are repudiation of femininity and controlling one's emotions (1994, 125–126). Men lure and trick women into having sex with them, thus demonstrating their superior knowledge and ability. For many young Chicanos, gender relations involve trying to bed females without any suggestion of longer-term relationships. They demonstrate their masculinity by not becoming emotionally involved with women and conquering more women than their friends do.

The epitome of such notions of gender relations is the "pimp-ho" relationship. The pimp figure is the ideal hypermasculine man. He obtains money his own way without recourse to the legitimate market economy and without fear of the law. Thus, some see him as a social bandit figure. He is clearly devoid of emotion as he has sex with many women but loves none. He does not shy away from violence and sees anything associated with femininity as weakness. He is aggressively heterosexual. He is stylish and intelligent. The women with whom he associates are inferior spiritually, emotionally, intellectually, and physically. They obey his every command and give their bodies and money to him.[19]

A small percentage of Chicano rappers discuss the "pimp-ho" fantasy world of popular rap. Chicano rappers refer to themselves and their friends as "pimps" or the related "player" figure. I found thirty songs (12 percent of those in the sample that discuss women) in which the idea of the pimp figures into the narrative. This relatively low percentage does not mean that only a few Chicano rappers represent male-female relations as emotionally distant and only for sexual pleasure. Nearly all representations of female-male relations in Chicano rap emphasize emotional detachment and sexual pleasure. Those who use the pimp-ho trope simply use the most hypermasculine, misogynist metaphors to discuss such relationships.

Women are used as gauges of male power in a different way. Feminist authors studying rape and sexual violence against women point out that in patriarchal societies, men see women as their property.[20] Men in their wars of domination with each other commonly struggle for control of women. Men often use women as instruments to defeat the enemy. Controlling women signals to other men that one is powerful and in charge and that other men are impotent and weak.

Examinations of wartime sexual violence help us understand the ways in which men use women as symbols of male dominance. Nikolic-Ristanovic, discussing violence against women during the war in the former Yugoslavia, writes that "for the rapist, rape of a woman in war may be as much an act against her husband, father, or brother as an act against a woman's body" (1996, 198–199). Rape during war, colonial conquest, or times of extreme ethnic or national conflict is a means of communicating defeat to an enemy. The powerful send a message reaffirming their dominant position over the subordinate (Dowd Hall 1983, 332). The subjugated male population receives the message that they are weak and incapable of protecting their women and their privilege as men (Hernandez Castillo 1998b, 139). Antonia Castañeda explains that rape "represents both the physical domination of women and the symbolic castration of the men of the conquered group" (1993, 25).

Control of women is a central means by which men maintain and understand their masculinity. Chicano rappers compete with other men by attempting to take away each other's women. This type of competition can be overtly discussed in the songs like Darkroom Family's 2001 "DRF por Vida" by asserting, for example, that an inferior man's woman ("bitch") is having sex with the superior man ("ridin' my dick"), or the competition can be inferred by the rapper boasting about the number of women with whom he has had sex. While the second type is nearly unquantifiable because of the sheer number of times rappers talk about women they have bedded, I found thirty-seven examples of Chicano rappers using women as competition between them and other men. In other words, in 14 percent of the songs that discuss women, Chicano rappers overtly use women as objects of competition between men.

Other rappers take dominance and repudiating femininity a step further by depicting misogynist violence. I found twenty songs in which violence against women is discussed. Only one, South Park Mexican's "SPM vs. Los," laments or critiques it. All seem to celebrate this type of violence as an example of male domination and their own superiority. For example, Street Platoon opens its misogynist "Pink (Pastrami Strips)" (2002) with a monologue by a young woman who begs to be raped, called dirty names, spanked, tied up, and choked during sexual intercourse. The entire song is laden with vitriol aimed at women who are described as "dirty bitches," "filthy sluts," "sexual cannibals," "snakes," and "dirty hoodrats." They describe women engaging in oral sex and other sexual acts with multiple partners and conclude that women were made for intercourse.

The need for young men to define themselves against women and to use women to demonstrate their dominance leads Street Platoon to argue that women love being abused. Misogynist songs, the pimp figure, and songs that use women as weapons in male competition provide evidence that dominant corporate popular cultural notions of masculinity as hypermasculinity influence Chicano rappers' understanding of gender. In their respective films with director Sut Jhally (1997a and 1999), hooks and Katz show that since the 1980s, misogynist violence has become commonplace in Hollywood movies and link its rise to the backlash against women. The ubiquity of hypermasculinity and misogyny in Chicano rap mirrors that found in movies, television, and other aspects of our communication and entertainment media. Chicano rap combines and rearticulates ideas of hypermasculinity and misogyny found in the dominant popular culture and patriarchal Black and Mexican male culture and tradition.

WOMAN AS SEX OBJECT

As noted, 37 percent of the songs in my sample that discuss women refer to their appearance. This finding is not surprising, given the narrow ways in which men are taught to see women, the fact that the authors of these raps are young men, and the history of sex as a proven money-maker in our popular culture. Young male culture (as well as that of older men) is replete with discussions of women's bodies and appearance. Young men's fascination with women's bodies, including touching and having sex with them, presumably accounts for most of young men's concerns with females. Robin Kelley astutely links misogyny in gangsta rap with a more general male youth culture, explaining that

> adolescent misogyny is characteristic of most male youth cultures, since male status is defined in part through heterosexual conquest and domination over women. Part of what distinguishes gangsta rap from "locker room" braggadocio is that it is circulated on compact discs, digital tapes, and radio airwaves. (1994, 185)

An important aspect of becoming a man in our contemporary society is to value women solely for their ability to satisfy male sexual desire. Other traits become unimportant and devalued. Women's intellectual, emotional, spiritual, and physical abilities are devalued by men because they pose a threat to men's access to women's bodies.

Intelligent, strong-willed women challenge men's attempts to have sex with them and to treat them as less than fully human (Rose 1990). Thus, young men create fantasy worlds in their music and accompanying videos in which incredibly beautiful women are theirs for the taking and strong-willed, intelligent women do not exist.[21]

As conquest of women is a central characteristic of contemporary masculinity, women can become a threat to firmly establishing one's masculinity. If a young man cannot conquer women, then his masculinity and heterosexuality become suspect in the eyes of his peers. Young men who find their sexual advances rejected feel the need to reestablish their masculinity by distancing themselves from women through name calling and other abuse (Rose 1990). Name calling is more common in Chicano rap than all other topics concerning women. I found 170 songs in which Chicano rappers refer to women by derogatory names; 65 percent of the songs that discuss women refer to them by epithets such as "bitch," "slut," "hoochie," "snake," "hoodrat," "ho," "freak," and "puta."

The work of Lil' Rob exemplifies the way in which Chicano rappers express both threat from and desire for women through name calling and seeing women as sexual objects.[22] In many of Rob's songs he pairs the male gaze with female name calling. In a common refrain, Rob refers to women using the words *chichonas* (big breasts), *nalgonas* (big buttocks), and *cabronas* (an epithet that translates as "old she-goats" and is used derogatorily for those who are disliked). In this short phrase Rob demonstrates the general attitude that most of the Chicano rappers in my sample express toward women. Women are valued for their large breasts and buttocks and rarely for any other traits. Moreover, even when they are valued for the visual and potential sexual pleasure that their bodies provide men, they are dehumanized and devalued through calling them *cabronas*.

While not all the Chicano rappers in my sample focus discussions of women on their beauty and voluptuousness, I found that of the sixty-seven rappers included in the sample, thirty-five had songs that discuss women's bodies as objects of male desire. This contrasts sharply with the relatively small number of rappers who speak of other aspects of women; for example, only eleven rappers in this sample had songs that discuss "good" women. The data clearly illustrate that Chicano rappers understand their masculinity in relation to womanhood in simple and degrading ways. For young Chicano rappers, as for many men in U.S. society, womanhood is valued for controlled sexuality and reproduction.

THE "GOOD" WOMAN: MOTHERS, WIVES, AND OTHER *FAMILIA*

In Chicano male culture and patriarchal culture generally women are not only valued for their ability to satisfy men sexually. Mothers, daughters, wives, and grandmothers are also highly valued. Thirty-one songs in my sample refer to women in seemingly appreciative ways as nurturers, loved ones, and loyal wives. While initially this seems like a positive trend in the music, further examination of the lyrics and the uses of the "good woman" archetype reveal that these images of women are often just the flip side of attempts to keep women in subordinate roles.

The cult of the Virgin of Guadalupe, or *marianismo*, has disseminated throughout Mexican society a gender ideology that allows for only two possible female roles (NietoGomez 1997, 48–49). Ideal women are the "strong, long-suffering women who endured social injustice, [and] maintained the family as a safe 'haven in a heartless world'" (A. García 1997b, 6). Women's proper role in family and in the community is one of subordination to husband and devotion to family.[23] Against this *mujer buena* or Ideal Woman, patriarchal Mexican culture created *la mujer mala*, the aggressive, independent, and "sexually loose" woman outside of male control (Rincón 1997, 26).

The Mexican woman is valued for her status as the wife and mother who assists the Mexican man and "nourishes and sustains [his] machismo" (Herrera-Sobek 1990, 11). Thus, her positive status results from her relationship to men. She has little value outside of these relationships. For ethnic Mexicans, the "good" mother is the most important person in the world, while the "bad" woman, *la escandalosa*, is among the most despised (Zavella 2003). The good-mother figure presents an ideal of womanhood that is almost impossible to fulfill. Young women, then, are socialized into a gender role that they inevitably fail to accomplish. Nonetheless, the pressures to comply are overwhelming, as they are found throughout all aspects of ethnic Mexican culture—in our religion,[24] oral and literary traditions, and music (Herrera-Sobek 1990).

María Herrera-Sobek has identified a central female archetype in the Western and Mexican literary traditions in the suffering mother, *mater dolorosa*. She finds that in the *corrido*, "the basic imagery is that of the weeping mother at the death of her son" (1990, 6). Even in death, the male hero of the *corrido* is supported by his mother. The weeping mother is the most common good-woman figure in Chicano rap. For example, South Park Mexican discusses this figure in five songs ("Ghetto Tales," "Filthy Rich," "Revenge," "Comin' Up, Comin' Down," and "Hustle Town"), and Latin Bomb Squad's first compact disc (1998) has three songs in which the figure appears. In "Temptations," "Deal with Tha Madness," and "Whatcha Missin'" the weeping mother image symbolizes a culture and a community that suffers from gun violence. In their laments about gang culture and macho Mexican and Chicano culture, Latin Bomb Squad (LBS) equates goodness with mothers and evil with irresponsible and violent men. They equate the young Chicano narrator of "Whatcha Missin'" with the irresponsible father figure when the rapper states that he is like his father ("Pops") because in his death he, too, abandons his mom. Throughout the CD the only moral figure and hope for the future is the mother. Every other character participates in violence, drug use, gang activity, or impersonal sex, and women are depicted as objects of the male gaze. LBS reiterates long-held Mexican beliefs that the mother is the repository of all that is good and that she is responsible for the future direction of the race—clearly an unfair burden that furthers male privilege and domination by allowing men to eschew responsibility for changing violent and misogynist behaviors.

Chicano rappers offer loving or emotional depictions of females other than their mothers. These, unfortunately, are few in number. SPM mentions his love for his daughter, Carley, in several songs ("All Cot Up," "Filthy Rich," "Comin' Up, Comin' Down"); Sir Dyno has a conversation with his daughter on "I Can't See Through the Rain"; Angel Loco offers praise and advice to a young Chicana who has just turned fifteen ("Fifteen Down"); Frost dedicates "Para Mi Abuelita" to his grandmother; and Conejo ("Till Death Do Us Part"), Frost ("Diamonds and Pearls"), and SPM ("Miss Perfect") talk of their love for their wives or girlfriends. The relatively small number of affectionate depictions of girls or women is overshadowed by the number of bad-woman representations and lyrical attacks on women. Moreover, even the good-woman discourse in Chicano rap fails to decenter men as the active subject in Mexicano/Chicano patriarchal culture. Men are valued more than women in the culture. Women are understood to be of value only when they fulfill the needs of men as their mothers, daughters, wives, and sexual partners.

CONCLUSION

Chicano rappers are products of their environment. The depiction of men and women in rappers' lyrics indicates a close relationship to patriarchal Mexican culture, especially as evidenced by its expressive culture. The uses of the pimp, player, and ho figures and Chicano rappers' musical and lyrical style are evidence of the role that intercultural exchange with young urban Black men has had in the development of Chicano rap. The use of R&B-derived vocal styles, samples of funk, soul, and R&B songs, and homages to important Black cultural and musical figures also points to the strong influence of African American culture. Hypermasculine depictions of violence and an arguably obsessive orientation toward it links Chicano rap with hypermasculinity in popular culture and our current crisis in masculinity. Chicano rappers and music producers reference violent characters and sample dialogue from Hollywood action movies. Their depictions of women as objects of the male gaze place their music squarely within the tradition of displaying women established by the dominant, corporate-controlled media.

Examination of Chicano rap lyrics reveals that each of the propositions about representations of gender in Chicano rap music has some degree of validity. First, if indeed men have responded to our contemporary crisis in masculinity by creating hypermasculine fantasies and a hypermasculine ideal of manhood and this has affected young Chicanos, then we should find similar depictions of violent manhood in the lyrics. The great majority of the songs in my sample— 71 percent—discuss violence in ways that mirror Hollywood movies and the general societal discourse that links violence to manhood. Popular media present a model of manhood in which men are required to be hypermasculine and dominant. In fact, male value is judged on propensity to violence, toughness, emotional distance, and emphasis on physical strength. The hyperviolent, domineering man wins in the end of many Hollywood blockbusters. So, too, in the majority of Chicano rap songs.

Michael Kimmel argues that key traits of manhood are aggressiveness and repudiation of femininity (1987, 1994). When these traits combine, we should expect to find Chicano rap representations of manhood closely related to domination over women. In pimp-ho depictions of the use of women for sex, violence against women, and objectification of women in struggles between men, we find Chicano masculinity defined, in part, as domination over women. Rarely are male-female relationships depicted in loving or affectionate ways. Even in these cases, women are valued predominantly for their service to men. Herrera-Sobek and others help us understand how "positive" depictions of women in Mexican and Chicano culture also constrain women, reinforce their servile roles, or portray them as the hope for the future of Chicano males.[25] The weeping-mother archetype found in *corridos* has its equivalent in Chicano rap songs. Several songs show mothers as the burden bearers of the problems in our communities. They weep for the sins of Chicano men and are burdened with the role of saving our culture from irresponsible male behavior.

Women in Chicano rap songs are most often represented as sex objects or objects of the male gaze. Seeing women solely for their physical attractiveness dehumanizes them and further distances them from men, who are represented as intellectually, physically, and otherwise superior. More than half of the rappers represented in this sample have songs in which they refer to women as sex objects. The Chicano rap discourse concerning male identity and its relationship to seeing women as sex objects evokes the depiction of women in advertising, movies, and popular music.

Chicano rap lyrics are created by young men socialized in a patriarchal environment. The discourses of masculinity and misogyny in Chicano rap are articulated within a social, political, and cultural environment that relies on and requires unequal gender relations. The dominant, corporate-controlled media foster a model of gender roles in which men are dominant and hypermasculine and women are subordinate. Further, Chicano rap as a hybrid form borrows from various aspects of Black and Mexican (American) cultures. Traditions of hypermasculinity and misogyny in these cultures are also part of the cultural milieu that created misogyny and violence in Chicano rap. Given the cultural, economic, and political models available to young Chicanos in our society, it should not surprise us that their depictions of men and women are violent and misogynist.

Chicana rappers are also socialized in a hypermasculine, patriarchal environment. They, like other Chicanas, are often the victims of male domination—physical, mental, and symbolic. Chicana responses to patriarchy are varied. Some resist, while others are resigned to what they see as their fate, while still others internalize the sexism of our broader society. In the next chapter I compare two distinct types of gender politics found in Chicana rap lyrics.

SEXUAL AGENCY IN CHICANA RAP

JV Versus Ms. Sancha

Several Chicanas have recorded songs and CDs over the past decade. Their lyrics cover a broad range of themes. Their styles, delivery, and music differ widely. From Ms. Sancha's explicit lyrics over heavy funk bass and drum production to Sista D's fun and party lyrics accompanied by Midwestern and Southern musical production to JV's straight hip hop, Chicanas show depth and diversity in their music. While they speak on many topics, this chapter will focus on Chicana rappers' representations of sexuality and sexual politics. Two types of sexual politics commonly occur in Chicana rap lyrics. One speaks of female sexual and personal empowerment. This type of discourse on sexuality invokes "powers of the erotic" to provide an empowering identity and sense of self for artists and fans alike. This sexual politics presents intimate male-female relations in more egalitarian, mutually gratifying, and democratic ways. Agency, creativity, and control over one's self (in other words, out of male control) characterize the sexual and personal politics represented in this type of Chicana rap.

JV's work is exemplary. The image of women in most of JV's work differs markedly from the depiction of women in Chicano rap lyrics. The second type of sexual and personal politics found in Chicana rap lyrics closely aligns the fate of women to that of the dominant presence of men. Female identity and worth are determined by the needs, wants, and desires of men. Such lyrics present Chicana bodies for the taking. They are sexual objects designed for male pleasure and control. Many of the depictions of female sexuality and identity found in the lyrics of Ms. Sancha present women through this patriarchal gaze. In her raps Ms. Sancha defines herself as a "gangsta bitch" who finds power and pleasure in violence, criminal hustles, and pleasing men sexually.

POWER OF THE EROTIC

Xicanistas have shown how both the dominant and Mexican cultures teach Chicanas to don the lenses of patriarchy and view themselves as subordinate. Chicanas' gender subordination within a male-dominant society often results in a "colonized identity" characterized by an internalized sexism (Córdova 1999). Yarbro-Bejarano writes that developing "Chicana feminism as a political movement depends on the love of Chicanas for themselves and each other as Chicanas" (1996, 214). Teresa Córdova adds that an important project is "to love ourselves—free from the need to obtain patriarchal approval" (1999, 23). So, instead of taking whole-cloth ethnic Mexican patriarchal history that makes women visible only through seeing them as inactive, passive objects, Chicana feminists have utilized the power of the erotic to redefine themselves.

Xicanistas theorize about and help women reclaim their bodies from pornographic patriarchal definitions. They use the erotic to empower themselves socially, culturally, and politically (Castillo 1994). Audre Lorde opens her essay "The Uses of the Erotic: The Erotic as Power" addressing the maintenance of patriarchal domination:

> In order to perpetuate itself, every oppression must corrupt or distort those various sources of power within the culture of the oppressed that can provide energy for change. For women, this has meant a suppression of the erotic as a considered source of power and information within our lives. (1984, 53)

The erotic is a source of empowerment that can be accessed to improve women's lives and to oppose male domination. The erotic "is an assertion of the lifeforce of women; of that creative energy empowered, the knowledge and use of which we are now reclaiming in our language, our history, our dancing, our loving, our work, our lives" (55). The erotic is a positive, sensuous, internal feeling that encourages personal excellence in all matters of life. It is a form of knowledge that "becomes a lens through which we scrutinize all aspects of our existence" (57). Once accessed, the erotic within will not allow for external control and domination of the self.

Moreover, the erotic act of sharing deeply with another empowers and bridges differences between people. The joy that comes from such sharing can be employed to collectively challenge heterosexist, phallocentric suppression of the life force. Similarly, Chicana cultural workers use the redemptive power of the exotic to redefine and reclaim their sexuality while challenging the patriarchal gender order.[1] The recent telling of the extraordinary life of Sor Juana Inés de la Cruz by Alicia Gaspar de Alba (1999) serves as a powerful example of the empowering qualities of the erotic.

Alicia Gaspar de Alba's historical novel of the life of early *mexicana* icon Sor Juana Inés de la Cruz exemplifies the ways in which the Xicanista cultural worker has "retrieve[d] mexicana cultural symbols of resistance that will help her (re)invent and (re)define identity in her own terms" (Huaco-Nuzum 1996, 262). Through careful historical research and a keen sense of drama and attention to detail, Gaspar de Alba recreates the trials, tribulations, and triumphs of a highly gifted and creative intellectual who because of her gender and sexuality could only counter the misogyny of a repressed and repressive Spanish colonial Mexico by entering the Catholic Church to become a nun. Sor Juana develops intellectually and sexually in the tense environment of the convent. In this community of women she can be free from unwanted sexual advances and direct control of men while at the same time avoiding the fate of Saint Catherine. In one scene from the book (1999, 21), young Juana Inés is speaking to her benefactor, La Marquesa:

> "What a fascinating image," said La Marquesa. . . . "Tell us what it means, Juana Inés." "It's Saint Catherine of Alexandra's Wheel, Señora, on which the Roman emperor was going to torture her for refusing to marry him. It's the symbol of her resistance to his will."

Sor Juana's explorations of her own sexuality, fantasies, desires for self-definition and control, intellectual capacity, and resistance to male authority are a model for the uses of the erotic. Under an extremely repressive and misogynistic patriarchal rule, Sor Juana refuses to be contained. She accesses the erotic in order to edify herself emotionally, spiritually, and intellectually. Sor Juana and Saint Catherine's Wheel become symbols for women who choose to reject heteronormative sexuality and male domination. Gaspar de Alba's retelling of Sor Juana's life is one of the latest in a number of Chicana texts that point to the possibilities for the reconstitution of Chicana sexuality and identity outside the gender order in Chicano and U.S. society that relegates women to very few roles (Madonna/whore) that all serve to maintain male privilege and domination. The erotic, self-love, community building, collective work, and complex stories and images of women challenge patriarchal dominance and present useful corrections and alternatives to sexist representations of women.

JV'S *XICANISMA*

In her songs, L.A.-based rapper JV defines herself and takes control of her identity. On *It Gets No Reala* JV speaks about male-female relationships, sexuality, and sex among other topics. Her discussion from an empowered female perspective continues the tradition established by first-wave Chicana poets and other artists. Like early Chicana poets who express solidarity with Chicanos *and* criticize them for their sexist and misogynist behaviors, JV emphasizes the potentially powerful relationships between Chicanas and Chicanos. Like her predecessors, JV warns men to treat her properly or else be prepared for resistance. JV's songs continue the critique of Chicano patriarchal behavior presented by Bernice Zamora, Inés Hernandez Tovar, and Naomi Quiñonez during the 1970s and 1980s. Her declarations of sexual independence and control over her body and self reflect the work of Xicanistas including Ana Castillo, Sandra Cisneros, and Cherríe Moraga. Importantly, JV's lyrics also often slip into dichotomous notions of gender and use sexist language to express power over others.

"Women's Lib"

JV defines herself as a physically, mentally, and lyrically strong woman on the song "Women's Lib" from the *It Gets No Reala* CD. As a woman and rapper she has special talents and powers that allow her to control herself and challenge men and others who believe themselves to be superior to her.

> I got a woman's touch
> don't play with me
> see it's no problem puttin' suckas in check
> don't like it?
> suck my left tit.

In this lyric from the first verse, JV warns people ("suckas") not to challenge ("play with") her because she will resist and defeat them ("put suckas in check"). To those who object to her setting the rules of interaction, she says "suck my left tit," a paraphrase of the expression "suck my dick" that men use to disparage others and allude to their own sexual superiority and dominance. This taunt symbolically places one's foe into a sexually submissive posture of giving unreciprocated oral sex. In the patriarchal imagination, the passive sexual partner, the woman, "sucks" the man's "dick," demonstrating the dominance of the male. JV reverses this phallocentric expression and centers her sexual pleasure and agency by putting the man in the position of providing unreciprocated sexual pleasure to her.

JV, in typical hip-hop style, goes on to speak of the numerous abilities and talents that set her apart from other less talented, skilled, and powerful men and women. She describes herself as "classy, classy," a "magnifico hip-hop creation," and "gourmet" as opposed to "fast food." Like many MCs, she claims her superiority through unmatched verbal ability. In one passage JV claims, "I flow better than 'bout, oh, a hundred percent / of all these MCs claimin' they represent." Quite simply, according to JV, she is the best MC in the business. JV claims a positive self-identity and wit displayed by her poetic and performative skill. Her rhyming and rapping deserve respect and recognition, or as she says: "gotta give it to myself cuz my demonstration, hands down deserves a standin' ovation."

JV is a skilled MC and lyricist. She demonstrates confidence in her intelligence and skill. She also claims that many are awestruck by her beauty. She raps, "the sexy new girl's got the world's fascination." In contrast to typical patriarchal, sexist understandings of women as passive, inferior beings, JV claims agency, subjectivity, and power. As the title of the song and some of the lyrics suggest, part of her positive identity and unique skill and worth result from a positive and empowering definition of womanhood. Unlike Chicano rappers' "hoodrats," "putas," "hos," and "chichonas" who are valued only for their sexual abilities and physical beauty, JV presents herself as multidimensional. Her intelligence and talents transcend her sexual self, though her poise, beauty, and sexiness obviously fascinate men as much as her music intrigues them.

"He Can't Get None"

Continuing the theme of her female superiority, JV describes a man's attempts to impress and woo her in the song "He Can't Get None." JV claims that "he wants to slide up in [have sex with her] but he can't get none." She says she will refuse the man's advances and stop his attempt at bedding her. Taking the sexual upper hand, JV tells the man, "I guess I been blessed / you can't slide up in but you can lick my breasts." While she denies the man sexual gratification, she will use him for her own. Like Chicana lesbian writers such as Moraga (1983) and Trujillo

(1991a,b) and female African American rappers such as Lil' Kim,[2] JV decenters phallocentric fantasy and male sexual prerogative by opting out of coitus and instead having the man stimulate her sexually.

She criticizes men who cannot satisfy her sexually, rapping that they "couldn't last a minute let alone two or three." Since she is "precious from mother nature / God's gift to this world," men who wish only to use her to fulfill their sexual desires "can't get none." To them she says that she

> won't be getting' tossed [having sex]
> so take your jim hat [condom] off
> use your four fingers and thumbs to jack off [masturbate]
> then get lost or tossed
> from in front of my face.

Further, JV calls men to task for their treatment of women. She confronts men who use sexist epithets, asking "who you callin' a ho or a tramp?" JV critiques "lame men for not havin' a clue" about her or women generally—they are shallow, selfish, and overly macho men who are too concerned about their own sexual satisfaction and sexual conquest to know the true, multifaceted value of women. Instead of passive, easily duped sexual objects, JV portrays herself and other women as in charge and in control. She is able to "crush" men's plans, make them do as she wishes, and defeat them in battle.

"Can't Live Without It"

JV is not willing to give control of herself over to men who mistreat women. Throughout the album, though, she makes it clear that she wants egalitarian, mutually gratifying relations with strong, intelligent men and will sexually please such men who engage in reciprocal affection and unselfish, respectful sexual relations with her. The men with whom she considers having sexual relations must be special. These men, in contrast to the "lame" guys she addresses in "He Can't Get None," are strong and able to make her feel loved and safe. In "Can't Live Without It," JV describes her man in the following terms:

> My man's a high roller
> with the weight of the world on his shoulders
> Girls, he ain't a punk
> I got a soldier

> and when he hugs me I melt in his arms
> secure cuz nobody can't do me no harm

JV likes her men "rough" and macho and "not a man in the palm of my hand like a punk / I can make wipe my ass like my personal chump." JV does not want a weak "chump" or "punk" but rather a "soldier" equal to her in intelligence, beauty, and talent.

While JV "disses" (rejects) "chumps" who "can't get none," she is happy to have passionate sex with the man who possesses all the necessary traits:

> I love my man so much
> five minutes is too long away from his touch
> so when he gets back in town
> I'm gonna ride his stuff [have sex with him]

To alleviate the stress her man feels from living a dangerous street lifestyle, JV makes her home a "luxury suite where I sweep my number one off his feet / doing the freaky deek [having sex] to a slow jam beat."

In "Can't Live Without It," JV rejects hierarchical relationships based on domination and submission. She does not want someone inferior to her, nor does she want someone to abuse her. JV desires an egalitarian relationship in which each attends to the needs of the other and improves the life of the other. JV illustrates the advantages of a cooperative partnership as opposed to the antagonistic, conflictual relationships described by male rappers. The male-female relationships enacted under the patriarchal dominance paradigm are based on deception, dominance, and mistrust. The more egalitarian relationships described by JV produce interpersonal relationships devoid of violence, dominance, and bad feelings. Love can flourish only in egalitarian relationships in which women and men interact with one another as equals and view each other with affection and respect.

Patriarchal Language

While JV calls for egalitarian relationships throughout her album, she often uses the language and ideals of the patriarchal dominance paradigm. Her description of her man and the roles each of them plays in their relationship in "Can't Live Without It" is typical of patriarchal notions of gender roles and identity. Her man is a strong and hypermasculine "soldier." He is the patriarch who goes out to work. She provides a home for him to come back to after hustling in the streets trying to make money presumably in illicit ways. In their relationship, JV feels secure because she has a man. Here JV plays the weak damsel in need of a man for protection. Describing the dangerous street culture and work of her man she says, "I feel like a cop's wife." Like wives of police officers who often worry over their husbands' safety, JV portrays herself as the concerned, helpless partner.

JV uses the language of patriarchy in describing other women as "hos" (whores). While she challenges men who call her a "ho," she does not hesitate to belittle other women by using the same epithet. The title of one song exemplifies her use of language that men throughout the hip-hop community commonly use to undermine women and distance themselves from the opposite sex. JV's song "Takin Hoes Men" is a boasting rap. Here she demonstrates her ability to take men from other women. In an interesting turn of the tables, men become the commodity over which women compete. Male bodies are turned into objects that JV uses to demonstrate her power. In her need to identify herself as powerful, though, she engages in competition with women whom she demeans through misogynistic language.

The language, symbols, and codes of the hip-hop community rely on violent, hypermasculine metaphors such as those of the soldier, warrior, war, and battles and on patriarchal notions of gender such as describing women as hos or bitches. Most rappers, including popular female rappers, have not avoided such language and codes. They speak in the metaphors of war and hypermasculinity even when they attempt to critique violence, poverty, discrimination, and gender inequality and representation. This, perhaps, calls into question rap as a truly liberating art form. To overcome the violence and misogyny epidemic in Chicano and other rap lyrics, a new system of language and symbols is required. The contradictions in JV's work point out how difficult such a project is.

MS. SANCHA, SEX OBJECT

In contrast to JV's subjectivity, San Diego–based Ms. Sancha presents herself as a sexual object valued for her ability to please men. In *Taking It Doggystyle: The X-Rated Album* (an album title intended to evoke images of female sexual exploitation and pornography), Ms. Sancha portrays herself as someone who exists for crime, violence, money,

Krazy Race, © 2006. Courtesy of Sal Rojas Photography
(www.salrojas.com) and Krazy Race.

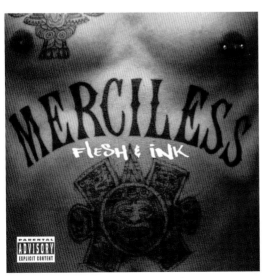

Cover of Merciless CD *Flesh and Ink*, © 2006. Courtesy
of Marco Parada.

Delinquent Habits in concert, © 2006. Courtesy of Sal Rojas
Photography (www.salrojas.com) and Kemo.

Big Citric representin' for Pueblo Café, © 2006. Photo by Alberto "Beaver" Alvarez.
Courtesy of Brenda Ponce and Anthony Campos.

2Mex in concert, © 2006. Courtesy of Sal Rojas Photography
(www.salrojas.com) and 2Mex.

Lil' Uno, © 2006. Courtesy of Sal Rojas Photography
(www.salrojas.com) and Lil' Uno.

Krazy Race in concert, © 2006. Courtesy
of Ayotl Xicana and Krazy Race.

Shysti and JDubs, © 2006. Courtesy of Sal Rojas Photography
(www.salrojas.com), Shysti, and JDubs.

Los Nativos, © 2006. Courtesy of Sal Rojas Photography
(www.salrojas.com) and Felipe Cuauhtli.

Rock-rap group Los Tumbados, © 2007. Courtesy
of Phase Loco and Estevan Oriol.

Pony Boy of Los Marijuanos. 2006. Courtesy of Sal Rojas
Photography (www.salrojas.com) and Rafael Ochoa.

Yaotl of Aztlán Underground and Kemo the Blaxican of Delinquent Habits, © 2006. Courtesy of Sal Rojas Photography (www.salrojas.com), Yaotl, and Kemo.

Almas Intocables in concert, © 2006. Courtesy of Jehuniko.

and sex. She is the perfect bad girl for macho, hypermasculine gangsta rappers. She is the Chicano macho's "slut" fantasy who allows easy access to her body. She offers no resistance to patriarchal dominance and is valued almost exclusively for her voracious sexuality.

Under Royal Male Control

In the minds of patriarchal Chicanos, women should be under male control. Characteristics of good women include caring for men, pleasing men, and sacrificing themselves for men. The rapper and rap persona Ms. Sancha embodies these characteristics in a new age and new environment. For many in the postindustrial working-class barrio, women remain under the control of men. The character Ms. Sancha developed under the control of Low Profile owner, artist, and producer Royal T. Royal is credited with composing all of Sancha's lyrics. As such, he owns her music and receives royalties based on sales and radio or other airplay. On the cover of *Taking it Doggystyle*, Ms. Sancha appears in a camouflaged G-string and half T-shirt. Her buttocks are prominently displayed, inviting men to look and, perhaps, take. A cursive "Royal T" is tattooed on her left side. With the tattoo Royal T boasts of his ownership over Sancha's body. This status symbol or brand lets all know that Sancha is his woman and under his control.

Royal T created Ms. Sancha's persona for adolescent Chicanos desirous of a woman who willingly offers her body to those who prove themselves to be real macho men. She, like most women depicted in mainstream rap lyrics and music videos, poses no threat to the young male ego. She, unlike real women, does not reject his sexual advances.[3] She is the imaginary easy conquest who confirms the young man's masculinity. In Sancha's lyrics, those who engage in criminal activity and gangbanging can have their way with her. She will do anything for them. She will engage in freaky sex with them, back them up in criminal activity, and protect them from danger. Ms. Sancha is sexual fantasy and "gangsta chick" in one petite package; or as she claims on "She's Dirty," she is into "shootin', suckin', and fuckin'."

The Slut Fantasy

> We could have a gangsta fiesta
> taking turns shootin cum on my tetas [tits]
> yeah, you can put it in my mouth

just let me be the one to clean you out
I'll make you feel so good
doin all the freaky shit your girl should

—Ms. Sancha, "Get It, If Your [*sic*] a Rider"

It appears that part of the pornographic imagination of young (and old) men involves humiliation of the sex object (Jensen 2002). Hypermasculinity requires distancing oneself from the passive, feminine Other. In male fantasies this is commonly done through unemotional sex with a variety of women. Robert Jensen argues that in today's pornography (in which we should include the music of Ms. Sancha), humiliation and violence push the boundaries of this sexual othering of women. Choking, slapping, calling names, unwanted anal and oral sex, gangbangs (multiple men having sex with one woman), and ejaculating on sex partners provide pleasure to many men who conflate sexual intercourse with violence and domination.

The violent lifestyles of gang members similarly blur the lines between sex and violence.[4] Gangsta-type rappers such as Low Profile and Darkroom Familia artists speak of sex in violent and humiliating ways. Ms. Sancha's "gangsta fiesta" involves members of Low Profile records engaging in a gangbang ("taking turns") in which they ejaculate on her ("shooting cum on my tetas"). Further, she offers herself as a sex toy, telling gangstas that she will do "all the freaky shit that your girl should." Ms. Sancha offers herself as a sex object upon which gangstas can play out their sexual humiliation fantasies. In "Get It," she says that she needs a "gangsta dick" and implies that all one needs do to have sex with her is be a ruthless gangsta. Throughout the compact disc she claims that she will let them do things to her that their girlfriends will not, including humiliating sex acts and rough sex. For example, she opens her song "Give It a Smack" with these lines: "Don't be shy / be a man / smack that shit [her body] / I like it rough." The domination and rough sex fantasy is repeated throughout the CD. On "Freaky Tonight" she raps, "I love it when you pull my hair and call me slut." With these lines Ms. Sancha, the sex fantasy, is asking men to act out their desire to be sexually dominant and hypermasculine.

Ms. Sancha plays the role of slut fantasy for her mostly adolescent and young adult male audience. One of the primary characteristics of the slut fantasy in adolescent minds is that the girl or woman be "easy," meaning that it does not take much money or other coaxing to get her to have sex. On the CD, Ms. Sancha implies that she is easy and will have sex anywhere at any time. For example, on "Do You Wanna," she raps: "1, 2, 3, 4 / I'm at the door / Ms. Sancha's here and it's time to bone [sex]." She continues, "Tanqueray and Alizé / give me a sip of that / that'll get you laid." With these lines Sancha suggests that whenever she is around, it is time for sexual activity and that simply buying her fashionable drinks allows one easy access to her body.

In a skit titled "LPG Interview," Sancha speaks with two Cheech and Chong stoner imitators. She claims to be working on CDs, pornographic movies, and burglary. Later in the mock interview she offers to have sex with both interviewers, to "suck him while you fuck me." In many songs, Sancha describes in great detail how she is willing, able, and ready to engage in all sorts of sexual activity. On the opening track, "Freaky Tonight," the chorus claims that Ms. Sancha is "so freaky," meaning she will do many different kinds of sex acts. Throughout she provides detail to this claim. She raps,

> you can do me in the back of the club
> in the back of the truck
> I don't care Papi
> I just wanna fuck
> a little lickin' on my clit
> a little suckin' on your dick . . .
> even take it in the butt
> you know what's up . . .
> [I will] deep throat
> these Low Pro gangstas know

The compact disc *Taking it Doggystyle* dresses up the male sexual domination fantasy in gangsta clothing. Ms. Sancha plays the "freaky slut" under male control who will do anything to please men. Of course, because she associates herself with a gangsta lifestyle, her men must be "down," or willing to engage in violent criminal activity. She does not challenge male authority, nor does she have any problems with letting men engage in violent and humiliating sex acts such as pulling her hair, performing anal sex, smacking her, and having multiple partners at once. Ms. Sancha, the gangsta rapper, was created to appeal to many young men's fantasy that equates sex with power.

Robert Jensen comments on rape as the ultimate consequence of this association:

> Feminist research long ago established that rape involves the sexualization of power, the equation in men's imaginations of sexual pleasure with domination and control . . . rape is about the fusion of sex and domination, about the eroticization of control. And in this culture, rape is normal. . . . Sex is a sphere in which men are trained to see themselves as naturally dominant and women as naturally passive. Rape is both nominally illegal and completely normal at the same time. (2004, 54–55)

The Ms. Sancha persona is very nearly a rape fantasy in which men can vicariously dominate a sexy woman who claims to enjoy, even live for, male domination. The fantasy claims that as long as the man is powerful and violent, he can extend his authority to the sexual realm with Ms. Sancha. He can prove his masculinity through two of the pillars of hypermasculine activity: violence and impersonal sex. Young men, often with few other ways to prove their masculinity, can fantasize about their "natural" dominance and women's "natural" inferiority. Ms. Sancha's debut compact disc proves to be about the eroticization of control.

Violent Female Agency

Ms. Sancha claims to be in control of many of the situations recounted in her lyrics. She is tough and violent, and she does not allow anyone to harm her. However, her control is derived almost exclusively from giving men pleasure. She never demonstrates her subjectivity through discussions of her creativity, spirituality, kindness, or intelligence. Ms. Sancha does not only have sex. In songs such as "Try Me," "Gotta Get the Money," and "Blow," Ms. Sancha also fights, robs, and kills. In her words she is a "gangsta chick" and challenges those who have a problem with her. In "Big Capone and Ms. Sancha," she confronts an imaginary detractor with the question "[you] got a problem / I'm a gangster with a pussy?" With this challenge she is establishing herself as a female gangbanger who is just as tough and dangerous as her male counterparts. In "Try Me," she claims that "never ever have you knew a bitch as bad as me / I ride around with them hustlas and them down ass G's [gangbangers]."

These lyrics are standard gangsta-rap fare with a female twist. Like her male gangsta rapper counterparts, Ms. Sancha claims a certain type of power in a society that often denies power to people of color, especially women of color. Sancha repeats the patriarchal dominance paradigm that equates power with power over others. A feminist vision of power argues that power does not have to be a negative power that destroys some in order to maintain the dominance of a few. Instead, power can be a positive force. We can think of power as empowerment that supports and aids instead of harming. This vision is far from the gangsta understanding that realizes that in today's postindustrial United States, power is vested in those who are willing to use military might and other violence. Most Chicana/o gang members have been denied even the most basic power. Brown argues that they are essentially denied full citizenship rights (2002). Their alternative is to take what power they can. This means terrorizing the displaced, marginalized, and unrepresented in their communities. They use guns to threaten people in their communities and gain a sense of personal empowerment.

Ms. Sancha's lyrics diverge only slightly from the basic gangsta lyrical formula of guns, drugs, and money. She is a woman who can use her femininity and sexuality to lure unsuspecting men to their doom—the archetypal treacherous woman or Malinche figure. In "Gotta Get the Money," Sancha discusses how she uses her sexuality to rob men:

> It's a shame how they make it so damn easy
> their minds start to flip when I start talkin' sleazy
> got 'em blind every time
> believe me
> flash that pussy I got 'em hooked
> next thing you know they been took

Since men are so preoccupied with sex and since she is so sexy, all she has to do is "start talkin' sleazy" and show her body, and they drop their guard ("got 'em blind"), and she robs them. These "levas" or "chavalas"—weak men—have little possibility for retaliation because she will use her guns, and she is part of a gang, the Low Pro Gangstas. Those who have just been robbed fear for their lives if they attempt retaliation ("they know they're getting' shot up if they try to find me").

Like many men who watch violent pornography, Sancha draws a direct line linking sex and violence. As feminists have pointed out, for men sex is often about power. This theme is common in popular culture and especially in gangsta culture.[5] Sancha makes this equation more explicit than most on her song "Gotta Get the Money." After robbing a man at gunpoint, Sancha raps:

this kinda shit makes me wet
my skirt up, throw up my set [gang sign]
head back to the LPG hideout
show these fools what I'm all about
I break bread that's got em all worked up
now we're fuckin' like we're breakin' the bed
    [sounds of moaning and a bed creaking] . . .
a little hustle
a little gunplay
a lot of fuckin'
today was a good day

Sancha claims that violence and robbing get her sexually aroused. She goes to her gang's hideout and shows them the money from her aggravated robbery. This gets the male gang members aroused, and Sancha engages in aggressive sex with one or more of them, capping an overall good day.

Ms. Sancha attempts to set herself up as "not your average chick." She claims to be superior to other women. She is smarter, sexier, better sexually, and tougher than most women. Like many women, she refuses to be controlled. Sancha wants power over her life, but the agency she seeks is steeped in the patriarchal dominance paradigm that values dominance over others and characterizes women as objects of domination. Her agency remains within the paradigm that not only undermines and devalues women but also is authoritarian and violent. In the end, Sancha's persona and lyrics reinforce violent patriarchal notions of power, gender, and sexuality.

POWER OVER VERSUS POWER TO

The different visions of power and sexuality discussed by JV and Ms. Sancha speak to the tension between female sexual objectivity and sexual subjectivity and between patriarchal notions of power as dominance (power over) and the feminist notion of empowerment (power to). JV challenges simplistic notions of female subjectivity presented in the dominant male culture in the United States. Her visions of herself, her sexuality, and her relations with men and others are democratic and loving. As a woman JV wants to control the definition of self while at the same time engaging in male-female relations that are mutually gratifying and empowering. She is not always a feminist or Xicanista, but she is not under male control, either. Sancha and Royal T. present her as a woman who is in control of the ways in which she pleases men. Her self-identity, relationships to men and others, and sexuality are framed by a hypermasculine and hyperviolent version of the patriarchal dominance paradigm. While Sancha claims that she is in control, ultimately violence and misogyny determine the content of her songs. She envisions power as domination. Ms. Sancha discusses exploitive relationships in which the central goal is to deceive, lie, rob, and steal using sexuality and violence.

CHAPTER FIVE

VIOLENCE IN CHICANO RAP

Mirror of a Belligerent Society

The rhetorics of violence in Chicano rap are part of the spread of a culture of violence in the United States (Giroux 1996). To properly understand the numerous images of violence in Chicano rap lyrics, we need to properly situate them within the contemporary violent society in which we live. I use articulation theory as a framework for analysis to examine the myriad ways in which Chicanos rap about violence. Expanding upon the discussion of articulation in previous chapters, I discuss an aesthetics of violence, interpersonal violence, and the politics of violence as part of the cultural field from which young Chicanos draw to develop their discussions and analyses of violence. The socialization of young urban Chicanas/os within a larger culture of violence in the United States has led to representations of violence in a significant proportion of Chicano rap expressions. In this chapter I explore the ways in which the lyrics of Chicano rappers mirror, comment upon, or critique the ubiquitous violence found throughout U.S. society. Often going beyond simple news media and Hollywood representations, Chicano rappers have developed sophisticated and nuanced analyses of the causes and consequences of war, state violence, and interpersonal violence.

In my sample of 470 songs I found that 71 percent included violent themes. This figure approximates Gerbner's finding (1993) in the Cultural Indicators Project that 63 percent of Latino television characters were victims or perpetrators of violence.[1] Chicanos rap about violence in myriad ways. In one song a Chicano rapper might threaten others with violent behavior while questioning his decision and grieving over loved ones killed or affected by barrio violence. In the next song he might provide a detailed description of superhuman violent exploits à la Arnold Schwarzenegger's movie characters and other macho Hollywood superheroes. On another cut the character might hit a woman or call on Chicanos to unite and violently overthrow Anglo or capitalist oppressors.

THE AESTHETICS OF VIOLENCE AND
VIOLENCE AS ENTERTAINMENT

> Violent movies are targeted at the young, both men and
> women, the same audience the military has determined
> to be most susceptible for its killing purposes. Violent
> video games hardwire young people for shooting at hu-
> mans. The entertainment industry conditions the young
> in exactly the same way the military does. Civilian soci-
> ety apes the training and conditioning techniques of the
> military at its peril.
>
> —Dave Grossman, *On Killing* (1995, 323)

Lieutenant Colonel Dave Grossman describes himself as a "killologist"
trained by the U.S. military in the arts, sciences, and psychology of
killing. His years of training and experience with killing and training
young men and women to kill for the military led him to the conclusion
that the violence we consume in our popular culture is a training ground
for real-life violent socialization and behaviors. Grossman argues that
at the movies young people are conditioned ("à la Pavlov's dog") "to
associate killing and suffering with entertainment [and] pleasure"
(302). Violent interactive video games reward killing with points, extra
games, high scores, and other positive feedback. These games are a
form of operant conditioning ("à la B. F. Skinner's rats") whereby
a child is rewarded for performing the task of murder (312–314).
Grossman argues convincingly that social learning takes place through
children observing and imitating hyperviolent movie heroes (317–322).
According to Grossman, through such societal operant and classical
conditioning, social learning, and physical and emotional distance from
others (victims), we have a society that encourages the "systematic
process of defeating the normal individual's age-old, psychological
inhibition against violent, harmful activity toward one's own species"
(304). Thus movies, music, video games, and other aspects of popular
culture have enabled a desensitization of U.S. society, allowing for high
rates of violence.

Grossman's insights provide a useful way of thinking about the
effects of an aesthetics of violence in our entertainment media. Still,
experts continue to debate the degree to which violence in popular
culture increases violent dispositions and behaviors. While most mental
health experts agree that increased exposure to violent entertainment
leads to increased aggressive and violent behaviors and attitudes, the

degree to which this is true or not remains controversial. There is no doubt, however, that our exposure to certain ideas present in popular culture affects our worldview. The American Academy of Pediatrics' Policy Statement on Media Violence (2001) states emphatically that "the strength of the correlation between media violence and aggressive behavior is greater than the correlation between calcium intake and bone mass, or the correlation between lead ingestion and IQ." Statements by other professional organizations representing physicians, psychologists, and school counselors likewise indicate their concern that violent media images correlate closely with aggressive behavior.[2]

According to Johnson, Jackson, and Gatto, "Social science researchers have generally shown that exposure to media violence tends to increase the probability of subsequent violent behavior in children and adults" (1995, 28). Many studies have tried to determine how rap music affects those who listen to it.[3] Most have argued that violent lyrical content leads to a greater acceptance of the use of violence and that those exposed to violent lyrics are more likely to engage in violent behavior or have violent thoughts. The evidence weighs heavily in support of the idea that violent media content— including rap lyrics—leads to an increase in violent thoughts and actions in the short term. Studies have not yet established whether there are long-term effects of exposure to rap music. Others question whether the music leads to violence or whether violent behaviors due to poverty, family dysfunction, crime-ridden neighborhoods, or mental illness lead to their discussion in the music. Could it be that the music "is a reflection of the social environment of its target population, or market . . . and simply reflects already existing adolescent sentiments back to the youth subculture?" (Epstein, Pratto, and Skipper 1990, 382). A complete analysis of the effects of violent rap music examines how different groups of people, especially young people, interpret the music. As Hansen explains,

> It would be extremely naïve to assume that subjects from very different racial and cultural backgrounds necessarily share a common interpretation of the 'street language' typical of rap. On the other hand, there may be few, if any, important differences among cognitive representations of violent means to ends because of homogenization produced by shared aspects of the socialization process and pervasive mass communication of mores and cultural values. (1995, 51)

While we are not empirically certain that a violent rap lyric will cause a young person to think or act violently, we do know that media act as agents of socialization and that continued exposure to violent media content socializes young people into the values expressed by such content. Young children, the most vulnerable to media socialization, are spending increasing amounts of their time with media.[4] Violent media content often shows violence as fun and honorable and shows that the person willing to engage in violence is rewarded monetarily or socially. The younger a child is, the less he or she is able to distinguish reality from media fantasy. And identification with violent heroes can create a violent value system in young people.[5] When a young person is exposed to violent content in the context of a broader culture of violence in the United States, it is hard to imagine that they do not begin to see violence as acceptable, natural, or even laudable.

We learn from movies and other media (Kamalipour 1995). We learn what the lives of others are like. White Americans learn about life in the barrios and ghettos from movies and television. For many Whites in our highly segregated country, their underlying notions about people of color form through the movies. Few Whites live in predominantly Chicana/o or African American neighborhoods, and fewer have intimate contact with people of color, our communities, or our institutions. I fear that movies such as *Boulevard Nights*, *Colors*, *American Me*, or *Blood In, Blood Out* overly influence White America's understanding of Chicana/o experiences. Furthermore, how many young Chicana/os "learn" about themselves from the movies? How many adolescent Chicanas/os see an image of themselves reflected in movies that is violent, bloody, and immoral? How many male children learn to become men through hypermasculine displays in the movies, on sports fields, in gangsta rap lyrics, or through video games?

In preparing to write this chapter I began documenting violence that I experienced in pop culture. I examined the violent imagery in popular music, television, movies, and news media. I was particularly struck by the wide offering of an aesthetics of violence at my local Blockbuster video store. It seemed to me that every other movie included violent imagery. Even more alarming was my observation that movies that included large African American or Chicana/o casts or themes about people of color were overwhelmingly violent and devoid of other topics. Was I becoming hyper-aware of violence in rental movies? Maybe it was just me. Maybe I was focusing too much on violence in movies. After all, I have my two young sons to worry about and protect from the euphoria of violence that much of our society seems caught up in. To dispel any notion that I was in a paranoid state of seeing violence everywhere, I decided to conduct a quantitative analysis of Blockbuster movies. Over a six-month period (October 2003–April 2004), I checked the new movie releases section at my local Blockbuster in Milledgeville, Georgia, once each month. I timed my observations to coincide with new release dates. I focused on movie advertisements on video cassette and DVD covers. I examined the cover imagery and the movie descriptions. I reasoned that since Blockbuster is the largest video rental chain in the United States, a trip to Blockbuster is a common aspect of leisure-time activity for many U.S. residents.

My local Blockbuster in Middle Georgia rarely received new movies dedicated to Chicana/o or Mexican themes or with more than one vaguely Latino character. No more than two movies with Chicana/o content were displayed simultaneously in the prominent New Releases section during my six-month study. Their content is predictable, if we know the history of Chicana/o and Mexican representation in Hollywood. Gary Keller's history *Hispanics and United States Film* (2004) shows the limited number and types of Mexican/Chicana/o representations in U.S.-produced films. Two prominent types are violent criminals and funny-men or buffoons. My Blockbuster carried one of each of these types of movies during my examination. *The Latin Kings of Comedy* is a quite well-conceived set of four stand-up routines hosted by Cheech Marin, and *Power Movez* is part of the "gang genre" of film in which pathological, ultraviolent Chicana/o youth engage in multiple acts of violence.

African Americans fare only slightly better in how they are represented in the New Releases section at Blockbuster. This more than likely has to do with the larger number of African American directors, producers, writers, and actors in Hollywood (Wilson and Gutierrez 1995). On average the Blockbuster New Releases section displayed 127 movies. On average, 50 of the 127 movie advertisements included violent content such as prominent displays of guns. At the Milledgeville Blockbuster, half (58) of the movies in the New Releases section featured Black themes and/or casts. Of these 58, nearly half (27) featured guns and violence. While half of all Black-themed or Black-cast movies focused on violence, other themes were also addressed. Comedies were also common, represented in 23 of the new releases.[6] A small proportion of Black movies were dramas or romances.

While violent roles are the most common for Blacks and Latinos in popular Hollywood movies, violent themes tend to dominate all

Hollywood productions. Because I live in a small town with a population that is slightly more than half Black, our Blockbuster carries many Black movies (and few Latino/Chicano movies); thus, due to sheer numbers there are more opportunities to see Black men and women in varying roles. The few movies dedicated to Latino/Chicano themes make generalizations about these characters difficult. However, with such a small Latina/o population in middle Georgia and with few opportunities for people, especially young people, to participate in Latina/o cultural institutions or have intimate contact with Latinas/os, such popular movies take on greater significance. For some, including most of my students at Georgia College and State University, the movies are the only source of "knowledge" about Chicanas/os and other Latinas/os. In this case, unrealistic and stereotypical representations take on enormous power to define the Other.

The idea of violent or buffoonish Chicanas/os has a long history in popular culture. The movie industry has only contributed to false and damaging notions of Chicana/o and Mexican people. These images are damaging because they are the "controlling images" of people of Mexican descent. That is, they serve political and economic as well as cultural ends. Patricia Hill Collins in *Black Feminist Thought* (1990) and Marlon Riggs in the documentary film *Ethnic Notions: Black People in White People's Minds* (1987) illustrate how images of African Americans over the centuries have served to justify racist behaviors, attitudes, and legislation that continue to set African Americans back and have damaged race relations. Examinations of the representation of Chicanas/os show similar occurrences. In our highly segregated society, popular images of minority others "control" the minds and worldviews of White Americans and the life chances of members of subordinate ethnic groups who suffer under racist institutions.

Movies are not the only source of an aesthetics of violence. As an eight-year-old in 2006, my son's exposure to violent movies and television was limited by a lack of access. He loved to spend time at his friend's house playing Nintendo. While his best friend had some games without violent content, they inevitably played their two favorites, *World Wrestling Federation* and *Teenage Mutant Ninja Turtles*. These two youngsters are clearly not the only ones who play such games. According to the *Nintendo 2002 Annual Report*, for fiscal year 2001 Nintendo declared $4.2 billion in net sales. It had net unit sales of its four gaming systems of $175 million. It sold more than 749 million games to go along with its gaming systems in 2001–2002. Millions of children in the United States alone spend hundreds of dollars each to play games that leading video game analysts have shown can lead to increased aggressive behavior, thoughts, and feelings and decreases in pro-social activities, especially among adolescent males.[7]

While these stories of an aesthetics of violence are not "proof" of a causal link between pop-culture violence and violence in Chicano rap, I believe that we cannot understand violence in Chicano rap without reference to popular culture. Chicano rappers often reference pop culture through samples of dialogue, nicknames, reenactments of scenes, and quotes from Hollywood blockbusters. They use monikers associated with historical and Hollywood bad guys as a means of demonstrating their lyrical and physical prowess. Capone, Capone-e, Bugsy, and Rhyme Poetic Mafia recall the criminality and "badness" of organized crime figures who have become larger-than-life legends as a result of the Italian-mafia film genre. Others name such figures in their lyrics; for example, Conejo refers to Al Capone several times on his album *City of Angels* (1999a). Other bad guys are invoked through visual and audio images. Psycho Realm samples Travis Bickle, the psychotic central character in *Taxi Driver*; Mr. Shadow prominently displays an advertising poster for Al Pacino's Cuban gangster hit, *Scarface*, in the video for the song "Bounce, Rock, Skate, Roll"; Rhyme Poetic Mafia liken themselves in "Violent by Nature" on *The Ollin Project* (2000) to the title character in the movie *Spawn*; in "Interrogated Cuzz I'm Brown" (*Mexican Power*, 1992), Proper Dos refer to policemen who have stopped them as "John Wayne"; and Conejo compares himself to the pathological killer Jason of the *Halloween* movie series. The Funky Aztecs cleverly use the names of Hollywood bad guys such as Jason, Freddy Krueger, those of *The Lost Boys*, Pinhead, and Candy Man and refer to the Chicano prison movie *American Me* on the song "Nation of Funk."

The rap music industry is little different from many other divisions of the entertainment industry in its use of violent imagery. Corporate recording labels, radio stations, and television stations prefer to sell violent and consumerist images to our youth rather than images that challenge the imperialist hypermasculinity of U.S. life and culture or those that reject a consumerist lifestyle in favor of life defined by joy, peace, dignity and love.[8] Hollywood has led youth to consider violence as fashionable and easy. Young men of all races easily purchase guns in inner cities and rural areas alike. Often, they do not carry guns simply for protection or hunting but also because Hollywood and other major media have glorified gun violence. Chuck D, leader of the political rap group Public Enemy, points out that after the movie *Colors* became a big hit, Black adolescents throughout the country decided to become either Crips or Bloods:

> They're heavily influenced by the news media coming from the bigger cities. The copycat gangsterism occurs in places like Kansas City, which is the wildest situation that you ever want to confront because in Kansas City you have people that have become Crips and Bloods from just choosing sides after seeing the movie *Colors*. (1997, 245)

Psycho Realm echoes Chuck D's analysis, rapping on "Street Platoons" (1999) about young men using guns and "joining street platoons like it's some fashion."[9] Thousands became gang members not solely for protection or economic necessity but because it had become fashionable. The popularity of gangsta rap and the Hollywood action genre contributed to the idea that macho and gangsta styles, attitude, clothing, language, and behaviors were cool.

Brownside's second CD, *Payback* (1999), is dedicated to violence. In all but one song ("Rest in Peace"), the rappers describe extremely detailed images of Brown-on-Brown violence, and "Rest in Peace" is a lament and eulogy upon the death of a friend. We are not told how he died. Could he have been a victim of violent crime? In the context of an entire album that places violence at the center of their lives, we can easily read his death as another instance of violent crime. In every other song, Brownside discusses explicitly how, who, with what, and when characters kill their enemies and how much fun they have doing it. The rappers exploit media images of themselves as criminals ("Do or Die") and gang members ("Eastside Drama"). Almost every song discusses "gangsta life in the city" and the inner-city conditions that make enemies out of other young Chicanas/os from nearby barrios.

While other songs dedicated to an analysis of violence briefly describe violent images in order to address the real subject matter of pain, despair, and psychological trauma caused by it, Brownside focuses on violence for the sake of violence. The group follows the Hollywood model of depicting hyper-real violence. Brownside is not alone in this, as many groups take the Hollywood formula to the extreme as they package their rap CDs in equally violent and criminal images. The front and back CD covers of *Payback* depict a blurry pistol in the center, held by a hooded homeboy. Similarly, the back cover of the 2001 Low Profile Records compilation *Califa Thugs* has an image of four Chicanos spread-eagle against a wall waiting to be searched by police. Even the title of this CD sells the criminal image of Chicanos. Most of the CDs from Darkroom Familia have front and back covers depicting guns, knives, blood, and the masked faces of gangbangin' Chicanos.[10]

In this era of hyper-real violence, it is not enough to insinuate a violent act. To outsell the competition, violence in media must go to extremes. It is not enough to shoot someone once. Instead, people must be shot several times with large-capacity automatic weapons, and the audience must see blood and/or hear the impact. Chicano rappers such as Brownside and the artists of Low Profile Records and Darkroom Familia follow the increasing trend in U.S. society toward ever more detailed and gruesome violence.[11] These rappers are socialized in our violent culture (as is evident in the similarities between their music and Hollywood action movies), and they recognize that many young Chicanas/os are also. On the one hand, then, the rappers are part of an entertainment industry that sells violence, and on the other hand, their artistic expression results from their maturing in a society that values and practices violence in many ways.

INTERPERSONAL VIOLENCE

Our violent culture does not stop at representation. Real violence is common in the United States. From wife abuse to road rage to school shootings, real physical violence surrounds us. Most U.S. citizens have experienced some form of violence. Women bear a disproportionate amount of the interpersonal violence in U.S. society. According to a Center for the Advancement of Women study, "Progress and Perils: New Agenda for Women" (2003), 92 percent of all women rank domestic and sexual violence as their main concern. A full one-third of all women surveyed reported experiencing at least one physical assault by a partner in her lifetime. This number is likely not to reflect the actual number of women assaulted by partners, as 77 percent of acquaintance rapes go unreported to police (USDJ 2002).

Arrest and incarceration rates reveal that the United States is one of the most violent societies on earth. From fraternity parties to sports arenas to our own homes, one can easily become a victim or perpetrator of a violent act. In our contemporary society, simply driving can become cause for perpetrating a violent crime.[12] Gang violence is another example of interpersonal violence found in U.S. society. Mike Davis reports (1990, 269–270) that the resurgence of Chicana/o gang violence in the late 1980s resulted from the introduction of the crack cocaine economy as well as the loss of jobs and the "juvenation of poverty" (40 percent of Los Angeles County children were poor in the 1980s). By the mid-1990s, gang violence was decreasing across the country. Grassroots efforts to stop gang violence as well as aggressive policing contributed to the decline. The Office of Juvenile Justice and Delinquency Prevention reported on this trend in March 2001. The report, "Youth Gang Homicides in the 1990s," noted a 15 percent drop in gang violence between 1991 and 1996. A review of National Youth Gang Surveys between 1996 and 1998 revealed that the trend continued in the late 1990s. The surveys reported that gang homicides declined from 1,293 in 1996 to 1,061 in 1998 in the largest 237 U.S. cities. Los Angeles and Chicago reported the most gang homicides, but even in these cities we have seen a drop in gang violence (Curry, Maxson, and Howell 2001).

Nevertheless, when 1,000 young men of color die each year from gang violence, this should be understood as an epidemic. Tom Hayden found (2003) that at least 25,000 people had died from gang violence since the 1970s. This epidemic of interpersonal violence found in the contemporary United States is often represented in the lyrics of Chicano rappers who relate stories about, revel in, and lament violence against women and gang violence. The following sections discuss these aspects of violent representations in Chicano rap.

MISOGYNIST VIOLENCE

Misogynist messages are common in the media (Barongan and Nagayama Hall 1995). The consequences of misogyny in the media continue to be debated. As with violent representations in the media, the effects of misogyny differ depending on the person and the types of misogynist images. However, most agree that representations of misogyny have harmful consequences for women.[13] For example, Barongan and Nagayama Hall found that "cognitive distortions concerning women facilitate men's sexual aggression toward women" (206). In other words, misogynist rap music can cause its audience to have distorted ideas about women, how men should treat women, and women's value that increase the potential for men to be sexually aggressive and violent toward women. Given that our social landscape is replete with distortions about women's value, including misogynist representations of them in popular culture, it is no surprise that violence against women is so common in our society and that young Chicano rappers would more often than not depict women with degrading language.

Chicano rap is, for the most part, misogynistic. Images of sub ordinate, passive women abound in Chicano rap. The image of the sexy woman who is sexually available and dangerous dominates the Chicano rap discourse on women. Women in rap serve men and are objects to be manipulated for male pleasure.[14] Chicano rappers refer to women with such epithets as bitch, ho, hoodrat, freak, slut, *chichona*, *nalgona*, hottie, and *puta* (prostitute). Representations of women as whole, complex beings are few and far between in Chicano rap. This is due, in part, to the fact that the community of Chicano rappers consists almost entirely of young men who are creating a fantasy world. In this world Chicano men control and dominate. In the fantasies of Chicano rappers, women do not challenge men, and rarely do they reject male sexual advances.[15]

Armstrong found violent misogyny in 22 percent of the gangsta rap lyrics of the popular African American artists he examined (2001),[16] while only 4 percent (19) of the 470 songs I analyzed for this study made any mention of violence against women. While we see a relative lack of misogynist violence in Chicano rap, the pleasure that some Chicano youths find in hearing and telling stories of violence against women is alarming.

Duke of the Darkroom Familia raps that he is going to beat Alyssa Milano with his penis and make her bleed in his song "Alyssa Milano." Two other Darkroom Familia rappers, K.I.D. and Oso, rap in "Players 4 Life" (*Smile Now, Cry Later*, 2001) that they will smack a "bitch" if she is ugly or smack her on her buttocks during intercourse if she is sexy. Others who celebrate misogynist violence include Brownside, SPM (*Never Change, Time Is Money, 3rd Wish*), Royal T (*Southsiders, Chp. 13, Crónica 2013*), Knightowl (*Baldheaded Kingpin, Knightmares*), Lil' Rob (*Crazy Life*), the Funky Aztecs (*Day of the Dead*), Street Platoon ("Pink"), and La Clika (*Thump n' Chicano Rap*).[17]

GANG VIOLENCE: CELEBRATION AND LAMENTATION

While gang violence was decreasing in the United States, representation of it in the media increased substantially. Gangsta rap became the best-selling genre of music in the early 1990s, and Hollywood continued to produce gang exploitation films such as *New Jack City* (1991), *Menace II Society* (1993), and *Juice* (1992). Critics often link gangsta rap and gang violence. Gabe Morales, a gang specialist and owner of Gang Prevention Services (GPS), wrote in "Chicano Music: An Influence on Gang Violence and Culture" (2006, 3) that "the growing violence in the lyrics in these songs also seems to indicate a trend toward willingness on the part of gang members to commit violent acts directed at law enforcement officers." He suggests a direct relationship between gangsta rap lyrics and gang violence that should cause law enforcement officers to scrutinize such music. Like most critics of gangsta rap, though, Morales' analysis is selective and overly simplistic. While many Chicano rappers celebrate gang violence, many others report complicated and complex attitudes and feelings toward gang violence.

Critics of gangsta rap have continually misunderstood how many in this genre discuss violence in complex and revealing ways. Many, I suspect, have not listened to entire songs or CDs and only understand the occasional gunshot and violent phrase. Critics unfamiliar with rap and hip-hop vernacular and the conditions in the barrios and ghettos that create a unique understanding and ethos of violence fail to understand that the authors of these narratives decry violence as well as celebrate it. Critics interpret the lyrics too literally and simplify the complex understandings Chicano and Black youth have concerning violence. Latin Bomb Squad addresses this point in asking after a triple homicide which morality is superior—that of the streets or that of the majority of U.S. citizens who do not inhabit the violent streets of the inner city.[18] Moreover, many Americans who do not regularly listen to rap have been influenced by exaggerated representations of rising youth crime in the corporate media;[19] the fallout from police protests against Ice-T's song "Cop Killer," which was written as a protest against police violence;[20] Tipper Gore's Parental Music Resource Center;[21] and C. Dolores Tucker's campaigns against rap.[22]

More complex popular and scholarly analyses of violence in rap and youth culture are needed. Cornel West's discussion of "nihilism in black America" helps us understand one important aspect of the discussion of violence in Chicano gangsta rap. West argues that the major enemy of Black people is "the lived experience of coping with a life of horrifying meaninglessness, hopelessness, and (most important) lovelessness" (1994, 22–23). He argues that nihilism is debilitating in that feelings of hopelessness can become self-fulfilling prophecies that cause apathy and, worse, violence. The result of nihilism for Blacks "is a numbing detachment from others and a self-destructive disposition toward the world" (23). Much of the fratricidal gang violence in Brown and Black America might be attributed to nihilism. LBS argues that nihilism often causes the rappers themselves and fellow Chicanos to not care about the lives of others. Narratives from Chicano gangsta rap also suggest that violence among young urban Chicanos is caused by what West calls a "self-destructive disposition toward the world." South Park Mexican, in "Land of the Lost" (1999), narrates stories of violence that result from the poverty-stricken environments that inner-city Chicanas/os endure. Poverty, lack of opportunities, and a degraded sense of self foster the violent outlook toward life and society that SPM often finds among young Chicanas/os. His experiences in the harsh urban environs of Houston cause him to attribute Chicano violence to nihilism. He argues that a lack of self-love causes violent young Chicanos to live "sick." Sir Dyno from the San Francisco Bay Area echoes LBS and SPM. On "I Can't See Through the Rain," he attributes violence in the barrios of the Bay to urban decay and a sense of nihilism that results—the crazy life that makes *locos* (crazies) out of Chicano boys. He raps that violence is so common in his community that he has learned to love and accept it. Yet, on the other hand, he wishes for a funeral so he can have peace and silence.[23]

De Genova persuasively argues (1995) that in discussing nihilism as the biggest threat to Black existence (instead of racist U.S. institutions), West simply rewords the "culture of poverty" thesis, which attributes little agency to the Black working classes and pathology to their social institutions. De Genova argues that Black gangsta rap is not merely an illustration of these young people's hopelessness and social pathology. Instead, a more complex notion of nihilism sees it as a struggle with death, as a response of some Black youth to their experiences as its victims and perpetrators.

Approximately 11 percent (53) of the songs I analyzed fit with De Genova's theory of nihilism in gangsta rap. For example, many tracks on LBS' CD *Neighborhood Creepas* involve extended discussions of violence and thoughtful critiques of it. Often the narratives seem ambivalent, as violence is both lamented and celebrated as a way to overcome one's enemies. In these songs one can read the authors' attempts to come to terms with the violence that surrounds them. In "Deal with tha Madness" LBS laments the proliferation of gang violence and the pain it causes Chicana/o families and friends. They open the song asking how many of their friends must die and how many family members must grieve because of the violent mentality fostered on urban streets. Their lyrics decry the unnecessary lives of Chicano youth lost to gang and other violence and many young people's ambivalence toward violence in their neighborhoods.

Many Chicano rappers do not simply promote gang violence.[24] Often, they use their raps/poems as cathartic devices to sort out their feelings about violence and cope with the loss of loved ones and the resultant siege mentality they might feel. More than a celebration of crime, gangsterism, and violence, I argue that violence in Chicano gangsta rap exhibits the multiple ways in which young urban Chicanas/ os attempt to make sense of death, the sacredness of life, and other existential questions and adolescent frustrations and violence that they must endure as subordinated, racialized subjects in postindustrial urban "America." Thus, while Hollywoodized representations of the threat posed by urban youth of color have influenced many rappers to celebrate interpersonal conflict such as misogynist and gang violence, others use the backdrop of gang violence to criticize the consequences of Brown-on-Brown attacks.

THE POLITICS OF VIOLENCE

Real, physical violence is not limited to its interpersonal manifestations. Our country's history is rooted in violence. The United States was established through the bloodiest genocide yet known in human history. The conquest and decimation of millions of native peoples surpasses that of even the Nazi genocide against Jews. If we add the millions of deaths of Africans during the Middle Passage and after their arrival to the United States, the establishment of the United States is far and away the most bloody series of events in history. This murder tally does not even count the thousands of murders of Chinese workers and the burning of their businesses and villages in the last half of the nineteenth century or the state-sponsored murder and terror that Mexican Americans in the Southwest faced during the same period.[25]

While this violence is often erased from our collective memory, the continued violence of the United States during the twentieth century and so far in the twenty-first, in its zeal to become the only superpower and most dominant country on earth, is regularly celebrated and honored. Over the past 110 years, the United States has waged war (declared or not) on dozens of countries. In Latin America the United States has invaded or supported violence in Puerto Rico (1898, not to mention the regular practice bombings of Vieques), Cuba (1898, early 1960s), Guatemala (1954, 1960, 1967–1969), Peru (1965), Chile (1973), El Salvador (1980s), Nicaragua (1980s), Grenada (1983), and Panama (1989). The United States has a long history of violence in Asia as well. Beginning in 1898 with the invasion of the Philippines until the Vietnam War between 1961 and 1973, the United States has waged war on Asian countries including Korea (1950–1953), Indonesia (1958), Laos (1964–1973), and Cambodia (1969–1970), all following perhaps the single most violent attack in human history, the nuclear bombings of Nagasaki and Hiroshima, Japan, in 1945. Africa and the Middle East also have felt the wrath of our government. The Congo suffered from U.S. intervention in 1964, and the Sudan was attacked in 1998. Most recently, the Middle East has been the region coveted by the United States for its natural resources, especially oil. This desire to control the Middle East oil-producing region has led to open warfare and covert operations against countries, peoples, and leaders of the Middle East, as witnessed in the attacks on Lebanon (1984), Libya (1986), Afghanistan (1998, 2002–), and Iraq (1991–1999, 2003–).[26]

This brief catalogue of the bellicosity of United States governments during the twentieth century does not include U.S. support of terrorist regimes, arms and military technology sales, and training of foreign militaries at places like the former School of the Americas. Violence has been the central tactic of U.S. foreign policy. Through media spin and the distortion of history in our textbooks, the violent overthrow of governments and the seizure of economies and resources is justified and celebrated. We are taught as children to be kind and peaceful but that violence in the name of our country is always right. We have made the world safe from communism and are killing hundreds of thousands of children in the Middle East to eradicate terrorism. We are told to be proud to be Americans in this day and age of the benevolent empire. And if not, well, President Bush said it best: "You are either with us or against us." While Bush and current political elites evaded "serving" in Vietnam, they continually send young people to face death and taunt people in the Middle East and Muslim countries with statements like "bring 'em on" when referring to the resistance to the U.S. occupation of Iraq.[27] Thus, while on the domestic front Black and Brown men are the violent enemy and threat to the United States, on the international front, bearded, turban-wearing, Muslims are to be feared. This rhetoric has allowed for the justification of the state killing of Black and Brown men (for example, the seventeen Black men murdered by the Cincinnati police between 1995 and 2001),[28] and the unexplained "disappearances" of thousands of Muslims and Arabic-looking people in the United States after the 9/11 tragedy.

This sordid history, rather than a warning, has been spun by the government and the media as the proper way to deal with international dispute. I cannot think of a better example of the dominance paradigm in action: violence as foreign policy, violence as social relation. The militaristic language and posturing of our governmental elites is lauded as bravery. These elites are real men who protect our families and our country. What red-blooded American boy would not want to emulate this behavior on a smaller scale?

One finds similar attitudes of violent posturing and honoring violence as bravery in the streets of many ghettos and barrios. A violent disposition toward the world is not only part of the U.S. government's foreign policy; it is also part of a larger complex of factors and behaviors that constitute street socialization.[29] Most of the artists I earlier described as working within the gangsta genre present a violent façade in which dominance and submission define social and personal relations.

Other Chicanos have assimilated the militaristic language and posture toward the world exhibited in U.S. military history and current foreign policy but speak from the perspective of the subaltern and colonial subject. They see the government and Anglo elites as the dominant forces that suppress them as racialized, colonized subjects. Aztlán Underground's work exemplifies this perspective. In its "Lyrical Drive-By" on *The Ollin Project* (2001), a compilation CD produced by Digital Aztlán media company, Aztlán Underground accuses the United States of stealing land from native peoples through colonization and argues for retaliation and retribution. They rap,

> The wetback's Uncle Sam
> stealin' and killin' from the red man . . .
> we got our AK huntin'
> a lil' blam, blam, blam to Uncle Sam
> cuz that colonizer straight jacked our land

In ways similar to Black counterparts such as Tupac Shakur, dead prez, and Master P, many Chicano rappers argue that they are under siege and at war with the police, the education system, and other key institutions. Many refer to themselves and their groups of friends as soldiers. Chicano rappers such as Psycho Realm, Street Platoon, and the contributors to *The Ollin Project* CD use vivid metaphors of war to describe the violent relationship between Chicano street youth and the police. Borrowing from pop culture, history books, and the nightly news, Chicano rappers talk about dropping napalm and chemical bombs and wearing camouflage, boots, and gas masks in their barracks.[30] They add sampled lines and sounds from war movies to their aural landscapes of hard-driving rhythms, eerie string and piano arrangements, and aggressive vocals.[31]

For Psycho Realm and *The Ollin Project* contributors, young Chicanos are at war with the agents of the U.S. government. On "Tha Strong Survive," the Brown Town Looters argue that the government holds Chicanos down through high prices and taxation. They implore Chicanos to stop killing each other and to unite in revolution. Krazy Race's "Dedicated" examines the links between contemporary Chicano disenfranchisement and a history of colonialism. Equating the Spanish conquest of Mesoamerica with current government treatment of inner-city residents, he raps about the slaughter of thousands of native Mexicans in the sixteenth century, comparing this to the oppressive conditions of contemporary project housing. He blames the government for inferior schools that only teach European history and values and Anglo business owners who place liquor stores on every barrio block.

The Psycho Realm devotes its entire second album, *A War Story, Book I*, to analyzing the violence in Los Angeles barrios as war between rival gang factions and with police and other governmental agents. Psycho Realm denounces Brown-on-Brown violence and instead urges Chicano gangbangers to become soldiers in a war against the true forces of their oppression. The police, government, National Guard, military, and intelligence services are all depicted as enemies of urban Chicanas/os.[32] Psycho Realm "schools" young Chicanos on the dangers of drugs, the Community Resources Against Street Hoodlums (CRASH) program and special police gang units, computer surveillance, and media misrepresentation.[33] They discuss and lament a false racial consciousness, arguing that young Chicano gangbangers who believe themselves to be rebelling against governmental authority are in reality participating in their own genocide. Psycho Realm asks gangbangers who sell drugs and commit violent acts to think about who profits from this activity. They answer that elite drug and gun manufacturers and traffickers are reaping the spoils of gang warfare stimulated by gun and drug trafficking. They then implore young Chicanos to take control of their lives and communities by organizing.[34]

The police are prime targets of Chicano rap critique and violence; 30 percent (144) of the songs I analyzed in this study discussed the police. In none of these songs are the police presented in a positive light. Chicano rappers contend that the police along with other governmental agencies oppress inner-city Chicanos. Violence against the police is common in Chicano rap and is seen as a way to rid the barrio of the primary agent of repression. This type of violence is celebrated because of the liberatory possibilities it engenders. In Chicano rap, perpetrators of violence against repressive agencies are seen as social bandits who reject societal mores and overcome oppression.[35]

Most Chicano rappers possess the same irreverence as the badman of African American folklore and literature. The ideal Chicano badman rejects all authority—the authority of the Church, the U.S. social and political system, police, and some aspects of Mexican and Chicana/o culture. Like the hero of the *corrido* who uses violence to overcome oppression, Chicano rappers offer a model of Mexican manhood in which the man is the often violent protector of family and strong head of household. In the impoverished postindustrial barrio, his enemies are often Chicanos from rival barrios. However, many Chicano rappers have developed a societal critique that lays the blame for Chicano marginalization and poverty on Anglos and our racist, capitalist system. While few of their raps focus on Chicano liberation, many young Chicanos follow in the tracks of *corridos* and other Chicano cultural expression in arguing for violence as a way to effect social change. Many locate the sources of violence in their neighborhoods with the government and its agents. For these rappers, the government and elites are the enemies of the Chicano people. Within many of their calls to revolutionary violence, Chicano rappers urge gangbangers and others to stop the Brown-on-Brown violence that has become so fashionable in recent decades.

CONCLUSION

To understand the violent discourse of Chicano rap we must recognize its embeddedness within a larger societal discourse and set of behaviors that celebrate violence and domination and that present it as the only way to resolve disputes and as the defining trait of manhood. We must critically examine the causes of violence in our barrios and in our world, while analyzing the violence in our popular culture that feeds the imaginations of our children. In this way we can understand that Chicano rap, like all cultural production, is articulated within a global cultural and political economy and not produced autonomously by a few hyperviolent youths of color. The violent discourses of Chicano rap are part of a larger formation of U.S. identity and culture bred for domination. The socioeconomic and political conditions in Chicano barrios and a history of celebrating violent heroes in Mexican patriarchal culture also contribute to the unique understanding of and response to violence that we hear from Chicano rappers.

Their hyperviolent lyrics inform us about the impact that our violent society is having on our youth. Whether fantasies, boasts, or street reportage, Chicano rap offers a mirror in which our violent society can see itself reflected. Chicano rappers critique our society's focus on violence as the means to solve social problems as well as its failure to alleviate poverty and crime through their tales of poverty, violence, and cynicism common in the most marginalized of our urban communities. The militarization of the inner city as the predominant governmental response to crimes of poverty and general societal unrest has failed miserably (M. Davis 1990), and Chicano rappers testify to it.

Violence in Chicano rap demonstrates how the spread of a culture of violence has influenced young people's thinking and orientation toward violence. For example, Chicano rappers often take the names of historical and Hollywood badmen. The rappers Bugsy and Capone take their names from notorious mobsters, while most Chicano rappers call each other "gangsta," "G" (short for "gangsta"), and "O.G." (short for "original gangsta") as they form their attitudes and orientation to the world based in part on the Italian-mafia genre of Hollywood movie.[36] Some Chicano rap producers introduce Chicano rap songs with dialogue from violent Hollywood movies, effectively linking this genre of rap to the larger culture industry controlled by upper-class white men. A great deal of the gratuitous violence found in Chicano rap, far from being produced from the pathological minds of Brown youth, results from copying the successful Hollywood formula of depicting macho superstars engaged in extremely violent superhuman feats. In their action stories, Chicano rappers replace the hypermasculine white superstars Bruce Willis, Arnold Schwarzenegger, and Sylvester Stallone with bald-headed Chicano gangstas, fully tattooed and Brown.

Chicano rap also reveals an important cultural interaction between Black and Brown men in the inner city. Of course, the fact that these Chicanos are rapping over rhythms and melodies from the Black musical tradition and not singing *corridos* or *tejano* music is testament to the important influence that the culture of Black men has had on inner-city Chicanos. Close examination of the vocal styles of some Chicano rappers reveals the influence of many Black rappers such as Tupac Shakur (Makaveli), Master P, E-40, Too Short, and Bone-Thugs-n-Harmony. The adoption of a language, style, and attitude developed among inner-city Black youth partially accounts for the pimp discourse on Chicano rap songs. That is not to say that Black patriarchal culture is to be blamed for young Chicanos' attitudes toward women. The Mexican/Chicano oral tradition is rife with misogynist attitudes that made the adoption of the pimp identity and style natural for this new generation of Chicanos.

The naturalization of violence toward women is a disturbing trend in our popular culture.[37] From the slasher genre to mainstream movies such as *Leaving Las Vegas* to gangsta rap, dominance over women is

being promoted through physical abuse, rape, and murder.[38] Scholars
such as Faludi, hooks, and Katz have linked this trend to a backlash
against the marginal advances made by women during the height of
the women's movement. Similarly, some Chicano rappers brag about
hitting women if they feel the women deserve it, or they make fun of
violence toward women. The "pimp slap" is the new weapon and threat
that Chicano rappers use to control women. The devaluation of women
in our larger society and Mexican culture's long history of misogyny
are reflected in the misogynistic violence and objectification of women
in Chicano rap.

The Othering process of the patriarchal dominance worldview leads
to antagonistic relationships with many men as well. Physical assaults,
road rage, school shootings, and gang violence reveal a contemporary
nation unprecedented in its violence. Chicanas/os in poor urban areas
endure interpersonal violence and the trauma and fear that accompany
it. The gang system has claimed the lives of many Chicana/o youth
over the past three decades. Many Chicano rappers have been affected
in countless ways by Brown-on-Brown gang violence. The shooting
that left Duke Gonzales of Psycho Realm paralyzed and the murder of
Steve "Cartoon" Rivera, both taking place after Chicano rap events, are
two prominent examples. Some seem to revel in the gangsta lifestyle.
They celebrate the power that can be found in a handgun or automatic
weapon. They live for the excitement of money, drugs, guns, and
sexually available women. Others lament the devastation wrought by
the proliferation of guns and gangs in urban Chicana/o communities.
Their lyrics tell woeful tales of friends and family killed by senseless
violence. They contemplate gun violence in order to gain better
understanding of the meaning and value of life. On "Drug Lab" (2001),
Street Platoon provides insight into the group's discussions of violence,
life, and death, rapping that their work is about "truth and freedom"
and asking God to "bless the process of death." Similarly, Frost, South
Park Mexican, Psycho Realm, Sir Dyno, LBS, O.T.W., and others rap
in ways that are critical of violence in our society and that help them
come to terms with everyday violence in their communities. In this
way, Chicano rappers provide important yet rarely heard discussions
of violence from those who live in violent urban barrios. Their critiques
of our country's focus on criminal justice and policing as solutions to
inner-city problems expand the dialogue about crime, poverty, and
violence.

Chicano rappers also reveal a sophisticated politics and critique of
power in our society through raps of liberatory violence. Chicano rap,

like *corridos* and the badman, turn the tables on racialized domination. Chicanos through fantasies of united uprisings against local and national agents of repression envision a new society in which Chicanos make the rules and govern themselves. But this new order is attained using a type of violence closely associated with patriarchal dominance. As a result, little has changed in their imagined worlds. Women are still second-class citizens, and governance does not occur through a more democratic process. Many Chicano rappers influenced by the rhetoric of the survival of the fittest envision a new social order in which the only variable that has changed is the ethnicity of those in power.

The media portray Chicana/o violence in simplistic and racist ways. Television and Hollywood sell it, and most of America fears it. Chicano rappers complicate our understanding of violence in the United States. Understanding violence in our country requires that we pay attention to Chicana/o and other youth who provide alternative interpretations of the causes and effects of violence. Without a serious discussion of how Chicano rap addresses violence, we will be doomed to commit the same mistakes in attempting to overcome it. As globalization increases inner-city poverty and violence, we are likely to continue to follow the same path of more laws, more prisons, more police, and less investment in the inner cities that we have followed since at least the early 1980s. The fact that Latinos are the fastest-growing population in both violent inner cities and prisons should cause us all to pause and reassess our society especially in light of the narratives of violence rapped by young urban Chicanos.[39]

Lest we get the wrong impression of Chicano rap music as being preoccupied with violence and perpetuating the broader stereotype that Mexicans are violent, I should note that while violence is the most common theme, it is not the only theme. Chicano rappers often discuss peace, love, and partying in the barrios. Artists such as Frost, Delinquent Habits, Slow Pain, SPM, Funky Aztecs, Sir Dyno, and even Brownside have recorded many songs that celebrate love of *raza* and barrio. Songs that depict scenes of homeboys and/or families gathering to enjoy each other's company to the sounds of Mexican music, oldies, and rap while drinking, smoking marijuana, eating Mexican food, and participating in joking and storytelling sessions are almost as prevalent as those that depict violent scenes. While beyond the scope of this book, the way in which Chicano rap, at times, rejects the individualized pleasures of capitalist-driven consumption for community-based love and joy must also be analyzed in order to have a well-rounded understanding of the music and culture.[40]

THE CHICANO RAP ON GLOBALIZATION

The Chicano rap and hip-hop explosion has taken place during a time of crisis in our barrios and throughout our world. Capitalist globalization has devastated developing countries,[1] while economic restructuring has led to increased poverty, epidemic incarceration rates, repressive criminal and immigration legislation, and disenfranchisement of youth and people of color in the United States.[2] In order to understand the types of stories told and analyses developed by Chicano rappers we must be aware of the impact that economic restructuring has had on Chicana/o barrios. This chapter uses the stories told by political Chicano rappers to develop a political economic history of U.S. criminal justice, the "War on Drugs," race, and imprisonment from the mid-1980s through the 1990s.

Chicano rappers articulate a criticism of capitalist globalization in their lyrics. Through their words we can see a different picture of the current economic and political situation in the United States. Their analyses of economics, the prison system, policing, and the media should be seen as a part of a larger set of critiques developed by academics and activists who argue that the politics and economics of the "New World Order" have had positive impacts only for the rich, while the rest of us have seen our quality of life diminished. Rappers such as Psycho Realm, Krazy Race, Cypress Hill, and the Funky Aztecs put faces on the statistics that many have used to condemn globalization and demonstrate how many in our communities are dissatisfied (to say the least) with economic and political decisions made by elites over the past three decades.

Gustavo Esteva and Madhu Prakash in their path-breaking work, *Grassroots Postmodernism (1998)*, focus our attention on evidence that while "the social majorities" or "two-thirds majority" of the world toil under the yoke of globalization, they have not given up hope.[3] They are resisting the dehumanizing effects of capitalist globalization and are struggling to advance alternatives to it. Stories from numerous places throughout the world suggest an emergent "grassroots postmodernism" through which the world's marginalized resist the logic, structures, and behaviors associated with globalization and the New World Order and construct alternative institutions based on the cultural logic of their local traditions and customs. An examination of grassroots struggles from environmental justice movements to indigenous and land struggles indicates that many of the seemingly most destitute among us are theorizing and practicing new ways of living while critiquing and resisting the intrusion of the global market into their homes and communities.[4] Esteva and Prakash contend that we must listen to these voices and engage in dialogue with them if we hope to stem the tidal wave of globalization and survive the coming globalization decades. In agreeing with them, I assert that the voices of Chicana/o youth present a particular, localized critique of globalization through the narration of their experiences in urban America. Chicano rappers have taken the lead in presenting this critique to the rest of us through recorded stories of inner-city life that if read carefully can contribute to our understanding of the effects of globalization, especially as concerns questions of violence, xenophobia, and economic powerlessness. I will focus here on a small sample of Chicano rappers from California.

CHICANO RAP NARRATIVES ON THE
CONSEQUENCES OF GLOBALIZATION

Chicano rappers serve as an organic intellectual class for the young, Brown, urban disenfranchised.[5] They theorize, represent, and give voice to the cares, concerns, desires, hopes, dreams, and problems of young inner-city Chicanas/os through their poetics rapped over the aggressive, transgressive rhythms conceived in the smoke-filled rooms of recording studios and private dwellings of the musicians.[6] In this chapter I discuss a sample of this Chicana/o poetics read against the backdrop of capitalist globalization and economic restructuring that has wreaked havoc on Mexican immigrant and Chicana/o communities.

Since Kid Frost released his CD *Hispanic Causing Panic* in 1990, Chicano rap has chronicled the effects of globalization and Chicano youths' resistance to it. By the late 1990s, Chicano rap critiques had matured, and many have developed poignant, poetic, and precise critiques of the consequences of globalization in their communities.

MEDIA AS PROPAGANDA IN THE NEW WORLD ORDER

Ever since you seen *American Me* / you scared of me.

— Funky Aztecs, "Nation of Funk"

Northern California's Funky Aztecs ingeniously use popular media to comment on the state of their postindustrial barrio. In "Living Forever" they compare themselves to Hollywood criminals and psychopaths to communicate their badness and masculinity. On "Nation of Funk" and "Prop 187," they point out how popular movies and other media have created stereotypes of Chicanos and Mexican immigrants that have swayed public opinion against immigrants and gangs or Chicano barrio youth generally. Such propaganda has caused most to turn a blind eye toward the violence experienced by immigrants on the border. Few citizens know, much less care, that 1,450 immigrants died on the border between 1996 and 2000 (M. Davis 2000, 41). In the decade after President Clinton initiated new "get-tough" policies on the border in 1994, "more than 2,600 have died—more than ten times the number who died trying to cross the Berlin wall during its three-decade history."[7] As immigration from Mexico and anti-immigrant feelings have increased, so too has the aggressive and violent policing of immigrants. Christian Parenti shows that the border between Mexico and the United States has become increasingly dangerous, with many more Border Patrol agents using sophisticated military technology (1999).[8] Others including Mike Davis emphasize the concomitant rise of vigilante groups on the border who take the law into their hands and engage in acts of violence against those they perceive to be illegal immigrants.[9] The upsurge in vigilantism led to the Minuteman Project during the spring and summer of 2005 in which more than one thousand civilians patrolled the U.S.-Mexico border.

The Funky Aztecs use their voices as rapped on their CDs to provide information that corporate media and Hollywood neglect. Over a haunting beat, the Funky Aztecs play short news clips about the supposed problems posed by large-scale immigration from Mexico and Latin America juxtaposed with citizen comments illustrating their racism and ignorance concerning immigrants and immigration. As well, the Funky Aztecs continually repeat the phrase "Secure the border" throughout the song "Prop 187." The song suggests that the average citizen's anti-immigrant attitudes and desires to secure the border from further illegal immigration stem directly from the misinformation provided by corporate media.

Much of America views the world of gangbanging Brown youth through media images and the endless refrain of the criminal justice system's discourse that we need more cops and prisons, more military technology and logic, to contain the threat posed by gangs (Escalante 2000). News stories, yellow television journalism, and the gang genre in film render the horrors of inner-city living that have the propagandistic effect of creating an enemy, an Other, out of youth of color. State and federal legislative bodies increasingly pass draconian legislation that disregards the human and civil rights of urban youth with the approval of middle-class Americans who lock themselves behind walled communities with neighborhood patrols and purchase the latest surveillance and deterrence equipment to protect themselves from the new "Brown scourge" (M. Davis 1990).

Two important points are left out of this hyper-real depiction of the Chicano gang threat: most youth of color, including most inner-city Chicanas/os, are not members of gangs and do not partake in its violent subculture; and analysis is needed of the roles of globalization, economic restructuring, and increased state violence directed at young people of color. But propaganda is never intended to present all of the facts. The role of propaganda is to establish the legitimacy of those in power and their acts of violence (physical, economic, symbolic, or other) and to illustrate the righteousness and benevolence of "our side" and the evil of the enemy (Pease 1992). So, it is left to the organic intellectuals, the urban poets, of the barrios to include an analysis of globalization and illegitimate violence on the part of the state in our imaginary of urban warfare.

On their second release, *A War Story, Book I* (2000), Sick Jacken and Duke of Psycho Realm address the relationships among barrio violence, draconian criminal justice legislation, and the media. The rappers hail from the barrio of Pico-Union. Since their arrival onto the hip-hop scene in 1997 with their self-titled debut, *The Psycho Realm*, they have focused their poetics on the violent environments found in many Los Angeles neighborhoods. They testify, document, and analyze the violence in their barrios and locate the cause of that violence in illegitimate state policies.

They assert that the propagandistic function of the media furthers intra-ethnic violence and masks damaging state policies. In "Order Through Chaos" they rap:

> chaos serves as smoke repeated hoax to screen
> we lose control confused in the midst of staged scenes
> media invented unrelented reports presented

often enough to make us think our world's tormented
sentenced by momentous news of feuds we side and
    choose
use weapons and step in the trap we lose . . .
all because the broadcast flashed ghetto stars
how much television you watch you tube whores? . . .
through tv set nonsense
we sit and fit as the face of violence.[10]

Psycho Realm argues that "invented" media reports convince us that "our world"—and specifically that of our barrios—is "tormented," violent, and dangerous. The effect for barrio youth is that they "side and choose, use weapons and step in the trap" of violent gang and criminal behavior. The propaganda, or "hoax," convinces white Americans and other "tube whores" of the new Brown scourge. Chicanos have become "the face of violence." The phenomenon of media depiction of Black and Brown youth as violent superpredators has been noted also by many media analysts and criminal justice critics.[11] Even police and drug enforcement agents recognize how eager the media have been to cover drug and drug-crime stories. Parenti (1999, 56) quotes the head of the U.S. Drug Enforcement Agency's New York office as stating that "the media were only too willing to cooperate [in running drug stories] because as far as they were concerned, crack was the hottest combat reporting story to come along since the end of the Vietnam war."

Economic restructuring beginning in the 1970s caused high Chicano youth unemployment and the drastic reduction or elimination of citizen entitlement programs like Aid to Families with Dependent Children (AFDC) and Social Security. Many young people found jobs in the illicit and illegal economies. The police militarized postindustrial barrios, while the corporate media publicly convicted entire Chicana/o communities. The solutions to the drug, gang, and poverty epidemic in Los Angeles became more police, more prisons, and longer prison sentences.

OF PIGS AND PRISONS

They keep order by making street corners gang borders
Beating down King and setting the theme for riot starters
Cop quarters can't maintain the disorder

So they call the National Guard to come strike harder
Rolling deep headed for Florence and Normandy where
   all you see
Buildings on fire chaos on Roman streets
Hope is cheap sold by the local thief relief from the
   common grief
Served on a platter shatter your smallest dreams
Pig chiefs are referees on gladiator fields
We're too busy dodging the sword truth stays unrevealed
Sealed all filled in the federal cabinets
Classified order through chaos for world inhabitants . . .
We go to the streets at night
And fight in the sick-ass side show of mine
We play the government role
And straight up fuckin' smoke the rival.[12]

The Psycho Realm song "Order Through Chaos" analyzes the multi-ethnic Los Angeles rebellion that followed the 1991 verdict in the case of the police beating of Rodney King and places it squarely within a context of violent globalization that creates "chaos for world inhabitants." Cedric Robinson argues similarly (1993) that understanding the not-guilty verdict in the "pavement lynching" of Rodney King requires analysis of racism, capitalism, and anti-democracy that characterized U.S. politics and economics during the Reagan years. The members of Psycho Realm locate the violence associated with the uprising as well as that of everyday violence in many L.A. barrios in the state strategies of containment of poor people of color. In saying "they keep order by making street corners gang borders," the authors offer a firsthand critique of the police practice of exacerbating neighborhood tensions.[13] They go on to state, "We play the government role and straight up fuckin' smoke the rival." Psycho Realm presents a vivid critique of how the powerful use the divide-and-conquer strategy to undermine potential revolt by focusing people's anger on one another. This strategy has the added benefit of causing people to be "too busy dodging the sword" to see the "truth," thus maintaining elites' claim to legitimate rule. Psycho Realm suggests that in busying themselves with fighting each other, many barrio residents remain uninformed of the true nature of their oppression at the hands of the state and the transnational bourgeoisie. In the song "Enemy of the State" (2000) from the same album they make this argument even more strongly:

> we're killing family tragically
> the enemy dividing those fighting against it
> weakening our infantry
> we caught on to your big plan
> separate us into street gangs
> infiltrate the sets [gang subsets] put some battles
>   in effect
> to distract from your dirty outfit, yeah

Psycho Realm suggests that those fighting against global capital are becoming weaker ("weakening our infantry"). The age-old divide-and-conquer tactic is used "to distract from your dirty outfit," a reference to global capitalist elites and their policing institutions that serve as the frontlines against revolutionary activity.

Psycho Realm offers the following in "Conspiracy Theories":

> the masterplan don't include us so they shoot us
> supply weapons, coke, crack and buddha
> keep track of who took the bait through computers
> enslave and regulate the 'hoods through the *juras*
> we're all victims as the plot thickens
> better recognize the big plan the clock's ticking

"Buddha" is hip-hop slang for marijuana. The reference to computer surveillance alludes to the practice of authoritarian states to continuously monitor its citizens, especially rebels and "criminals." In the barrios of the United States this takes the form of gang databases and a sophisticated national FBI data center. *Jura* is Chicana/o slang for police.

In "Order Through Chaos" the Psycho Realm reveals another common theme in Chicano rappers' analysis of global urban violence—animosity toward and conflict with the "pig," or police officer. Many barrio residents, like poor people worldwide, have had disastrous interactions with law enforcement agents including unwarranted stops, searches, and seizures; harassment; "planting" of evidence; physical abuse; and even murder. Increasingly we hear reports of police officers stopping and harassing Latinas/os for infractions such as "driving while Brown" and talking with friends. Repressive legislation and police policies have been used to deal with the rebellious Chicano youth. Examples are the proliferation of gang databases in police departments and a 1997 court order that placed a curfew on "members" of the Eighteenth Street Gang in Los Angeles and made it illegal for more than two identified gang members to congregate, even though some of the supposed gang members were family members who lived in the same house. Such measures have promoted further animosity between Chicana/o youth and police officers.

Moreover, since economic restructuring and job loss have increased in working-class inner-city communities, so too has the police presence. The federal Violent Crime Control and Law Enforcement Act of 1994 added 100,000 new police officers during the mid-1990s (Parenti 1999, 65). Further, the 1984 crime bill allowed police to more easily seize assets of suspected drug criminals. As a result, local police units formed special squads to seek assets from narcotic arrests. "Nationwide the gross receipts of all seizures shot from about $100 million in 1981 to over $1 billion by fiscal year 1987. By 1990 . . . a total of between $4 and $5 billion worth of cash and property had been forfeited since the 1984 crime bill" (51). The police with increased incentive to aggressively patrol inner-city communities added to their poor reputation in Chicana/o communities.

> this pig harassed the whole neighborhood
> well this pig worked at the station
> this pig he killed my homeboy
> so the fuckin' pig went on vacation
> this pig he is the chief
> got a brother pig, Captain O'Malley
> he's got a son that's a pig too
> he's collectin' pay-offs from a dark alley . . .
> an' it's about breakin' off sausage
> do ya feel sorry for the poor little swine?
> niggas wanna do him in the ass
> just ta pay his ass back
> so they're standing in line
> that fuckin' pig
> look what he got himself into
> now they're gonna make some pigs feet outta
>   the little punk
> anybody like pork chops?
> how 'bout a ham sandwich?

These lyrics are from the song "Pigs" on the 1991 album *Cypress Hill*. "Pigs" reflects two common themes associated with young Chicana/o barrio dwellers' understanding of the police: police harassment of Chicana/o barrios and police violence directed at Chicana/o youth. Further, this song plays out a violent fantasy of some Chicana/o and Black youth who wish to retaliate against their oppressors. For many barrio youth their most immediate oppressor and symbol for all oppressors is the pig. In this song Cypress Hill tells of a police officer who gets convicted of drug trafficking (another common theme in barrio lore about the police) and gets sent to prison, where he will not have his gang (other police officers) to protect him, nor will he have the protection of the state. Cypress Hill raps,

> 'cos once he gets to the pen
> they won't provide the little pig with a bullet-proof vest
> to protect him from some mad nigga
> who he shot in the chest and placed under arrest

The fantasy continues as they discuss paying the pig back for crimes he has committed against barrio and ghetto youth. They liken their revenge to cutting up a pig into pig's feet, pork chops, sausage, and ham. As well, they mention what is perceived to be the ultimate act of vengeance—rape—when they say "Niggas wanna do him in the ass."[14]

This song introduces the next theme associated with the relationship between Chicana/o barrio youth and police officers: the criminality of cops. First, the rappers suggest that cops are murderers and then go on to discuss their role as drug traffickers: "he's collectin' payoffs from a dark alley . . . / this pig works for the mafia / makin' some money off crack." In another song from their album *IV* (1998), they discuss the dark world of the police officer. "Looking Through the Eye of a Pig" presents the ravings of a fictional cop who in his twenty years on the force has become "worse than some of these motherfuckers [he] put away." Cypress Hill talks about the presumed tendency for many cops to use cocaine for the purposes of getting "wired" enough to meet barrio streets with a battle mentality: "Bad dreams all up in my head / No lie / Sometimes I got to take a sniff so I could get by." They also accuse cops of abusing alcohol and other drugs, rapping in this song from the point of view of their fictional cop: "Fuck I need a drink and I'm almost off / At the precinct it's like an AA meeting all gone wrong." Moreover, Cypress Hill understands the cops' criminality and drug use/abuse to be sanctioned by the state and sees cops as a tight-knit group, or "gang," whose members protect one another from external enemies such as "criminals" and "gang members" as well as from the law. Reflecting barrio lore about the police, Cypress Hill raps in this song:

> I'm in the biggest gang you ever saw
> above the law
> looking through the eyes of a pig
> I see it all . . .
> I.A. [Internal Affairs] got an eye on my close friend,
>   Guy
> for takin' supply from evidence
> a bust on a buy
> that doesn't concern me
> we never rat on each other
> we went through the academy
> just like frat brothers.

The Internal Affairs office has a mandate to investigate the criminal activities of police officers, and the "supply" they mention is drugs stolen from police evidence rooms.

The song ends with the police officer pulling over a truck because it has been modified, customized, in the lowrider style popular among Chicana/o youth. Again, these formerly illegal searches and seizures have become increasingly common, standard practice in ghettos and barrios as police regulations and new custom allow for searches in many more circumstances. As it turns out, the victim of "driving while Brown" is Cypress Hill rapper B-Real, who gets "framed" by the criminal cop. They end the song rapping:

> what's this a dark green truck
> tinted windows
> dually modified
> probably a drug dealer
> "Pull over to the curb
> take your key out of the ignition
> raise your hands out the windows
> get 'em in a high position
> don't move or I'll blast your fuckin' head off
> don't give me that bullshit
> I've heard about your raps
> all you're talkin' about is slangin' and shooting off your
>   straps [guns]
> okay Mr. B-Real get the fuck out of the truck
> I love it how all you fuckin' rappers think you're
>   so tough

get your ass out
I don't need no probable cause
you got a big sack of coke
so take a pause"

This ending illustrates a common problem for Chicana/o youth who participate in a subculture characterized by their style—baggy jeans, baseball hats, short hair or shaved head, lowrider cars and trucks, tattoos, and rap music. The song suggests that the vehicle occupants are innocent and are pulled over and framed simply because they are barrio youth. Cypress Hill connects drug use by police officers with police brutality and harassment of Chicana/o youth. On their 2000 release "Earthquake Weather," Psycho Realm takes a step further in its analysis of the connection between police cocaine abuse and police violence. They link police drug abuse to murder. They rap, "split second in time life becomes short / courtesy of LAPD psycho / inhaling white coke straight snort." While I have only discussed the work of Psycho Realm and Cypress Hill concerning their raps about the police, the reader should be aware that negative attitudes toward the police are abundant in Chicano rap. Of the songs in my 470 song sample, 30 percent deal with police–Chicano youth relations. None of them discuss these relations in positive ways, and some label this relationship as one of warfare and call upon youth to violently resist police abuse and violence.

The poor economic situation for Chicanas/os caused in part by economic restructuring and globalization contributes to new criminal legislation and policing practices and technologies. The results are an expanding Chicano prison population. For Psycho Realm it is as if the prisons are being especially built for young Brown and Black men. In the "Palace of Exile" from their third full-length CD, Jacken and Duke liken prisons to "palaces of exile" where "everybody lookin' like us" (Chicanos/Latinos) ends up due to a corrupt legal system. In the first verse Jacken examines the economic system that has elites living "fabulous" while working-class Chicanos "are the broke and scandalous / who'll never know what lavish is." He raps that police and other authorities

flood the street with cannabis
crystal-meth handle this
get you fucked up
then serve you guns with high calibers . . .

got cops ready to serve you just waiting
to take you to the palace exiled from your baby mama
you could be clean as a whistle homey but still
the palace was built for you, that's real

Here Jacken argues that the legal system that "establishes rules for savages" and the drug economy are two aspects of a larger strategy of containment and isolation of the young Brown and Black.

The prison-industrial complex that gains profit for a number of private corporations was one of the fastest-growing industries in the United States during the 1990s. A. Davis reports that between 1990 and 2000, "351 new places of confinement were opened by states" (2003, 92–93). While education, housing, job training, and other social programs were being defunded by state and federal governments, policing and prison construction were growing. Christian Parenti points out that "in 1996 alone contractors broke ground on twenty-six federal and ninety-six state prisons" (1999, 213). During the fifteen-year period of increased economic restructuring and the expanded prison population (1984–1999) twenty-one prisons were opened in California (A. Davis 2003, 12–13). As commentators such as Angela Davis and Parenti point out, economic restructuring and the disinvestment in human capital push people into the illegal economy of drug selling, robbery, and prostitution. With 2,100,146 people incarcerated in the United States in 2001 and a disproportionate number of these being Black and Brown men, it is hard to argue with Davis and Parenti, who conclude, like Jacken, that prisons are being built for the people, especially working-class people of color, who are being discarded by the new economy.[15] Without jobs, education, or a social safety net for those who need assistance, ever more poor people will be warehoused in prisons.

Moreover, the drug economy stimulated by the FBI's Counter Intelligence Program (COINTELPRO) operations designed to undermine the Black Power and militant Chicano movements and other revolutionary organizations and CIA funding to the Contras in Nicaragua flooded barrios and ghettos with drugs such as marijuana, heroin, and cocaine. As many scholars and Black and Chicana/o community leaders have pointed out, the government's role in the drug trade has been the decisive factor in the drug epidemic of the past three decades. Ward Churchill briefly describes how government agencies flooded urban streets with heroin in the early 1970s as a way to counter the successes of the growing revolutionary movements of people of color. The CIA and FBI imported high-grade heroin into the United States in the late 1960s and early 1970s, resulting in the "great heroin epidemic of 1971–1972." Churchill argues that this influx of heroin "appears to have been calculated to narcotize the country's then-burgeoning black liberation movement in much the same way that LSD and other hallucinogens were employed to undermine the white 'new left' movement a few years earlier."[16] The effects of this illegal governmental activity continue to be felt in our ghettos and barrios. As a result of the money that could be made in the drug trade and the dissolution of the Black Power movement, gangs grew in number and intensity, and gang activity became a full-blown epidemic by the 1980s. In addition to the violence of the drug trade and gang warfare, the 1980s and 1990s saw the development of crack cocaine, children born addicted to crack, the swelling of the prison population of poor people of color convicted on drug use and trafficking, the institution of an even more repressive penal code that disproportionately affected poor and minority offenders, and the government's further abandonment of human capital and social services programs in the inner cities in favor of increased policing and surveillance technology.

As more people of color go to jail for longer periods of time, not only do our communities suffer the loss, but corporate elites gain a windfall. While private-prison construction and management have grown rapidly, other corporations have also begun to feed at the incarceration trough. In the 1990s prison reform activists began to comment on the use of prisoners as a captive workforce being paid well below minimum wage to sew, answer phones, make furniture, build computers, and myriad other tasks. Corporations that once paid "free" workers union wages began to move their operations inside prison walls. In 1998 the federal government through Unicor (Federal Prison Industries) employed 18,000 convicts to make 150 different products, while private corporations employed 2,539 convicts (Parenti 1999, 231). What better incentive to eliminate entitlement programs and at the same time create harsher policing and sentencing codes. This practice is well known by many barrio residents and convicts. Psycho Realm comments on it in "Palaces of Exile." Jacken raps, "If in jail get petty money for labor skills / while stock holders sell and make money off shit you build." With policing and criminal justice practices such as these, it is no wonder that I have found so many Chicano rappers who are fed up with the system and willing to engage in and/or encourage criminal or otherwise rebellious activity.

The prison-building binge has important economic effects for many rural towns that have also suffered from job loss and general economic depression as a result of economic restructuring. Many small, mostly White, rural towns have benefited from the prison economy.[17] Some Chicano rappers recognize the wealth generated by the prison-industrial complex. On "Merry Maladies," Rhyme Asylum connects the growth of the prison industry to repressive criminal justice legislation, rapping that the "three strikes law is like job security."[18] Lengthy prison sentences provide more jobs for correctional officers (COs) and in industries that serve prisons. As well, politicians have carved out entire careers by "being tough on crime" and delivering much-needed prison-industry jobs to their impoverished districts.

ECONOMIC RESTRUCTURING AND CRIME

Chicano rappers tell stories of the devastation caused by economic restructuring from the perspective of those who confront job loss, educational inequity, the prison-industrial complex, and racism. Academic critiques of the U.S. political economy over the past twenty-five years provide readers with illustrations of the degree of social crisis caused by economic restructuring and globalization. Job exportation, the weakening of union power, the dismantling of the social safety net, and other such consequences of economic restructuring and global-ization have led many to turn to illicit economies. As a result, many feel they have little choice but to engage in crimes of poverty that may lead to violence and jail. Nicaraguan-born, L.A.-raised rapper JDubs presents a vivid picture of the "Catch 22" in which some barrio youth find themselves. He begins the song "Distorted Nights" (2004) rapping:

> I'm under pressure as the family's only breadwinner
> so I'm runnin' out the liquor store with fresh booze
> I'm hopin' to survive this attempt to get paid
> but as I run around the corner I proceed to get sprayed
> unfriendly fire from all around me
> and with three convictions over my head
> this is my destiny

JDubs recounts the story of a Latino male head of household having difficulty providing for his family. He chooses to rob a liquor store, all the while fearing death or a long prison sentence (perhaps life imprisonment) due to his previous convictions. The character's fears are probably common among a group of Chicana/o and African

American working-class poor who "under pressure as the family's only breadwinner" have engaged in petty crime and face three-strikes laws or long mandatory-minimum sentences. Parenti discusses such laws in his examination of the prison-industrial complex. The Anti–Drug Abuse Act of 1986 began a rash of legislation that imposed lengthy mandatory-minimum prison sentences for an increasing number of crimes, extended the death penalty to more crimes, and extended sentences if a convicted person was deemed a gang member.[19]

Later, JDubs delivers a line that connects him to a long history of social bandits in Mexican and Mexican American history, folklore, and song who engage in armed rebellion against discriminatory policing agencies and elites who get rich from the labor of working people:

> this is my destiny
> to make neighborhoods hot with gunshots
> on those that make money without ever giving us props

He links his destiny to the disempowerment and struggles of his community (note his use of the first-person plural "us") and like Robin Hood or Joaquin Murrieta "stalks his prey," those who "make money without ever giving us props" (proper respect, which would undoubtedly include fair wages, health care, and safe working conditions, all of which have slowly eroded under economic restructuring). JDubs essentially argues that he is engaging in acts of armed class warfare that results from a racist and unequal economic system.

Like many of his fellow underground rap artists, JDubs sees one of the consequences of racism, economic restructuring, and the resultant Chicana/o–Latina/o poverty as warfare between state agents—especially local police and sheriff's units—and working-class Chicanas/os. Like the Funky Aztecs and Psycho Realm, JDubs sees the media as a propaganda tool of the elite classes. He argues that "no mass media can change all the facts / we are the hunted ones and we need to react." The media portray inner-city youth of color as "superpredators" who prey on innocent communities, disrupting lives and livelihoods. Chicano youth and activists of color find the opposite to be true. The predators are financial and government elites who use militarized police forces to do their "hunting." JDubs argues that we need to react to this war, rapping that he is "aiming the nightscope [of his weapon] at government." He uses "city hall" as a metaphor for all government, rapping "I'm coming back with bats, knives and glocks / stop at city hall and level three shots."

In response to state violence against Chicanas/os, JDubs advises armed resistance. In the second verse to "Distorted Nights" he continues:

> Sticks and stones get thrown at microphones in front
>   of politicians trying to feed us deception
> they getting scared cuz we comin' hard like an erection
> kidnap nominees during elections
> treat these United Snakes like an infection . . .
> they tryin' to kill us real slow
> I'm sending out a call to arms with this flow
> look around and wake up to the facts
> refuse and resist and then attack

Much can be made of JDubs' lyrics as advocating violence, and perhaps he is doing just that. However, we should keep in mind that rap is poetry. It is literature that uses literary devices such as metaphor, simile, double entendre, and exaggeration. So, for example, he raps, "I use these rhymes like heavy artillery." Not as literal artillery but as knowledge, so that "when our seeds [children] grow they'll never know misery."

Whether or not he truly advocates armed insurrection is perhaps less important than the critique of government abuse he offers and "the call to arms" that he is sending out to young Chicanas/os. This call to arms again should not only be taken literally but also figuratively. The call to arms is a wake-up call, a plea to young Chicanas/os to critically analyze their environment. His call to arms is as much mental, psychological, and emotional as it is a call to violence. Evidence comes from other lyrics to this song. He raps, "As I revolutionize I get wise." His verbal artillery is used to "fill that space [lack of knowledge] with raw intellect."

JDubs' struggle as manifested in the lyrics to this song is both physical and mental. He recognizes and stylizes the feelings held by many who wish to change the status quo, what he calls the "new battleground," using violent means while hoping that through music young people can begin to struggle against enemies of working-class Chicanas/os, i.e., the government, politicians, and the police. In the end he raps that "the time has come to be in defense of the Earth and the sun," and he closes the song hoping that "one day we will all live as one."

CHICANO RAP'S "GREAT REFUSAL"

At the beginning of Krazy Race's underground hit "Dedicated," former President George H. W. Bush is heard repeating his infamous phrase "New World Order." Krazy Race connects Bush's and fellow elites' economic policies with problems in his East Los Angeles barrio. For Krazy Race and his community, the "new world order" means substandard housing, propagandistic education, and ultimately "global genocide."[20] In "Premonition" (1997), Psycho Realm samples parts of a speech in which the orator denounces the "new world order": *La orden del nuevo mundo, no, nunca!* (The New World Order, no, never). These brief statements summarize the attitude that many in the Chicano hip-hop community have toward the late-twentieth-century economic policies of the U.S. government. They, more than almost any other group, have seen how "free-market," "supply-side" economics have affected the working class and people of color. Chicano hip-hop youth are among those people of color who have seen schools fall apart because federal dollars have gone to increasing the ranks and the firepower of the police and the military. Chicano youth have been harassed by police who have new mandates to suppress young people because they wear "gang-style" clothes or have brown or black skin. Many Chicano youth await the "palaces of exile" that have been built at increasing rates to deal with the epidemic of poverty occasioned by economic restructuring. Chicano youth have lived in dilapidated housing projects and urban areas that have been neglected by our government. Many are speaking out about it. Chicano rappers are among the leaders of this movement for justice in Chicano barrios and other communities of color.

Chicano rap narratives vividly illustrate the consequences of urban decay resulting from globalization. Their stories of violence, murder, drug use and trafficking, police repression, and poverty contribute to a theorization of globalization from barrio streets. Their narration of urban dystopia puts brown faces on statistics concerning urban neglect, decreased job opportunities, and hopelessness in Chicana/o U.S.A. Their "armed-with-words" response to the war waged by the transnational bourgeoisie and their conscious rejection of the middle-class lifestyle reflect a Great Refusal shouted by many throughout the two-thirds world.[21] This Great Refusal and the eloquence with which many in the Chicano rap community express it can also be a warning and a lesson for the rest of us. Because as Howard Zinn quotes in his important work *A People's History of the United States* (2003, 10), "the cry of the poor is not always just, but if you don't listen to it, you will never know what justice is."

In the place of globalization and the violence attending it, Chicana/o rappers and other members of the Hip-Hop Nation are building a multiracial community based on love for one another and free expression. This utopic model is, of course, not always followed by practitioners and enthusiasts of hip hop. Rappers have often illustrated racism and virulent hatred toward other members of the Hip-Hop Nation, resulting in a few isolated acts of violence. Further, the pervasive sexism and homophobia in rap turns the utopic Hip-Hop Nation upside down for women and gays and lesbians. Nevertheless, Chicano rappers have begun to illustrate ways in which to unify people of color and other marginalized people through "love for the hood."[22]

CONFRONTING DOMINANCE AND CONSTRUCTING RELATIONSHIPS WITH YOUTH

Misogyny and violent hypermasculinity seem to be everywhere in the late capitalist period. The cultural field in the postindustrial United States is dominated by hyperviolent images and attitudes and hypersexualized and exploited bodies, especially female bodies. The capitalist cultural and economic order has commodified and devalued life, sexuality, and human relationships. The New World Cultural and Economic Order profits from exploitative, controlling images of women and criminalized hypermasculine representations of youth of color. The dominant cultural attitude in the United States views our youth as dangerous and as such devalues their lives. This attitude leads to legislation that erodes justice and community nurturing for our working-class urban youth of color. This environment contributes to disfigured self-concepts among a large sector of our youth and a self-fulfilling prophecy in which young people assume the misogynist and violent traits attributed to them by the dominant culture. Cultural workers, teachers, activists, and parents can challenge the socialization and education emanating from the media, popular culture, advertising, and politics. Careful attention to youth culture and examples of democratic, anti-authoritarian, loving relationships and institutions can help youth overcome the patriarchal dominance paradigm and related damaging self-images. Community members, elders, and teachers can develop empowering and caring pedagogies utilizing the movies, literature, and criticism of Xicanistas and other feminists and the caring art of many Chicano rap artists.

XICANISTA CHALLENGES TO THE DOMINANCE PARADIGM

Few female voices exist in Chicano hip-hop culture to challenge the male-centered perspective. However, other elements of Chicana expressive culture present a Chicana feminist critique of female images and of the patriarchal dominance paradigm and new, complex discussions of gendered subjectivity and alternative institutional and interpersonal relationships. Xicanista (Chicana feminist) cultural production challenges racism and sexism and presents an alternative knowledge base that imagines and demonstrates the possibilities for racial, economic, environmental, and gender justice rooted in practices of collectivity, cooperation, and peace.[1]

Controlling images of Chicanas such as virgin/whore, *mujer buena/ mujer mala*, suffering mother, and sex object find fertile ground in postindustrial patriarchal Chicano cultural production. Most striking about the representations of women found throughout the Chicano rap lyrics I sampled is their one-dimensionality. These images fail to grasp or value women's complexity and humanity. Rap lyrics focus on women as Other and sexual object to be conquered. Men highlight female bodies for the pleasure they can give and ignore other aspects of their beings. When Chicano rappers represent good women, they are mothers and girlfriends or wives valued for their service to men. Rarely do Chicana or other female characters have a voice or subjectivity within Chicano rap discourses. While few Chicanas in rap culture counter the force of controlling, one-dimensional images of women, Xicanista artists have been challenging patriarchal representation since at least the 1970s.

Chicana authors, activists, and artists have developed an important critique of images stemming from the patriarchal dominance paradigm. Xicanistas challenge patriarchal images by showing women in myriad roles and refusing to relegate them to simplistic stereotypes. Xicanistas present complex female perspectives, characters, and images in their work.[2] For example, early Chicana filmmakers challenged the male-centered perspective of Chicano movement art by placing women at the center of a broad historical narrative, as in Sylvia Morales's *Chicana* (1979), or in depicting women's everyday lives, as in Esperanza Vásquez's *Agueda Martinez* (1977). Both films center on Chicana power, creativity, and autonomy. *Chicana* counters the male-centered revisionist history created by scholars and cultural workers of the Chicano movement. Morales' film examines five hundred years of ethnic Mexican history linking the various epochs by examining both the continuity and change in women's struggles, home life, and culture. She reexamines important historical figures such as La Malinche and Sor Juana Inés de la Cruz from a Xicanista perspective. She argues for a positive Chicana identity by uncovering a Chicana lineage (Fregoso 1993a, 18).

Agueda Martinez contributes to the development of a new language and new stories by depicting the life of a Chicana elder in rural New Mexico. Vásquez represents Agueda Martinez in an unapologetic and dignified manner. She composes a metaphor for Chicana logic and power as she follows Martinez around her ranch filming her daily routine. Martinez describes her life and worldview, which can serve as a model of healthy Chicana self-identity and autonomy. Vásquez also contributes to a new aesthetic language by marginalizing men and men's worldviews in the film. Martinez's is the only voice we hear and the only character we see in the film; men simply do not appear. Thus, part of the new language being created suggests that Chicanas do not need men to care for them, protect them, or make decisions for them. While Xicanistas often want to create community and families with Chicanos, they also want to highlight women's abilities to live independently (as in this film) or within a community of women (as suggested by *Chicana*).

Loving depictions of women as valuable for the entirety of their beings are uncommon in the male-centered expressive culture of Chicanos. Females are subordinate to men in public and private life as well as in the realm of cultural expression. This subordination can cause a "colonized identity" in some women who internalize the sexism they see around them (Córdova 1999). Many young women, especially adolescents, see themselves in hateful or unloving ways, begin to accept the patriarchal perspective as natural, normal, and correct, and see themselves as less valuable and, perhaps, less lovable.

Today, love rarely appears as the subject matter of Chicano rap lyrics. The rappers I examined occasionally spoke about their "homeboys," "homies," "crews," and other groups of friends in caring ways. A few songs do discuss loving male-female relationships. A pedagogy that strives to have young women and men "love ourselves—free from the need to obtain patriarchal approval," as Córdova suggests (1999, 23), should encourage the study of Chicana cultural producers who critique the patriarchal worldview and present new images, ideas, and interpretations of womanhood, manhood, and relationships.

Xicanistas often reexamine history for models of democratic, caring, and strong women and social practices and institutions that reflect these values. Many Xicanistas have examined pre-Columbian indigenous spiritual and social practices in the Americas. They have "resurrected every pre-Conquest and Catholic icon, ritual, [and] symbol possible" to develop new epistemologies, ontologies, and interpretive schemes (Castillo 1994, 94). With these symbols and ideas and their experiences as Chicanas, Xicanistas have created new spiritualities and identities that reinterpret and recontextualize the religious, social, and gender orders of pre-Columbian mother-goddess worship.[3] Writers such as Gloria Anzaldúa, Ana Castillo, and Alicia Gaspar de Alba and artists such as Yolanda López, Ester Hernandez, and Alma Lopez have reclaimed Mexican, *indígena*, and Chicana icons and identities in their work.[4] These representations can provide a counter discourse that helps young boys and girls see women in different ways than the depictions in Chicano rap or the dominant, corporate-controlled popular culture.

Xicanista artists have remade the image of La Virgen de Guadalupe from their perspectives. Against the patriarchal controlling definitions of La Virgen, Ester Hernández redefines her as a contemporary martial arts expert defending Chicanas/os. In her 1975 etching "La Virgen de Guadalupe Defendiendo los Derechos de los Xicanos," La Virgen dressed in a martial arts uniform breaks out of her passive, solemn stance with a side kick. Similarly, Yolanda López is "removing the traditional figure from the halo of rays and replacing it with powerful images of family and self. . . . López's Guadalupes are mobile, hardworking, assertive, working-class images" (Mesa-Bains 1991, 137). In her 1987 "Portrait of the Artist as the Virgin of Guadalupe," López depicts herself breaking out of the ideal woman as defined by the patriarchy. She bursts forth from Guadalupe's rays wearing running shoes and stomping on the red, white, and green colors of Mexican/Chicano nationalism. The new Guadalupe is not the sacrificing, passive, virgin mother of Christ but the powerful and brave athlete clutching a serpent (Gaspar de Alba 1998). These artists and other Xicanistas show the importance of new, empowering identities based in community building and a reexamination of history, as opposed to Chicano identities rooted in the xenophobia of the dominance paradigm.

A PEDAGOGY OF THE EROTIC

Chicano rap and most of male culture view female sexuality pornographically. Through young male discourse, including rap, they fantasize about unfettered access and dominance over women's bodies. Extending older patriarchal notions and newer pornographic representations of women, Chicano rappers who discuss sex and sexuality almost always depict women as objects of domination and pleasure for men. Women have no agency, sexual or otherwise, and are valued for the pleasure their bodies can give men. Pornography and domination are the central characteristics of Chicano rap lyrics about women and sexuality.

The pornographic imagination steeped in the patriarchal dominance paradigm devalues and dehumanizes women. Using pornographic images the rapper attempts to illustrate his dominance, his manhood. In the absence of alternative narratives from Chicana rappers and few examples of female self-representations in the dominant popular culture, young Chicanas/os are assaulted by pornographic depictions of women. Such images contribute to patriarchal, heterosexist gender socialization for both young men and women (Jhally 1997a). Community members, elders, and family members concerned about violence and misogyny in youth culture and expression should challenge patriarchal gender socialization using a pedagogy that empowers young women in myriad ways.

A pedagogy of the erotic can access the inner power of young women, and creative discussions and examinations of it can change the understanding of our young men toward women. The erotic helps free female bodies, minds, and sexuality. The life force accessed through the erotic can change self-image and empower young women to challenge sexist acts and images. The erotic rejects capitalist and racist domination as well (Lorde 1984), and thus it can have a strengthening influence on young Chicanas/os.

Many Chicanas redefine Chicana sexuality and identity, reclaiming them from patriarchy. Sandra Cisneros unashamedly "confesses" that she has broken the gender conventions imposed by Catholicism and Chicano, Mexicano, and European patriarchy. In her preface to *My Wicked, Wicked Ways* (1992, ix), Cisneros announces,

> Gentlemen, ladies. If you please—these
> are my wicked poems from when.
> The girl grief decade. My wicked nun
> years, so to speak. I sinned
> Not in the white-woman way.

With these opening lines Cisneros simultaneously confronts oppressive religious, patriarchal, and racist practices while establishing herself as a Brown woman. Her book provides material from which to develop an empowering pedagogy of the erotic. Her poems discuss love, desire, lust, pleasure, doubts, mood swings, relationships, and the fears that accompany them. In short, she presents a complex picture of herself and other women that male culture including Chicano rap rarely represents.

In several poems Cisneros discusses her own desire for men and her admiration for beautiful male bodies. In "Beautiful Man—France" (47) she writes,

> I saw a beautiful man today
> at the café
> Very beautiful

> But I can't see
> without my glasses.

After confirming that he is beautiful, she describes a flirtation with the man who catches her eye. In Cisneros' poems she is the agent in control of her sexuality. She approaches the man and exchanges a beautiful moment. Her desire is kind and active. It does not rely on sexualizing her partner, dominating or demeaning him. It empowers the woman without disempowering her potential sexual partner, friend, or acquaintance. In the "Postcard to the Lace Man—The Old Market Antibes," "Letter to John Franco—Venice," "To Cesare, Goodbye," "Ass," and "Trieste—Ciao Italy," among others, Cisneros describes beautiful men and mutually gratifying encounters with them. In these poems she examines gender and efforts to cultivate romantic relations that are ethical, kind, edifying, and egalitarian.

Perhaps even more forcefully, alejandra ibarra claims a powerful erotic voice for herself in *Santa Perversa and Other Erotic Poems* (2000). She introduces her poems with quotes from Audre Lorde, Sandra Cisneros, and Anaïs Nin that address the erotic, desire, and sexual subjectivity. ibarra feels compelled to address controlling images of women. The first lines of the book read: "shatter / I / tu idea / of womanness." In the opening poem, "jonesin' más ahh . . . (masa)," she begins to describe the "self love," "power," "shamelessness," and "sexual curiosity" that are central "elements of the erotic" (Rodriguez y Gibson 2000). ibarra has developed the concept of "sexesmiotroerótico": "the term translates to sex is my other erotic."[5] In emails she explains that "much of my work is influenced by feminists of color—[Audre] Lorde and [Cherríe] Moraga—who discuss the erotic as a power that emanates from lived experiences rooted in a spiritual realm. i created the term to reflect how the erotic is not always to be thought solely in sexual terms. yet, sexuality should be affirmed in positive terms."[6]

In "Sanctuary" ibarra connects sexuality and spirituality through ritual and the power of the erotic (9). She describes the place in which the ritual-like, powerful, and loving sex will take place as *el santuario,*

> where the candlelight
> blends with the aromas
> *del cedro* [of cedar]
> *copal* and
> sage

The lovers are "enveloped by the goddess' energy." "Routine encounters" in *el santuario* rejuvenate her and cause her to discover "renewed desires." ibarra's descriptions of sexual relations with men focus on the mutually gratifying, soul-edifying power of sex when erotic (as opposed to pornographic) power is present. Sexual relations in ibarra's poems resemble religious rituals more than the rapes and assaults described by many in Chicano rap and elsewhere in male culture.

ibarra shows that when women access the erotic within, they do not need men or heterosexual intercourse to express and experience a powerful sexuality. In "dancing silhouettes" she writes: "last night, / I wanted sexual stimulation / go to a boys club / jam with dancers to house music." She describes the erotic experience she has with a man in the second stanza: "silhouettes dancing to the seditious beats / taking us higher and higher / as we pray to the vinyl incantations." Her focus is not on heterosexual intercourse but rather an erotic experience that is mutually empowering and spiritual. ibarra describes an erotic encounter in which heteronormative, phallocentric sexuality plays no part. She goes to a gay male dance club where the meditative, aggressive, and "seditious beats" of house music allow her to have a spiritual, sexual moment without intercourse.

Cisneros' and ibarra's poems are examples of a number of Chicana texts that point to the possibilities for the reconstitution of Chicana sexuality and identity outside the gender order in Chicano and U.S. society. The erotic, self-love, community building, collective work, and complex stories and images of women challenge the patriarchal dominance paradigm of most Chicano rappers and present useful corrections and alternatives to narrow definitions of women and human relationships. Creative and innovative use of such Xicanista cultural work by teachers, elders, community leaders, and family members can inspire in young people new, powerful identities and behaviors. As Chela Sandoval explains, "For only in freeing our erotics as readers, writers, activists, thinkers, spiritualists, lovers, thinkers, bodies can we fully engage in this methodology of emancipation" (2002, 26).

RESISTING VIOLENCE AND CREATING COMMUNITY

Luis J. Rodriguez writes about "creating community in violent times" (2001). In his vision, people in our communities recognize their responsibility for young people's lives, understand youth, take their culture and concerns seriously, and commit firmly to nurturing and empowering them. He says, "We have a tremendous responsibility as members of the community for the condition of our young people" (106). The violence of our society is driving youth representations of violence in rap, violent situations in our communities, and hypermasculine behaviors and outlooks among a large sector of our youth. For this reason Rodriguez argues that "we can't see violence—or any crime—as just a law enforcement issue" (87). Violence is a societal problem that requires a broad strategy to combat. Instead of criminalizing youth and demonizing youth culture, for example, elders who work with youth should focus on young people's strengths and experiences and listen to their voices: "Listening requires taking in whatever is given, even if it seems like nonsense" (121). Much of youth culture seems foreign, ugly, criminal, or inane to many adults. Creating community and nurturing youth requires that we begin to listen to them.

Respecting youth cultural production and consumption can create open intergenerational communication pathways. We can find out what drives youth to produce and consume violent and misogynist art, and we can introduce alternative art and music.[7]

LOVE AND UNITY RAPS

> I'm fucking tired of this shit, man
> I'm tired of people just killing each other
> for what, man?
> dirty money man
> what's up?
> you gotta wise up
> take a stand.

> —5th Battalion, "Never Ending Battle"

Tom Hayden writes that the body count from gang wars of the past three decades is little mentioned, while "if 25,000 white people were killing each other in ethnic wars, you can be sure that Americans would pay attention" (2003, 6). Why do the lives of Chicana/o, Black, and other poor people of color merit little attention from the broader U.S. public? The casualty rate in poor urban communities is staggering. Hayden argues that the actual numbers of dead and wounded in gang-related violence is probably even higher than FBI and state crime data suggest. Yet few from outside these communities have intervened to stop the bloodshed. The state's only solution has been more prisons, more police, and longer prison sentences. Restorative justice programs, after-school programs, job creation, and social spending are rarely seen as options to control the violence among what many in the law enforcement and government establishments see as incorrigible youth of color. The attitude of many is "Once a gang member, always a gang member." There seems also to be quite a strong racist component to the lack of concern paid to this problem. Gang expert Glen D. Curry explains this from his viewpoint: "It is my opinion that gang homicides have not been tracked more carefully because selected presidential administrations don't really care about violent crimes where 99 percent of the victims are minorities" (in Hayden 2003, 14).

Yet, while few from outside poor urban communities of color have concerned themselves with gang and street violence, many victims and perpetrators of violence have organized to end the violence. Numerous strategies have been used to stem the tide of urban youth violence. Spirituality, anger management, mentoring, "scared straight" programs, and many other tactics have been employed by gangbangers-turned-peace-advocates and the families of victims who have had enough. In his chapter "A Handmade Life" (2001, 159), Luis Rodriguez writes, "Art is the most powerful means of dealing with violence." He discusses the work of Rock A Mole (rhymes with "guacamole") Productions, which "put[s] on grassroots cultural festivals (eight so far) that feature music, art, poetry, and film by or about at-risk youth, immigrants, the homeless, welfare recipients, and prisoners." The idea as described at the organization's website (www.rockamole.com) is that

> anyone who spends any time in the streets, the jails, or the homeless shelters constantly encounters talented artists of every kind—from painters to poets, from video wizards to musicians. These marginalized people are our sisters and brothers. They are demonized in the media as the ones who are responsible for our society falling apart. That is a lie. The volcanic flow of creativity in the streets of America challenges us all to unite around a vision of a peaceful America where everyone's needs are met.

Activists in the gang peace and unity movement—among them Barrios Unidos, Hands Across Watts Foundation, and the Community Self-Determination Institute—have made remarkable strides toward helping to create peace and social justice in working-class inner-city communities.[8] Many youth groups combine art and culture, anti-violence, and social justice as means of youth empowerment. Rodriguez has worked with Youth Struggling for Survival (YSS) in Chicago, whose young leaders and members have faced numerous obstacles to their peace and youth empowerment efforts, such as police interference and roadblocks and media disinterest. L.A. rap organizations, artists, and groups such as 5th Battalion, El Vuh, and Krazy Race rap about peace and social justice, and they perform for benefits and conferences, organize youth, and conduct creative writing and culture workshops. These efforts illustrate the possibilities for an empowering pedagogy that uses youth strengths and helps youth learn about community, justice, and peace.

My own work with youth in a high school pre-collegiate program, workshops with the community organization Ways Out Academy, and Chicana/o college students has confirmed for me the power and potential of combining socially conscious Chicana/o rap and youth culture with an active social change curriculum and agenda. My experiences with Chicana/o and other youth have demonstrated that when you take youth, their concerns, and their culture seriously and commit to empowering pedagogies, they begin to take an active role in examining and improving their lives and communities. For this reason a cornerstone of my teaching strategies with high school students and in college Chicana/o studies courses has been exploring rap music and hip-hop culture. Many Chicana/o youth, as well as youth of all ethnicities, embrace the sounds and values of hip-hop culture. However, the dominant culture, the corporate media, and many patriarchal aspects of Chicana/o culture teach violence and misogyny. As a result, much of youth culture reflects this socialization. Many youth carelessly produce and uncritically consume rap that depicts violence and sexism. Corporate-dominated rap bombards youth with pornographic sexuality and violent masculinity. To make money and seem cool, Chicana/o youth follow the lead of our violent culture.

More often than not, my students cite artists known for sexism and gangsta style and lyrics among their favorites. Taking their decisions to listen to certain types of rap seriously, I ask them to share their music and their thoughts concerning it. At the same time I present examples and analyses of rap that challenge sexism and violence. Class and workshop discussions of rap and hip hop can elicit fruitful conversations about our world, youth concerns, youth culture, and peaceful and just alternatives to an inhumane economy, a largely amoral postindustrial globalized culture, and lack of equality and democracy in their lives and in the greater world. Children as young as ten have shown a remarkable capacity for reflection and critical analysis when adult teacher-students frame conversations in respectful and accommodating ways. Young people can learn peace as well as violence.

Chicano rappers who have called for peace and love in their communities, even while the dominant current in youth culture has been violent, can play powerful roles in youth-elder relationships such as mentoring and working in nonprofit youth services and formal school settings. Among rappers using their art to call for peace, love, and unity in their barrios are El Vuh and Victor E, Kinto Sol, Delinquent Habits, Frost ("Nothin' but Love for the Hood," "La Raza," and "La Raza II"), and Krazy Race ("Dedicated").

Krazy Race's verse in "Up To Us" from *The Never Ending Battle* exemplifies the peace, unity, and social justice position within Chicana/o rap. He begins by saying that it is up to Chicana/o and other working-class youth to change their behavior. He shouts a question and the response:

> ain't it kinda strange
> those that bring pain look just like you and I
> with a different last name?
> struggling to see the light
> we need to break these chains
> cast the demons out our brains
> before we go insane

While he laments Chicano fratricide and says that only "we," Chicano working- and under-class youth and other community members, can change the situation, he does not simply blame youth for their violent environs and behaviors. Krazy Race connects youth violence with neglect and oppression when he tells his audience that "you need to recognize / we helpin' out the system / when it comes to our demise." He raps this solution, repeated often in the L.A. Chicano rap underground and those in the barrio peace movement: "my last words, my people / unite and rise."

El Vuh members view the situation of violence and social injustice in Chicana/o communities in ways similar to Krazy Race and offer an indigenous racial identity and spiritual tradition in their music. They recognize that the current political economic, spiritual, and cultural systems cause grief and despair in many of our communities. They

point to the colonialism of Spain and the United States as the catalyst for the destruction of indigenous spirituality and community. To
correct the wrongs of contemporary society, El Vuh argues that we
must return to the ancient wisdom of the Aztecs, Mayas, and other
indigenous peoples. Ceremony, ritual, and the recognition of multiple
gods and goddesses are central to El Vuh's philosophy. The lyrics to
their songs from *Jaguar Prophecies* (2003) demonstrate their beliefs and
strategies for change.

They contend that contemporary European-derived society is the
source of oppression. In "Heavy," members of El Vuh argue that many
of the ills in our communities result from European colonialism:

>we have been kept from our ancient wisdom
>torn away from our roots
>>that's why we have drug dealers, gang bangers and
>>>prostitutes
>identity lost
>spiritual death is the cost
>modern day holocaust
>since 1492
>>but no one is making a big deal about it like they did
>>>for the Jew
>you see, Hitler's roots go back to Columbus
>the first chance they got they started killing us
>to this very day the killings are continuous

Mexican indigenous wisdom derived from centuries of examining
celestial phenomena, nature, and human spirit allowed our ancestors
to place themselves within a natural and spiritual order in which
all life is respected. They observed a biocentric (life-centered) way
of life. After five centuries of colonialism, the children of native
Mexicans—Chicanas/os—have seen their "natural" ways replaced by
an anthropocentric (human-centered) value system whereby with
each advancement in technology we find a concomitant increase in
our distance from the natural world and each other. We have become
ruled by a consumer ethic in which we define our quality of life by our
relationship to things as opposed to our relationships with people and
other living beings. Examining the often destructive interplay between
technology, "progress," and the nature of humanity, in "m.i.n.d." on
Jaguar Prophecies El Vuh rhymes,

> technology has kept me under captivity
> not allowing me to be who I'm supposed to be
> a natural human
> surrounded by the technological demon in search of my
>   original origin
> but where do I begin?

E-Rise adds to this analysis in the first verse of "Spiritual Souldier," rapping that "our souls are controlled by the billfold." Money and the "mental penitentiary" control us and cause us to support corrupt politicians. We are blinded by material goods, causing us to

> back a beast who has us fighting wars to make his
>   pockets obese . . .
> hidden societies
> won't be pleased
> till we're all deceased
> or on our knees
> man-made disease
> and killer police
> run loose on my peeps [people]

For El Vuh and other indigenist-Mexica rappers and musicians, everything from police violence to greed, misogyny, prostitution, and drugs result from the loss of ancient wisdom caused by European colonization of Anahuac or Turtle Island, names that indigenous peoples gave the Americas.

Like Krazy Race and others, El Vuh suggests that unity among oppressed people in resistance to racist, capitalist, misogynist domination is the solution for our survival and the survival of all beings. El Vuh as Mexica focuses on the unity of indigenous peoples throughout the Americas as in this line from "Heavy": "Mexica, the day will come when all of Anahuac will be unified as one." Again echoing Krazy Race's stance that it is up to us to change our situation, El Vuh shouts that we need to return to an older way of life and worldview: "broken is the cycle once you decide to change your mind / unleashing the ancestry that was left behind." Like their elder Luis J. Rodriguez, members of El Vuh hail from the dangerous urban environs of Los Angeles where violence, poverty, and disillusionment are concentrated. Much like Rodriguez, El Vuh sees part of the problem as a loss of identity and an uncertain future for many youth. They rap and put music to the efforts of urban activists who are promoting new rituals and ceremonies as a way to provide a sense of identity, a pathway, and a future for youth. Lines in "Heavy" exemplify the way in which El Vuh sees a pathway out of the dire circumstances for many of our youth: "enter the circle and find your true identity / not a fantasy / brought over by a foreign mentality." Throughout the album El Vuh evokes images of ritual and ceremony such as entering a prayer circle, thanking "the four directions, Mother Earth and Father Sky," and praying to gods and goddesses such as "Tezcatlipoca, Quetzalcoatl, and Ometeoh." They rap that through ritual we can find healing and find ourselves.

TOWARD A CONSTRUCTIVE DIALOGUE

The oral tradition in Mexicano-Chicana/o culture continues to evolve and provide insights into Mexican-Chicana/o life. Chicano youth speak back to power using rap lyrics and music. They present important critiques of U.S. institutions and policies that impact Chicana/o-Mexican communities. In so doing they rely on the figures and symbols of previous generations of Mexican Americans. These symbols include the social bandit, hypermasculine figures, and female stereotypes. While these are not the only figures found in the Mexican-Chicana/o oral tradition, they are influential and are reinforced in the worldview of young Chicanas/os by dominant media that rely on sexist and racist stereotypes. The result is that the patriarchal dominance paradigm dominates the cultural and social fields, both Chicana/o and corporate, from which young Chicanas/os draw to develop their worldviews and identities.

In this cultural landscape the hypermasculine and misogynist aspects of Mexican cultural traditions have come to dominate young Chicano definitions of masculinity, womanhood, and justice. Stories of the "good" and "bad" woman influence young rappers' views of women, while more holistic representations of women such as the multifaceted and powerful stories offered by Xicanista cultural workers are left out of their lyrics. The male figure in Chicano rap is almost always brave, strong, rebellious, and violent. He is dominant, and most others, including racial and gender others, are objects of domination. His chief strategy for overcoming Anglo American racial and class domination is violent rebellion. Rarely does the male figure in Chicano rap engage in the difficult social-change work of institution building and/or other forms of nonviolent community empowerment. As a result the progressive politics of Chicano rap are often contradicted by a narrow vision of power, i.e., "power over" instead of "empowerment."

To reverse the progress of the dominance paradigm in the worldviews of Chicana/o youth, we require a dynamic constructive dialogue between feminist-oriented men and women and young Chicanas/os. Affecting the gender and political socialization process of our youth requires introducing Xicanista stories of female agency, creativity, and power and those who provide examples of collectivity, peace, and democracy. Since many of the ideas, symbols, and themes used by Chicano rappers and consumed by their young audiences derive from Mexican cultures, Xicanista redefinition and recontextualization of them can be useful starting points for dialogue. Xicanista cultural production can alter the worldviews of Chicana/o youth. Introducing Xicanista worldviews, ontologies, epistemologies, and values in critical discussions of rap and hip hop leads to empowering dialogues between youth and elders. The knowledge gained from such interactions can go a long way toward revolutionary change in gender socialization and identity among youth while expanding definitions of ethnicity, justice, democracy, and equality. The openings that a Xicanista pedagogy can offer a young boy or girl are tremendous. New identities and senses of self provided by such a pedagogy mean that hypermasculine attitudes and behaviors as well as misogynist worldviews can be effectively combated. However, we cannot be effective in this task if we are not literate in the language, symbols, and values of youth culture. We must respect their culture and them as individuals. Our dialogue with them must be conducted in an idiom they understand and respect. Hip hop is such an idiom.

OUTRO

Chicano rap is important to hundreds of thousands if not millions of youth. Thus, it requires scholarly understanding and research. The analysis of Chicana/o rap and hip-hop culture is beginning. A few scholars have begun to take notice of this important cultural phenomenon. In this book I have chosen to analyze two important aspects of Chicana/o rap—gender and violence—and their interrelatedness. Masculinity in our country and in Chicano youth culture contains two important elements: (1) violence, aggression, and domination; and (2) distance from female and homosexual others. Chicana/o youth definitions of "male" and "man" depend upon narrow, essentialist definitions of women as weak, passive, and subordinate.

Using articulation theory and the work of feminist cultural criticism we can see how Chicano rap does not develop in a vacuum and is influenced by myriad forces in our society. The images of violence and misogyny common in much of Chicano rap music reflect those images in the broader U.S. popular cultural, economic, political, and social fields. This analysis of nearly five hundred songs shows that many Chicano rappers pull directly from popular cultural images when discussing violence and gender. Hollywood action movies, video games, and actual, real-life violence in the form of war and street crime provide the primary material from which rap artists write their poetry. Pornography, Hollywood movies, and advertising show one-dimensional, misogynist images of women to young Chicanos. These, too, are part of the primary material cited by rappers in their lyrics. Without attention to this, critics and proponents of rap and hip hop will never understand this subculture.

It is also imperative that we examine the violence and misogyny of Mexican and Chicano patriarchal culture when critiquing, praising, or analyzing Chicano rap. The male-centered lineage in Chicana/o culture has produced limited notions of femaleness and maleness. Moreover, researchers must pay attention to the ways in which cultural exchange with African American youth and the popularity of misogynist and violent aspects of Black expressive culture as championed by the corporate culture industry have influenced Chicana/o gender socialization and, thus, lyrical representations of men and women in Chicano rap music.

This study has shown how myriad aspects of U.S. social, political, cultural, and economic life have influenced the attitudes of young Chicanas/os toward gender and violence as expressed in their music. It is my hope that this study can encourage in-depth, qualitative, audience reception-type analysis that will further our understanding of Chicana/o youth socialization. Moreover, examinations of other themes in Chicano rap lyrics can help solidify our knowledge about young Chicana/o lives in postindustrial barrios. How young people understand community, racial identity, and drug use requires scholarly analysis. The methodological approach for studying violence and gender used in this project can provide important insights into these areas of Chicana/o life.

Finally, my twenty-five years of experience with rap and hip-hop culture and more than fifteen years of formal study of Chicana/o culture have helped me develop a rap pedagogy that can go beyond criticism of youth culture. This rap pedagogy is a generative approach à la Paulo Freire's "pedagogy of the oppressed" that uses the themes, concerns, desires, and cultures of Chicana/o youth as the starting point to a critical analysis of U.S. society and youth lives. Young working-class Chicanas/os, more than most of us, know that something is tragically wrong with postindustrial society. While they sometimes are unable to express it or are not fully aware of it, they intuitively understand that racism, capitalism, and authoritarianism are undermining their lives. Their experiences and youth rebelliousness provide openings for elders, activists, and teacher-students of all sorts who care about developing anti-authoritarian, spiritual, and loving worldviews among youth. Without our guidance, however, youth and their culture can devolve into authoritarianism, sexism, and violence indicative of the patriarchal dominance paradigm and found in much of Chicano rap. Critical analysis of U.S. society, respectful attention to youth culture, and a focus on loving, democratic, and egalitarian aspects of our cultures and traditions can provide a basis for a rap pedagogy of emancipation that can change lives.

NOTES

INTRODUCTION

1. See Banes (2004) and Holman (2004) for examinations and explanations of breakdancing.

CHAPTER ONE

1. Jhally 1997, 1999; Kimmel 1994.

2. Giroux 1996; Jhally 1995, 1999.

3. In their song "Order Through Chaos" on *A War Story, Book I* (1999), Chicano rappers Psycho Realm critique this understanding, asking television watchers ("tube whores") how much television they watch and asserting that because of media focus on violence in the ghettos Brown men are seen as "the face of violence."

4. Kelley (1994) examined the rise in popularity of gangsta rap by the early 1990s.

5. Giroux defines "hyper-real violence" as a new "form of ultraviolence marked by technological overstimulation, gritty dialogue, dramatic storytelling, parody, and an appeal to gutsy realism" (1996, 64).

6. On the eve of the historic rap summit Taking Responsibility (June 2001, New York City), Treach of the important rap group Naughty by Nature appeared on *BET Live*, an interview program on the Black Entertainment Television network. The summit, which featured a speech by minister Louis Farrakhan of the Nation of Islam, was in part aimed at artists and black moguls to challenge them to analyze their position within the industry and reassess their commitments and responsibilities as high-profile members of the Black community. Treach, along with two rap industry executives and a representative of the Nation of Islam, discussed the proliferation of violent, misogynist, capitalist, and otherwise negative images in popular rap music. Treach argued that the recording industry was the primary culprit in the increasing volume of violent images in rap since the late 1980s. Artists recognize that violence gets recorded, promoted, played, and sold while other images receive less attention from the industry. This, according to Treach, results in the modification of their images, sounds, and iconography to satisfy the requisite gangsta image. This is, of course, not the first time Black artists and their cultural products

have been manipulated by the culture industry. See Mike Alleyne's discussion (1999) of the commodification and manipulation of Bob Marley's music by the Island Records company. On similar processes in the marketing of *salsa* music see Sánchez-González (1999). Extensive discussions of the commodification of expressive culture and its reactionary consequences can be found in many of the works of the Frankfurt School and of other critical theorists; see for example Adorno (1989a,b) and Lowenthal (1989).

7. Examples of the value placed on violent heroes such as Mexican revolutionary heroes and boxers can be found in numerous Chicano rap songs. Frost likens himself to Pancho Villa in his song "Bambseeya" and East Los Angeles boxing superstar Oscar de la Hoya in "La Raza II."

8. Limón defines the *corrido* as "a male narrative folk song of greater Mexico composed in octosyllabic quatrains and sung to a tune in ternary rhythm and in 3/4 or 6/8 time. The quatrains are structured in an *abcb* rhyme scheme with no fixed number of stanzas for any given song or performance" (1992, 10).

9. See J. Scott (1987) for the initial theorization of the concept "weapons of the weak."

10. In *Mexicano Resistance* (1981), Rosenbaum distinguishes between five types of rebellion throughout Mexican (American) history. He finds that "social banditry involves a small number of active participants and widespread support from the larger community" (53). The defining characteristic that separates the social bandit from the common criminal is community support. To oppressed Mexicans during the late nineteenth and early twentieth centuries, Mexican (American) social bandits like Gregorio Cortez, Tiburcio Vásquez, and Joaquín Murrieta were "heroes and defenders, remembered in story and song" (55). Social bandits are seen as resisting racist or other oppression that "common" people also suffer. Many Mexicans have seen them as heroic figures because they fight back, do not harm their community, and behave according to a community-defined ethos.

11. For collections of transcripts of *corrido* lyrics and music see Robb (1980), Paredes (1976), and Loeffler (1999).

12. The theme of the Mexican outsmarting the Anglo appears often in the Mexican American joking tradition (Reyna n.d.) and in stories about Don Pedro Urdemales, a trickster character in the oral traditions of many Latin American countries. Don Pedro represents the peasant and working-class Latin American who overcomes his situation through cunning and by outwitting the wealthy.

13. R. Saldívar writes that during the period "1850–1930 the number of Mexicans killed in incidents of racial violence in the Southwest was greater than the number of lynchings of black Americans during the same period in the South" (1990, 18).

14. Limón 1992; Herrera-Sobek 1990.

15. An emergent culture creates new values, meanings, and relationships from an unsatisfactory assimilation of two cultures, one usually dominant (Limón 1992).

16. M. Davis 1990; Kelley 1994; Rose 1994.

17. Bello 1994; Rose 1994; Valle and Torres 2000; Wilson 1987.

18. See Kelley (1994) for a thorough analysis of gangsta rap and its precursors.

19. For example, Ice-T's *Original Gangsta* (1991) and *Power* (1988); N.W.A.'s *100 Miles and Runnin'* (1990) and *Greatest Hits* (1996); Ice Cube's *Predator* (1992) and *Kill at Will* (1992); Dr. Dre's *The Chronic* (1992); and Snoop Doggy Dogg's *Doggystyle* (1993). The funk precursors to rap are exemplified by George Clinton's groups Parliament and Funkadelic, especially on *Parliament's Greatest Hits* (1984). Another important influence on "gangsta beats" is James Brown, notably on *Star Time* (1991).

20. This new free trade regime, or neoliberalism, is seen in treaties such as the North American Free Trade Agreement (NAFTA), the General Agreement on Trade and Tariffs (GATT), and the Multi-Lateral Agreement on Investment (MAI), which formalize economic cooperation between national bourgeoisies, especially those of the North.

21. W. Robinson reported the following United Nations figures on global poverty (1996, 22): Between 1990 and 1995 Latin American poverty increased from 183 million to 230 million people; the percentage of poor people in Latin America increased from 40 percent in 1980 to 48 percent in 1995; across the globe 1.3 billion people lived in absolute poverty. Commenting on the growing gap between the global rich and the global poor, Robinson concluded that "the ratio of inequality between the global rich and the global poor . . . was 1:150."

22. For more detailed discussions of the effects of globalization in Latin America see W. Robinson (1998); for its effects in Mexico see McFarland (1999).

23. For important discussions of changing Mexican American/Chicana/o urban communities in the 1980s and 1990s, especially concerning the impact that immigrants have had in remaking cities, see Mike Davis' *Magical Urbanism* (2000) and Victor Valle and Rodolfo Torres' *Latino Metropolis* (2000).

24. These changes began in the early 1980s. In the United States they include the following: weakening of union power, inaugurated and exemplified by the Reagan government's defeat of the Professional Air Traffic Controllers Organization (PATCO) in 1981; the change from a manufacturing to a service economy; the trend toward increasing reliance on part-time and temporary workers; the internationalization of production, leading to the exportation of well-paid manufacturing jobs; technological developments that replaced workers with machines or computers; deregulation of the workplace (halting or rolling back workplace safety standards, environmental regulations, worker benefits, etc.); changes in the tax code that placed a larger percentage of the burden on workers; and shifts in government spending to enrich business and military subsidies and cut investments in human capital (education and job training, health care, and welfare).

25. Churchill 2003; M. Davis 1990; Dunn 1996.

26. Aguirre and Turner (2007), using U.S. Census Bureau data, show that economic restructuring has disproportionately burdened Latinas/os: the 2002

poverty rate for Mexican Americans was 22.8 percent, more than twice the rate for non-Hispanic Whites (8.0 percent); and in 2002 few Mexican Americans (11.9 percent) worked in high-wage, high-prestige managerial or professional occupations, compared to 35.1 percent of non-Latino Whites. Mexican Americans were overrepresented in the ranks of the low-wage, unstable service industry (34.3 percent, compared to 22.4 percent of non-Latino Whites) and farmer-laborer sector (31.2 percent, compared to 13.3 percent of non-Latino Whites). Avalos found that in 1990 in every occupational category except "craftsmen," Latinas/os earned less than their non-Hispanic White colleagues did (1996, 35).

27. Chicano and Chicana LFPRs in 1991 were 80 percent and 51 percent, respectively, compared to 74 percent and 57 percent for non-Hispanic White males and females, respectively (González-Baker 1996, 13).

28. Eitzen and Zinn report that in 1995 the Latina/o unemployment rate was 9.4 percent, for African Americans 10 percent, and for non-Hispanic Whites 4.8 percent (1998, 303).

29. Median income in 1991 was $12,894 for Chicanos and $22,207 for non-Hispanic White men; it was $9,286 for Chicanas and $12,438 for non-Hispanic White women (González-Baker 1996, 15).

30. Census figures show that for the nation as a whole, Latino men made 64 cents for every dollar made by non-Latino males in 1988 and 63 cents on the dollar in 2002.

31. The incarceration rate during this period rose "from 163 to 529 prison inmates per 100,000 'Hispanic' residents" (Donziger 1996, 104). "Hispanic" is a term the U.S. Census Bureau has used to encompass people of Latin American descent residing in the United States.

32. See Watkins (2005, 163–189) for analysis of the growth of California's prison-industrial complex, with a special focus on the juvenile justice system.

33. For example, 1990 U.S. Census data show a poverty rate for Hispanic families in Los Angeles in 1989 of 22.3 percent. This translates to a Hispanic child poverty rate of 26.7 percent, or 61.4 percent of all children in poverty in Los Angeles. In 1990, among Hispanic households throughout the United States, 18.7 percent were headed by women; among these, 44.6 percent lived in poverty. An analysis of Census data of income by race reveals a wide gap: non-Hispanic White families in Los Angeles earned approximately $10,000 more than Hispanics in 1989 and $19,000 more than Black families. Economic restructuring in Los Angeles created many new service jobs that pay minimum and subminimum wages. Changes in the city's industrial landscape have caused native-born Mexican Americans to be relegated to these poorly paid jobs. As a result, journalist Harold Meyerson found, "native-born Mexican American men were making a lower percentage of the average white-male wage in 1989 than they were in 1959" (in Valle and Torres 2000, 108).

34. This astonishing phenomenon of military recruitment offices inside Chicana/o high schools was communicated to me (December 2003) by Fernando Escobar of the Chicano hip-hop organization 5th Battalion and discussed on the

Divine Forces radio show in 2003 and the *Democracy Now!* radio show of March 22, 2004.

35. The "hypermasculine" is related to Baudrillard's "hyper-real," which Boyd characterizes as "a situation where the contradiction between the real and the imaginary is effaced" (1997, 70)—that is, the contradiction between men as emotional, dependent, caring, nurturing, strong, vulnerable, and powerful and the popular notion of manhood as simply violent, competitive, and aggressive.

36. Ferber (1998, 21) quotes Elizabeth Spelman on how "crucial gender distinctions can be the maintenance of . . . race distinctions . . . [and] the study of gender relations is absolutely essential to the study of . . . race relations because it is pivotal to the study of how societies define and distinguish themselves." Discussing racial boundary policing, Ferber writes that "it is through the construction of boundaries themselves that identities come into existence" (1998, 24).

37. The commercial and artistic successes of Black female rappers such as Lil' Kim, Queen Latifah, Trina, MC Lyte, and Mia X demonstrate that women can master this art form. Nonetheless, women's voices are seldom heard unmediated. Discussions of women's place in rap and hip-hop culture from female hip hoppers can be found in McGregor (1997) and Raimist (1999). Among the numerous rap albums by women, see, for example, Lil' Kim's *Hardcore* (1996) and *The Notorious K.I.M.* (2000); MC Lyte's *Lyte as a Rock* (1988), *Eyes on This* (1989), *Act Like You Know* (1991), *Ain't No Other* (1993), *Bad as I Wanna B* (1996), *Badder than B-Fore* (1998), and *Seven and Seven* (1998); Mia X's *Good Girl Gone Bad* (1995), *Unlady Like* (1997), and *Mama Drama* (1998); Queen Latifah's *All Hail the Queen* (1989), *Nature of a Sista* (1991), *Black Reign* (1993), and *Order in the Court* (1998); and Trina's *Da Baddest B***ch* (2000). Two websites that detail female rappers' discographies and provide lyrics to their songs are www.OHHLA.com and www.allmusic.com.

38. Reasons include the following: rapping has been seen as a male form of expression; the male-dominated culture industry exploits women; sexism prevails in Black and Brown youth culture; and women generally lack resources to affect the dominant patriarchal worldview and culture of the United States. Pough (2004) expands upon Habermas' ideas to examine Black women's roles in and impacts on the public sphere.

39. hooks (2003) argues that African Americans learned patriarchal masculinity through imitation of White masters' patriarchal control over slaves, wives, and other property. Today, under the constraining forces of aggressive capitalism, whose central ethic is greed, Black men often exercise and practice their masculinity through the pursuit of money, women, and power. The same can be said for men of all races and ethnicities in the United States.

40. On gender as performance see Berger, Wallis, and Watson 1995; Butler 1990; and Kimmel 1994.

41. Kimmel calls this hegemonic masculinity "marketplace manhood." He writes that it is "a manhood that require[s] proof, and that require[s] the acquisition of tangible goods as evidence of success. It reconstitute[s] itself

by the exclusion of 'others' . . . and by terrified flight into a pristine mythic homosocial Eden where men could, at last, be real men among other men" (1994, 124).

42. For extended analyses of cultural exchange between Mexican-origin people and Black Americans see Loza (1993) on rock 'n' roll music and culture in the 1950s and 1960s, Mazón (1984) on zoot suit culture in the 1940s, and Yamaoka (1998) on lowriding beginning in the 1950s. Also see Boyd (1997, 92–95) and Johnson (2002).

43. Rap music and hip-hop culture are not homogeneous. Within rap there are many different styles, political philosophies, and religions.

44. For extended discussions of violence and the media also see Dixon and Linz (2000), Fishman and Cavender (1998), O'Keefe and Reid-Nash (1987).

45. The interested reader can view *Lowrider Magazine* and *Orly's Lowriding* magazine; Parsons and Padilla's book *Low 'n Slow: Lowriding in New Mexico* (1999); Yamaoka's film *The History of Hydraulics* (1998); and the Brown Pride website (www.brownpride.com).

46. In addition to Fregoso's film studies, the interested reader can examine analyses of gender representations in other Mexican/Chicano expressive cultural forms such as Broyles-González' study (1994) of *El Teatro Campesino*, Herrera-Sobek's critique (1990) of *corridos*, Gaspar de Alba's edited volume *Velvet Barrios* (2003), and Romero's examination (2002) of the *indita* music genre.

47. Herrera-Sobek 1990; Limón 1992; McFarland 2002; Paredes 1959; Romero 2002. Of course, to describe the Mexican oral tradition as simply patriarchal is overly simplistic. While patriarchal themes dominate, many others challenge the worldview expounded by Mexican patriarchy. Religious themes, discussions of rural life, humor, celebrations of community, and politics are also common in the Mexican oral and literary traditions.

48. See Herrera-Sobek (1989) for a discussion of representation of women in the *décima*.

49. The *Viejitos* collection has eight songs in which women are depicted as mothers, eight with depictions of them as religious figures, and six with representations of women as lovers or wives. The *Cancionero* collection depicts women as mothers in four songs, as lovers or wives in twelve songs, and as religious figures in two songs.

50. In the *Viejitos* collection (Loeffler 1999), the following songs (with page numbers in parentheses) have passing references to women in which women serve as the objects of the male gaze: "Frijolitos Pintos" (15), "Indita de Cochití" (33), "La Huerfanita" (90), "La Boda Negra" (94), and "Lupita Divina" (98). Songs in which women are represented as objects of the male gaze in *Cancionero* (Paredes 1976) include the following: "La Pastora" (7–9), "La Chiva" (126–128), "La Negrita" (137–138), "El Colúmpico (The Swing)" (142–143), "La Borrega Prieta" (144–145), "Bonita Esta Tierra" (161–162), and "Tex-Mex Serenade" (169–170).

51. Songs like "La Mancornadora" (Two-Timing Woman) (Loeffler 1999, 98–99), "La Canción de Carlos Guillén" (Paredes 1976, 107–108), "El Colúmpico"

(The Swing) (Paredes 1976, 142–143), and "Los Mexicanos Que Hablan Inglés" (Paredes 1976, 163–164) are part of the long history of *malinchismo* that sees women as potentially traitorous to their men, nation, and *raza*.

52. Paredes (1976, 107–108) presents the song "La Canción de Carlos Guillén," in which the archetype of the treacherous women appears. Guillén shoots his beloved and is sentenced to death. He claims, "A prisoner am I, because of a faithless woman."

53. Throughout the album, women are depicted as traitorous for having sex with more than one man, but male infidelity is celebrated as in the song "Mis Movidas." The male protagonist of this song describes his many female sexual partners (*movidas*), his ability to get money from them, and his skill at taking women from their men.

54. Paredes records the song "Elena," which ends with this warning: "Ladies, give your attention to what happened on this occasion/How her husband killed Elena because of her artful ways" (1976, 16–17).

55. See Watkins (2005, 136–140) for discussion of the consequences of media consolidation for rap music.

56. In discussing the uses to which the dominant society has put the image of the "bad black mother" Hill Collins writes: "Portraying African-American women as matriarchs allows the dominant group to blame Black women for the success or failure of Black children . . . such a view diverts attention from the political and economic inequality affecting Black mothers and children and suggests that anyone can rise from poverty if he or she only received good values at home. . . . Using Black women's performance as mothers to explain Black economic subordination links gender ideology to explanations of class subordination" (1990, 74). Another important controlling image is the "whore," or Jezebel: "Jezebel's function was to relegate all Black women to the category of sexually aggressive women, thus providing a powerful rationale for the widespread sexual assaults by white men typically reported by Black slave women" (77).

57. For in-depth discussions of Latina images in film see Fregoso 1992a and Wool 1980.

58. The treacherous or traitorous Mexican woman has a long history in Hollywood films. Keller writes that the vamp or temptress "was the most common female Hispanic type during the first decades of American film production" (1994, 44). The first Mexican temptress appeared in the 1909 film *Mexican Sweethearts*. Keller describes another important stock Mexican female character: "The cantina girl serves an ancillary function as the love interest of the Anglo hero. She seems either to be waiting for the Anglo to enter her life, or is quick to discard her Latin suitor in favor of the Anglo" (40).

59. In *From Dusk Till Dawn*, not only is Salma Hayek a body—she is a dangerous body, a treacherous bad woman, the new *malinche*, the latest cantina girl. After her seductive dance in a border cantina—a typical scene in Hollywood depictions of Mexican women (Keller 1994, 40)—she morphs into a vampire and literally sucks the blood out of the White protagonists.

60. In the film *Representation and the Media* (Jhally 1997), Stuart Hall discusses the relationship of images, creation of meaning, and behaviors.

61. Andersen and Hill Collins 1998; Hill Collins 1990.

CHAPTER TWO

1. In *Chicano Poetics* (1997, 10), Alfred Arteaga describes the similar language use of Chicano poets: "Linguistically, Chicano poetry often manifests some degree of interlingualism, employing English, Spanish, caló (Chicano slang), and perhaps Nahuatl."

2. A sample is a small part of a sound recording, used by a music producer as an instrument or a backing track or to add texture. A sample can be a beat, chorus, melody, instrumental riff, street sounds, movie dialogue, speech, or other sounds. It can be altered or unaltered. See Bartlett (1994).

3. Proper Dos also has made *We're at It Again* (1995), *Heat* (1998), and *Overdose* (1999).

4. For more on Chicano rock 'n' roll and Chicano and Black interaction see Steven Loza's *Barrio Rhythm* (1993).

5. Loza 1993; M. García 1998; J. Vigil 2002; Yamaoka 1998.

6. Rose locates the emergence of rap in New York during the economic restructuring beginning in the 1970s (1994, Chapter 2). Contributors to *In the Barrios* (Moore and Pinderhughes 1993) detail the effects of the deindustrialization process on working-class Latina/o communities. Mike Davis' (1990) account of power and racial inequality in Los Angeles documents police abuses in Los Angeles' communities of color. Brian Cross provides a detailed table that lists the race of police abuse victims in the years 1965–1991 in his *It's Not About a Salary* (1993). In *Real War on Crime* (cited in Donziger 1996), the National Commission on Criminal Justice criticizes the judicial system, detailing racial inequality and mistreatment of people of color at all stages of the criminal justice system.

7. For excellent descriptions of the West Coast sound from artists see the documentary *Rhyme and Reason* (Spirer 1997).

8. Between 1990 and 1999, Lighter Shade of Brown released three more albums: *Hip Hop Locos* (1992), *Layin' in the Cut* (1994), and *Lighter Shade of Brown* (1997).

9. Brown Pride Online 2001, "Another Latin Timebomb," www.brownpride.com/latinrap/latinrap.asp?a = alt/index.

10. Cross 1993; Ndlovu 2000.

11. Control Machete has since recorded three more albums: *Artillería Pesada* (1999), *Solo Para Fanáticos* (2002), and *Uno, Dos: Bandera* (2003).

12. In the important documentary film *Pass the Mic*, Jacken discusses their experiences with Sony Records and why they decided to go independent. On their album *A War Story, Book I* they also discuss their problems with Sony.

13. Jacken describes the event in his short essay "A War Story," at www.brownpride.com/latinrap/latinrap.asp?a = warstory/index.

14. The documentary film *Money, Power, Respect* (Hall 2003) provides more detail on the dispute between Royal T/Low Profile Records and Lil' Rob.

15. www.allmusic.com; www.40ouncerecords.com.

16. Sir Dyno's releases include *What Have I Become?* (2000) and *Through My Eyes* (2001).

17. See, for example, Crooked, *Then Fear Me* (2001); K.I.D., *Commitment to Excellence* (2001); Los Traficantes, *Matan Mi Gente/No Pararemos Hasta la Muerte* (2001); Oso, *Who Can I Trust?* (2000) and *The Hated One* (2001); and Young D., *The Mind of a Mexican* (2001).

18. www.babybash.com.

19. On May 6, 2004, Cuahutli wrote this brief piece of Los Nativos history on brownpride.com: "Los Nativos are straight OG's ["original gangstas," used here to mean original members of the label] of Rhymesayers. I have had people come up to me and say 'Oh that's tight that Rhymesayers hooked up with a latin rap group.' But the truth is RSE has always had a Chicano rap group since day one. We used to be called the Native Ones."

20. Latino Saint, personal communication, October 21, 2003; www.myspace.com/latinosaint.

21. For discussions of women in rap see the documentary film *Nobody Knows My Name* (Raimist 2000) and Guevara 1996, Keyes 2002, Pough 2004, and Rose 1990.

22. www.505underground.com.

23. Sista D, personal correspondence, February 27, 2004.

24. Interested readers can view cover art, photos, and related artwork at www.lowprofilerecords.com.

25. Krazy Race, phone interview, January 17, 2004.

26. Levine 1977; Walser 1998.

27. Joanne Nagel (1996) explains that an important aspect of any ethnic or other identity is that often one cannot choose his or her identity; instead it is forced upon the individual by a dominant group. It is ascribed to the person.

CHAPTER THREE

1. Eckes and Trautner 2000; Renzetti and Curran 1999.

2. See also Berger, Wallace, and Watson 1995, Bhabha 1995, Brittan 1989, Hatty 2004, and LaFrance 1995.

3. "Concerns about body image and athletic performance may be leading teens, as well as adult men and women, to use anabolic steroids, despite the serious side effects of these drugs"—heart disease, liver cancer, depression, aggression, eating disorders, acne, and HIV risk (NIDA 2000).

4. Jhally 1999; Kimmel 1994.

5. See Jhally 1999 for details. An American Automobile Association (AAA) study found that 90 percent of motorists surveyed in January 1995 had experienced a road-rage incident in the previous twelve months; reporting on the AAA study, Matthew Joint (1995) adds that "in the United States, unverified

figures of up to 1,200 road rage-related deaths a year have been reported." Jeff Siegel (2005) writes that the typical road-rage incident involves at least one eighteen- to twenty-six-year-old male.

6. Jhally 1999; Kimmel 1994.

7. Boyd 1997; Katz 1999; Lusane 1997.

8. Boyd 1997; Chuck D 1997.

9. Harper 1996; hooks 1994.

10. Castillo 1994a; A. García 1997; Limón 1992. For a different perspective see Mirandé (1997), who challenges the notion that the ideal man of Mexican descent is almost always figured as hypermasculine. G. Rodriguez (2002) uses the example of superstar boxer Oscar de la Hoya to complicate our notions of the boxing club and ring as arenas for the performance of hypermasculinity.

11. Yamaoka 1998.

12. Loza 1993.

13. Mazón 1984.

14. Rap music style is a theme in the documentaries *Pass the Mic* (Montes 2002) and *Money, Power, Respect* (Hall 2003).

15. M. García 1998; G. Johnson 2002.

16. On pimp imagery see George 1998 and Kelley 1994.

17. Denzin 2002; Schneider 2004.

18. Brownside 1999; Knightowl 1998, 1999, 2000, 2001.

19. Boyd 1997; George 1998; Kelley 1994.

20. Castañeda 1993; Castillo 1994, 130; Dette 1995; Dowd Hall 1983; Hernandez Castillo 1998; Nikolic-Ristanovic 1996.

21. Rose 1990; Jhally 1995.

22. The San Diego–based rapper, formerly affiliated with Low Profile Records, embodies Chicano street mentality, fashion, and music. Rob dresses in Chicano street youth (*cholo*) attire; loose-fitting usually khaki pants, Pendelton shirts or white T-shirts, tennis shoes or boots, and sunglasses. He wears his hair cut close to the scalp and assumes a cold, hard stare and a defiant stance. His CD covers often depict him surrounded by barrio iconography, lowriders, gang graffiti, and the like, with a marijuana cigarette in his mouth. His musical style epitomizes Chicano youth culture as it fuses hard-core rap sounds with oldies-style musical production, vocals, and samples, and Chicano street vernacular. His embodiment of contemporary *cholo* style was confirmed in 2000 when he was named the best Chicano rapper in an online poll conducted by Brown Pride.

23. Herrera-Sobek 1990; Rincón 1997.

24. Castillo 1994a,b; A. García 1994.

25. Castillo 1994a; A. García 1997; Herrera-Sobek 1990.

CHAPTER FOUR

1. Alarcón 1993; Castillo 1994; Trujillo 1991a,b.

2. Beauty Bragg, "Lil' Kim's Hardcore Subversion of Heterosexual Norms," unpublished manuscript.

3. Jhally 1995; Rose 1994, 1990.

4. Brown 2002; L. Rodriguez 1994; and Sanchez 2001.

5. Brown 2002; Jhally 1997, 1999; and Jensen 2004.

CHAPTER FIVE

1. In his 1995 article "Television Violence: The Power and the Peril," Gerbner explains that "being Latino/Hispanic or lower class means bad trouble: they are the most likely to kill and be killed. Being poor, old, Hispanic or a woman of color means double trouble, a disproportionate chance of being killed." See also Escalante (2000) for extended discussion of the politics of Chicana/o representation in television.

2. The American Psychological Association, American Medical Association, American Psychiatric Association, National Association for the Education of Young Children, the American Academy of Child and Adolescent Psychiatry, and the National Association of School Psychologists have all released similar statements regarding the damaging effects of violent entertainment on young people. For these statements, related research articles, and other information regarding violent entertainment and its effects see the Lion and Lamb Project website at www.lionlamb.org; although the project has ended, the site remains available for reference.

3. Barongan and Nagayama Hall 1995; Berry (1990); Fried 1999; Hansen 1995; Johnson, Jackson, and Gatto 1995.

4. Schrag and Javidi reported in 1995 that "the average child watches over seven hours of television programming a day" (212). They argue that "the content of television programs, when combined with high concentrations of exposure to that content, clearly influences the cognition, attitudes, beliefs, and subsequent behaviors of children."

5. See the insights into criminal behavior offered by Daniel Glaser's differential identification theories of crime (1956).

6. The problem of the Black male character as a clown or buffoon is as old as moving pictures themselves. Buffoons and gangstas or criminals remain the most common black characters in movies. For analysis of this problem see Jhally's films with hooks (1997) and with Katz (1999); Riggs' film *Ethnic Notions* (1987); and Wilson and Gutierrez 1995.

7. Anderson and Bushman 2001; Anderson and Dill 2000. The power and popularity of video games is not lost on the United States military. They have created their own "action" video games as recruiting and training tools. Matthew Schwartz reports (2002) that "the United States Army has begun to fund a game called 'America's Army' until 2007. 'America's Army' promises to have life-like simulation boot camp training as well as proper weapon functioning. 'The goal of the game,' according to writer Daniel Morris, is to 'realistically model the weapons, tactics, and experiences of the modern army.' This includes using weapons as they are used in real life, as well as planning attacks." Not only is the thrill of shooting guns and killing enemies made lifelike in these games,

but also the powerful draw of heroism and patriotism is insidiously made part of the experience. While the Army could stand to make a great deal of money from the sale of *America's Army*, it seems to have something more important in mind: recruits. According to Schwartz, "This violent simulation game is available free of charge to anyone who asks, although the Army hopes to market the simulation to the 'key recruitment demographic of 18-to-25-year-old males.'" Moreover, "it is clear that with this game's frightening accuracy, the Army is 'virtually training' its new recruits." This argument mirrors Lieutenant Colonel Grossman's claim throughout his 1995 work that the new generations of lifelike video games are training young people to become sharpshooters and killers of foreign-looking enemies at an increasingly efficient pace. See also Andrea Lewis' detailed discussion (2005) of the *America's Army* website (http://www.americasarmy.com/).

8. See Armstrong 2001.

9. In "Conspiracy Theory" (1999), Psycho Realm raps that young men are "desensitized with force through violence that's televised in spite of the cross / through news and other media we see homicides."

10. Examining the Darkroom Familia's website I found its catalogue of CDs. Many of the titles invoke violence. Examples include Duke's *To Live and Die in the Bay* (1996) and *Kill Them Slowly* (2000, whose cover shows a young Chicano slicing the throat of another); A.L.G.'s *Right to Remain Violent* (2000); N.K.A.'s *Northern Killa4nia Assassins* (2000); Dub's *My Way or the Die Way* (2000); Darkroom Familia's *Homicide Kings* (2000); Los Traficantes' *No Pararemos Hasta la Muerte* (We Won't Stop Until Death); and Crooked's *Violence Solves Everything* (2000).

11. Many Chicano rappers use violence in this way. The roster of the Low Profile Label features numerous rappers who specialize in gratuitously violent lyrics. Among them are Lil' Rob, Royal T, Proper Dos, Knightowl, Yogi, and Lil' One. Others similarly use violence, among them Slush the Villain, Mr. Shadow, Conejo, Capone, Frost, Cypress Hill, and Street Platoon.

12. In the late 1980s the term "road rage" came into the U.S. vocabulary as violence on the road became a more common problem and concern for drivers. In a survey reported by the American Automobile Association (AAA) Foundation for Traffic Safety (Mizell, Joint, and Connell 1997), drivers reported that their number one concern on the highways was road rage; drunken driving came in second. The report, *Aggressive Driving: Three Studies*, examined thousands of police and newspaper reports of road rage. It found more than 10,000 cases of road rage between January 1, 1990, and August 31, 1997. The AAA reported that the phenomenon was getting worse. Also see Rathbone and Huckabee 1999.

13. See also Donnerstein 1980; Donnerstein and Berkowitz 1981; Linz 1989; Sommers and Check 1987; St. Lawrence and Joyner 1991; Zillman and Bryant 1982.

14. Conejo repeatedly refers to women as dangerous on his albums *City of Angels* (1999a, "City of Angels," "I Need Money," "I Put It Down," and "You Ain't the Homie No More") and *Fallen Angel* (2001, "Tonight We Go to War").

15. See Jhally's film *Dreamworlds II* (1995) for an extensive discussion of music videos as a male fantasy world. Also see Rose 1994.

16. Armstrong analyzed 490 songs from the most popular gangsta rap albums from 1987 to 1993.

17. Particularly problematic regarding the misogynist violence expressed in Chicano rap is that few Chicanas have cut rap CDs. My sample contains only one song by a female rapper, JV, and I know of only a handful of others, including those mentioned earlier and Tamara, Diamonique, and Blanca la Chingona, none of whose music I have been able to find. Women rappers could potentially challenge Chicano rappers' representations of them as Black female rappers have done (Rose 1990, 1994).

18. LBS released its debut compact disc, *Neighborhood Creepas*, in 1998. Like most gangsta rap, the CD tells stories of barrio youth and the violent situations they encounter. The members of LBS hail from Los Angeles.

19. "Corporate media" is a term used to describe media governed by advertising, a pro-business ideological orientation, and conservative social values and racial understandings. Others have referred to these types of media as "dominant" or "mainstream." I choose the term "corporate media" to highlight mainstream media's close ties with corporations and capitalist logic and practices and to distinguish it from "alternative" or "underground" media sources that critique capitalist globalization, military violence, racism, sexism, and homophobia.

20. "Cop Killer" (1992, later dropped) is not a rap song but a "heavy metal" or "hardcore" song sung (not rapped) by Ice-T's group, Body Count. It narrates the story of a young man who goes searching for a cop to murder in order to avenge police brutality and harassment. In the chorus to "Cop Killer," Body Count repeats "fuck the police" for Daryl Gates, Rodney King, dead homies, and police brutality. Lyrics and more information on the song and Body Count can be found at www.bodycount.com/home.php.

21. The PMRC was co-founded in 1985 by Tipper Gore, wife of then-Senator Al Gore. The group was primarily responsible for the warning labels on compact discs with explicit, violent, or otherwise "inappropriate" lyrics for young people.

22. The late Congresswoman C. Dolores Tucker waged a decade-long campaign against gangsta rap through the National Political Congress of Black Women (http://www.npcbw.org/), which she helped found and once chaired. Lipsitz (1998) discusses C. Dolores Tucker's anti-rap efforts as well as several other incidents that demonized rap music in the public eye. He discusses controversies surrounding songs and incidents such as N.W.A.'s "Fuck the Police" and 2 Live Crew's *Nasty as They Wanna Be*.

23. This song is from his album *What Have I Become?* (2000). More lyrics and information on Sir Dyno can be found at http://www.brownpride.com/latinrap/latinrap.asp?a=sirdyno/index.

24. Among the Chicano rap artists who discuss violence in these ways

are Sir Dyno, Psycho Realm, SPM, Street Platoon, Frost, Slush the Villain, Delinquent Habits, Wicked Minds, Funky Aztecs, Johnny Z, Los Marijuanos, Knightowl, Clika 1, Proper Dos, and Lil' Rob.

25. On violence against Chinese immigrants see the documentary film *Chinese in the Frontier West* (Ding 1998) and Takaki's book *Strangers from a Different Shore* (1989). For more on violence against people of Mexican descent see Rodolfo Acuña's classic general Chicana/o history, *Occupied America* (1988).

26. See Ward Churchill's comprehensive review of U.S. military aggression since 1776 in *On the Justice of Roosting Chickens: Reflections on the Consequences of U.S. Imperial Arrogance and Criminality* (2003).

27. For example see *USA Today* 2003.

28. *Democracy Now!* 2003.

29. For a cross-cultural analysis of street socialization see J. Vigil 2003.

30. On *The Ollin Project*, Street Platoon's "Dead Lines" concerns chemical bombs, and Ill Fame's "Rules of Engagement" mentions barracks and war paraphernalia.

31. Among these are Los Tumbados' "U$" on *The Ollin Project* and all of Psycho Realm's music.

32. "Earthquake Weather," "Conspiracy Theories," "Sick Dogs," "Moving Through the Streets," "Enemy of the State," "Tragedy.Com."

33. "The Crazy Area," "Earthquake Weather," "Conspiracy Theories," "Tragedy.Com," "Order Through Chaos."

34. "Street Platoons" and "The Wind of Revolution."

35. Robin Kelley argues similarly (1994) that irreverence has long played an important role in Black oral culture. The badman and trickster heroes of many Black folktales challenge and reject authority. Most Black rappers to whom justice and equality are meaningless catch-phrases identify with the irreverent stance of these folk heroes and embody rebellious attitudes in their lyrics and style.

36. Chuck D 1997; Kelley 1994.

37. hooks 1994; Jhally 1997.

38. On films see Jhally 1997. On gangsta rap see Armstrong 2001, Kelley 1994, and Rose 1994.

39. Donziger 1996; Valle and Torres 2000.

40. All of (Kid) Frost's albums include many songs that touch on these themes, as do artists such as Delinquent Habits on *Delinquent Habits* (1996) and *Merry Go Round* (2001); Slow Pain on *The Hit List* (2000); SPM on *The 3rd Wish to Rock the World* (1999); Funky Aztecs in "Ribbit Part Deuz," "Nation of Funk," "Crazy Juice," and "85 Style" (1995); Sir Dyno in "Let's All Go Back to Charter Way" and "Pure Darkroom Funk" (n.d.); and Brownside in "Corona" (2000). For an important discussion of the distinction between individual pleasure as part of capitalist consumer culture and communal joy see Gina Dent's introduction, "Black Pleasure, Black Joy," to her *Black Popular Culture* (1992), 1–19.

CHAPTER SIX

1. S. Anderson 2000; Bello 1994; Brecher, Costello, and Smith 2000; Danaher 1994; Danaher and Burbach 2000; Green 2001; Hahnel 1999; Wallach and Sforza 1999.

2. Wilson 1987; L. Chavez 1992; Moore and Pinderhughes 1993.

3. Esteva and Prakash prefer the term "social majorities" to describe the majority of people in the world who "have no regular access to most of the goods and services defining the average 'standard of living' in the industrial countries. Their definitions of 'a good life,' shaped by their local traditions, reflect their capacities to flourish outside the 'help' offered by 'global forces'" (1998, 16). The authors compare the social majorities (or the two-thirds world) to the "social minorities" of "both the North and South that share homogeneous ways of modern (western) life all over the world."

4. Esteva and Prakash 1998; McFarland 1999.

5. In theorizing the concept of "organic intellectual" in contrast to the "traditional intellectual," Gramsci (1971, 5) writes that "every social group, coming into existence on the original terrain of an essential function in the world of economic production, creates together with itself, one or more strata of intellectuals which give it homogeneity and an awareness of its own function not only in the economic but also in the social and political fields." Excepting the vanguardist role that Gramsci reserves for the organic intellectual, this concept can be useful for understanding the role that rappers play in their communities. That is, Chicano rappers serve the function of solidifying a self-understanding for Chicana/o youth in urban America. I use the term "solidifying self-understanding" as opposed to the Gramscian-like construction of "giving an awareness to" because I contend that the intellectual material from which rappers or any other organic intellectual develops her or his knowledge of the world results from an embeddedness in the community and interactions and an interdependence with the community's customs and traditions (its epistemology, ontology, and social structures). While rappers may present new understandings that serve a pedagogical function for their constituencies, their cultural production owes a great deal to the community wisdom in which the rappers were socialized. Moreover, Gramsci's concept is apt, given that the aforementioned role of Chicana/o youth in the international economy allows us to conceive of urban Chicana/o youth as a class with a specific, unique, and "essential function in the world of economic production."

6. The use of marijuana in rap and hip-hop culture is well known and celebrated on songs too numerous to mention here. A cursory look at the lyrical content of the rappers discussed in this essay reveals several cuts devoted to the pleasures and politics of marijuana consumption. It is beyond the scope of this discussion to detail the use of marijuana and the uses to which it is put in the hip-hop community. Suffice it to say that we cannot underestimate the importance of marijuana to the evolution of this form of cultural production.

7. Cooper 2004, 22. Cooper notes that in 2003 alone, more than four hundred people died crossing the Mexican-U.S. border.

8. Parenti discusses the Violent Crime Control and Law Enforcement Act of 1994 that nearly doubled Border Patrol forces (1999, 66). The $3 billion allocated to the Border Patrol included monies to purchase high-tech weapons and surveillance gear and vehicles as well as money to incarcerate rather than deport undocumented immigrants. See also Tim Dunn's seminal work, *The Militarization of the U.S-Mexico Border* (1996), which describes how the Border Patrol began beefing up operations prior to the 1994 act.

9. M. Davis 2000, Chapter 4; also see Chacon and Davis 2006.

10. This analysis of the propagandistic function of the media to cause people to believe that "the face of violence" is a young and Brown one is illustrated in the lyrics from the Chicano rappers Funky Aztecs on their song "Nation of Funk" (*Day of the Dead*, 1995).

11. See, for example, Parenti 1999, A. Davis 2003, and Reeves and Campbell 1994, especially Appendix C, "Chronology of Kernel Events in the Cocaine Narrative."

12. These lyrics were posted at www.lyricsfreak.com/p/psycho + realm/ order + through + chaos_20111887.html. The Internet has been an important asset in the development of hip-hop culture during and since the 1990s. Besides posting the lyrics for thousands of rap songs, rap enthusiasts can discuss issues around their favorite artists (including the politics of their lyrics), read or write biographies of artists, and read about contemporary issues pertinent to the existence and survival of hip-hop culture including legislation, recent public debate on music, and insights into the recording industry.

13. The fine documentary *The Fire This Time* (Holland 1995) offers a similar critique of state practices that contribute to inner-city fratricide through exacerbating gang differences and allowing for and encouraging weapons distribution; the film examines the government's role in the crack-cocaine trade. See also Scott and Marshall 1998; Van Peebles 1995; Churchill and Van der Wall 1988.

14. I must note here that this form of domination stems from a deep homophobia and sexism in U.S. culture. The reason that this is seen as the ultimate act of vengeance is because the person committing the rape turns the raped into either "his bitch" or a "fag." In our sexist, homophobic society it becomes the ultimate expression of heterosexual male superiority through symbolically creating an inferior woman or homosexual out of the victim.

15. "At year end 2005, there were 3,145 black male sentenced prison inmates per 100,000 black males in the United States, compared to 1,244 Hispanic male inmates per 100,000 Hispanic males and 471 white male inmates per 100,000 white males" (USDJ 2006).

16. Churchill 2003, 146. On the origins of this tactic by the CIA, Churchill writes that in 1953 CIA Director Allen Dulles initiated a program known as MK-ULTRA, "designed to test the utility of LSD-25 an extraordinarily powerful hallucinogen, in achieving 'mind control'" (115). Fifteen hundred active-duty soldiers unwittingly took LSD as part of an experiment by the U.S. Army and in

order to pacify the counterculture population in the United States millions of hits were dumped into the streets.

17. Parenti 1999, 211–212; A. Davis 1997.

18. *The Never Ending Battle* (2004, 5th Battalion Entertainment).

19. Parenti 1999, 57, 65–66. Besides the 1986 act see also the Anti–Drug Abuse Act of 1988 and the Violent Crime Control and Law Enforcement Act of 1994.

20. In "Illuminati" (*The Never Ending Battle*, 2004), about George W. Bush's policies and secret society affiliations, Krazy Race begins with an explanation of genocide as "the mass extermination of specific groups of people to achieve specific political, racial and/or economic objectives constitutes genocide." He then shouts, "they're tryin' to keep this a secret from us but I'm about to enlighten a few of y'all." In the song "Fact of Fiction" he continues his analysis and critique of the Bush presidency.

21. Marcuse (1964) suggests that an important aspect of a revolutionary social movement is the rejection of capitalist society and its logic. He notes that art in its most "advanced" and political form serves as an important catalyst for social protest. See also Esteva and Prakash 1998; McFarland 1999.

22. Chicano rapper Frost uses this phrase in his song "Nothing but Love for the Neighborhood" on the compact disc *Smile Now, Die Later* (1995).

CHAPTER SEVEN

1. Alcalá 2003; Broyles-González 2002; Castillo 1994b.

2. Alarcón 1989; Barvosa-Carter 2000; Fregoso 1993a,b; Gaspar de Alba 1998; Griswold del Castillo, McKenna, and Yarbro-Bejarano 1991; Lomelí, Márquez, and Herrera-Sobek 2000; A. Ramírez 2000.

3. Castillo 1994; Córdova 1999.

4. Gaspar de Alba 1998; on Alma Lopez see S. Ramírez 2002.

5. Reina Prado (alejandra ibarra), personal correspondence, September 8, 2004.

6. Ibid.

7. See Paolo Freire's *Pedagogy of the Oppressed* (1973) for a complete discussion of "generative themes."

8. L. Rodriguez 2001, Chapter 14. See also Hayden 2003.

REFERENCES

The references are listed in two sections, one for primary sources and one for secondary sources. The "Primary References" section has five subsections: "Albums and Songs Used in Sample," "Chicana/o Rap Albums, General," "Films," "Personal Communications," and "Websites." The subsection "Albums and Songs Used in Sample" lists information on the 470-song sample from which the quantitative data are drawn. The "Chicana/o Rap Albums, General" subsection lists information on other music discussed in the book, including the history discussion in Chapter Two, the comparison of JV and Ms. Sancha in Chapter Four, and the in-depth inquiry into the overtly political lyrics found in the final two chapters of the book.

PRIMARY SOURCES
Albums and Songs Used in Sample

A.L.T. 1992. "Tequila." In *A.L.T.* East West Records.
———. 1993a. "17 Shots." In *Stone Cold World*. Par.
———. 1993b. "Audio 5000." In *Stone Cold World*. Par.
Brown Pride Riders. 1999. Various artists. Volume 1. Aries.
———. 2000. Various artists. Volume 2. Aries.
Brownside. 1999. *Payback*. Preuss Records.
Califa Thugs. 2001. Various artists. Low Profile Records.
Capone. 2001. "Barrio Dope." In *Barrio Dope*. Latin Jam.
Chicano Players. N.d. Various artists. PR Entertainment Group.
Clika 1. N.d. "Deadly Sins." In *Clika 1*. Artes.
———. N.d. "Mexican Mobsters." In *Clika 1*.
Conejo. 1999a. *City of Angels*. Aries.
———. 1999b. "Conejo." In *Neighborhood Vida*, volume 1. Aries Records.
———. 2001. *Fallen Angel*. Casualty.
Cypress Hill. 1991. *Cypress Hill*. Ruffhouse/Columbia.
———. 1995a. "Killa Hill Niggas." In *III Temples of Boom*. Ruffhouse/Columbia.
———. 1995b. "Locotes." In *III Temples of Boom*.
———. 1998. *IV*. Ruffhouse/Columbia.
———. 2001. *Stoned Raiders*. Sony.
Delinquent Habits. 1998. *Here Come the Horns*. RCA.

———. 2000. *Merry Go Round*. Ark 21.

Duke. 2000. "Alyssa Milano." In *To Live and Die in the Bay*. Darkroom (Familia) Studios.

Funky Aztecs. 1995. *Day of the Dead*. Raging Bull.

Keepin' It Gangsta. 2001. Various artists. Lideres.

(Kid) Frost. 1990. "La Raza" and "Homicide." In *Hispanic Causing Panic*. Virgin.

———. 1992. "I Got Pulled Over," "No Sunshine," and "Mi Vida Loca." In *East Side Story*. Virgin.

———. 1995. *Smile Now, Die Later*. Ruthless/Relativity.

———. 1997. "You're a Big Girl Now." In *When HelL.A. Freezes Over*. Relativity.

———. 1999. *That Was Then, This Is Now*, volume 1. Celeb Entertainment.

———. 2002. "I'm Still Here," "Still up in This Shit," "Para Mi Abuelita," and "Where's My Ese's At?". In *Still up in This Shit*. Koch.

Knightowl. 1995. "Brown to the Bone" and "Knightowl." In *Knightowl*. Familia Records.

———. 1998. *Wicked West*. Aries.

———. 1999. *Shot Caller*. Familia.

———. 2000. *Knightmares*. Aries.

———. 2001. *Baldheaded Kingpin*. Lideres.

Latin Bomb Squad (LBS). 1998. *Neighborhood Creepas*. Jeep Beat Society Records.

Latino Velvet. 2000. "Brand Nu Playa" and "Threesome." In *Velvet City*. Celeb Entertainment.

Lil' Rob. 1997. *Crazy Life*. Familia.

———. 2000. *High Till I Die*. Aries.

———. 2001. *Can't Keep a Good Man Down*. Lideres.

———. N.d. "4 Corner Room." In *DJ Supermix*. Bad Check Records.

Los Marijuanos. 1999. "Puro Pleito" and "Time to Get High." In *Puro Pleito*. Wicked.

———. 2001. "Mi Carnal," "Mr. Weedman," and "Marijuana para Mi." In *The Smoke Out*. Wicked.

The Ollin Project. 2001. Various artists. Digital Aztlán.

Proper Dos. 1992. *Mexican Power*. Rhino Records.

———. 1994. "Tales from the Westside." In *Mi Vida Loca Soundtrack*. Mercury.

———. 1999. *Overdose*. Aries.

Psycho Realm. 1997. *Psycho Realm*. Sony.

———. 1999. *A War Story, Book 1*. Sick Symphonies.

———. N.d. "Needful Things." In *Unreleased*.

Royal T. 1998. "Real MFs" and "Servin' Fools." In *Coast to Coast*. Low Profile Records.

———. 2000. "Chicanos Don't Dance" and "The Villains in Blue." In *Southsiders, Chapter 13*. Aries.

———. 2001. "2013," "Jackin' Ballers," and "Bump the Real." In *Cronica 2013*. Lideres.

Sir Dyno. 2000. *What Have I Become?*. Darkroom Studios.

Slow Pain. 2000. *Hit List*. East Side.

Slush the Villain. 2000. *Based on a Thug's Life*. Aries.

Smile Now, Cry Later. 2001. Various artists. Darkroom Studios.

South Park Mexican. 1998. *Power Moves*. Dope House Records.

——. 1999a. *The 3rd Wish*. Dope House Records.

——. 1999b. "City of Danger." In *Lone Star Ridaz*. Crushed.

——. 1999c. *Hillwood*. Dope House Records.

——. 1999d. "Hustletown" and "We Ain't Nowhere." In *Latin Throne II*. Jonathan Cape.

——. 2000. *Time is Money*. Universal.

——. 2001a. *Never Change*. Universal.

——. 2001b. "Tex to Cali Part 2." In *Shunny Pooh Presents 3rd Coast's Finest*. Down South.

Street Platoon. 2001. *The Steel Storm*. Sick Symphonies.

Tha Mexakinz. 1994. "The Wake Up Show." In *Zig Zag*. Wild West.

Thump N' Chicano Rap. N.d. Various artists. Thump Records.

We're in This Together. N.d. Various artists. Low Profile Records.

Chicana/o Rap Albums, General

2Mex. 2000. *Words Knot Music*. Meanstreet.

——. 2001. *B-Boys in Occupied Mexico*. Meanstreet.

——. 2003. *Sweat Lodge Infinite*. Temporary.

——. 2004. *2Mex*. Image.

5th Battalion. 2003. *The Never Ending Battle*. 5th Battalion.

A.L.T. 1993. *Stone Cold World*. Par.

Control Machete. 1997. *Mucho Barato*. Polygram.

——. 1999. *Artilleria Pesada*. Universal Latino.

——. 2002. *Solo para Fanáticos*. Universal Latino.

——. 2004. *Uno, Dos: Bandera*. Universal Latino.

Cypress Hill. 1999. *Los Grandes Éxitos en Español*. Sony.

——. 2000a. *Live at the Fillmore*. Sony.

——. 2000b. *Skull and Bones*. Columbia.

El Vuh. 2003. *Jaguar Prophecies*. Xicano Records and Film.

G-Fellas. 1999. *Crime Stories*. Celeb.

——. 2001. *Gangsta 4 Life*. Triple X.

JV. 1996. *It Gets No Reala*. Thump Records.

(Kid) Frost. 2001. *Frost's Greatest Joints*. Thump Records.

Los Nativos. 2003. *Día de los Muertos*. Rhymesayers Entertainment.

Ms. Sancha. 2003. *Taking It Doggystyle*. Low Profile Records.

Proper Dos. 1995. *We're at It Again*. SBA.

——. 1998. *Heat*. Rhino.

——. 1999. *Overdose*. Aries.

Psycho Realm. 2003. *A War Story, Book II*. Sick Symphonies.

Slow Pain. 1995. *Baby OG*. Thump Records.

——. 2001a. *Lil' Don Juan*. Thump Records.
——. 2001b. *Presents Old Town Gangsters*. Thump Records.
Sista D. 2003. *Rap Starr*. Kut-n-Kru Records.
Thugs and Soldiers. 2000. Various artists. Aries.
Victor E. 2004. *Knowledge and Wisdom*. Xicano Records and Film.
——. N.d. *Black and Red Ink*. Xicano Records and Film.
Xololanxinxo. 2003. *People Kill People*. Memo Records.

Films

Ding, Loni. 1998. *Chinese in the Frontier West: An American Story*. Part 2 of
    Ancestors in the Americas. Center for Educational Telecommunications
    (CET).
Hall, J. 2003. *Money, Power, Respect*. WEA Corporation.
Holland, R. 1995. *The Fire This Time*. Rhino Home Video.
Jhally, S. 1995. *Dreamworlds II*. Media Education Foundation.
——. 1997a. *bell hooks: Cultural Criticism and Transformation*. Media Education
    Foundation.
——. 1997b. *Representation and the Media*, with Stuart Hall. Media Education
    Foundation.
——. 1999. *Tough Guise: Violence, Media, and the Crisis in Masculinity*. Jackson
    Katz Series. Media Education Foundation.
Montes, R. 2002. *Pass the Mic*. Safada y Sano Productions.
Nemo, J. 2000. *Miss MC: Women in Rap*. V-12 Filmworks.
Raimist, R. 1999. *Nobody Knows My Name*. New York: Women Make Movies.
Riggs, M. 1987. *Ethnic Notions: Black People in White Minds*. Berkeley:
    California Newsreel.
Spirer, P. 1997. *Rhyme and Reason*. Miramax.
Valinia, Amir. 1999. *Latin Throne*. AV1 Productions.
Van Peebles, Mario. 1995. *Panther*. Polygram Video.
Yamaoka, J. *The History of Hydraulics*. 1998. Lowrider Magazine.

Personal Communications

Escobar, Fernando. 2003. December 9.
——. 2004a. February 1.
——. 2004b. February 22.
——. 2004c. February 23.
——. 2004d. May 22.
Krazy Race. 2002. December 6.
——. 2003. February 12.
——. 2004a. January 17.
——. 2004b. July 1.
——. 2004c. July 29.
——. 2004d. August 10.

Latino Saint. 2003. October 21.

Shysti. 2004. January 14.

Sista D. 2004a. February 2.

———. 2004b. February 20.

———. 2004c. February 27.

Zero. 2003a. November 11.

———. 2003b. December 9.

———. 2004a. February 9

———. 2004b. February 20.

———. 2004c. June 9.

Websites

5th Battalion. www.5thbattalion.com

40 Ounce Records. www.40ouncerecords.com

505 Underground Records. www.505underground.com

All Music. www.allmusic.com

Baby Bash. www.babybash.com

Brown Pride. www.brownpride.com

Chingo Bling. www.chingobling.com

Divine Forces Radio. www.divineforces.org

Dope House Records. www.dopehouserecords.com

El Vuh. www.elvuh.com

Groundkeepers. www.groundkeepers.com

Krazy Race. www.krazyrace.com

La Familia del Sol. www.myspace.com/lafamiliadelsol

Low Profile Records. www.lowprofilerecords.com

Mañosas. www.manosas.net

The Original Hip Hop Lyrics Archive. www.ohhla.com

Rhymesayers Entertainment. www.rhymesayers.com

Rock A Mole. www.rockamole.com

Thump Records. www.thumprecords.com

Xicano Records and Film. www.myspace.com/xicanorecordsandfilm

SECONDARY SOURCES

Acuña, R. 1988. *Occupied America: A History of Chicanos*. 3d edition. New York: Harper and Row.

Adorno, T. 1989a. "The Culture Industry Reconsidered." In *Critical Theory and Society: A Reader*, ed. S. E. Bronner and D. M. Kellner, 128–135. New York: Routledge.

———. 1989b. "Perennial Fashion—Jazz." In *Critical Theory and Society*, ed. Bronner and Kellner, 199–269.

Aguirre, A., and J. H. Turner. 2007. *American Ethnicity: The Dynamics and Consequences of Discrimination*. 5th edition. Boston: McGraw-Hill.

Alarcón, N. 1989. "Chicana Writers and Critics in a Social Context: Towards a Contemporary Bibliography." *Third Woman* 4:169–178.

——. 1993. "The Sardonic Powers of the Erotic in the Work of Ana Castillo." In *Chicana Critical Issues*, ed. N. Alarcón, 5–19. Mujeres Activas en Letras y Cambio Social (MALCS). Berkeley: Third Woman Press.

Alcalá, R. C. 2003. "A Chicana Hagiography for the Twenty-first Century: Ana Castillo's Locas Santas." In *Velvet Barrios: Popular Culture and Chicana/o Sexualities*, ed. A. Gaspar de Alba, 3–16. New York: Palgrave Macmillan.

Allen, E. Jr. 1996. ""Making the Strong Survive: The Contours and Contradictions of Message Rap." In *Droppin' Science: Critical Essays on Rap Music and Hip Hop Culture*, ed. W. E. Perkins, 159–191. Philadelphia: Temple University Press.

Alleyne, M. 1999. "Positive Vibration?: Capitalist Textual Hegemony and Bob Marley." In *Caribbean Romances: The Politics of Regional Representation*, ed. B. Edmonson, 92–104. Charlottesville: University Press of Virginia.

Alvarez, L. 2002. "Zoot Women: Pachuca Bodies, Gender Style, and the Politics of Dignidad in Wartime America." Paper delivered at National Association for Chicana and Chicano Studies meetings. Chicago, March 23–27.

American Academy of Pediatrics. 2001. "Policy Statement: Media Violence." *Pediatrics* 108, no. 5 (November 2001): 1222–1226. http://aappolicy. aappublications.org/cgi/content/full/pediatrics;108/5/1222.

Andersen, M., and P. Hill Collins. 1998. "Shifting the Center and Reconstructing Knowledge." In *Race, Class and Gender: An Anthology*, ed. M. Andersen and P. Hill Collins, 3d edition, 11–19. Belmont, CA: Wadsworth.

Anderson, C. A., and B. J. Bushman. 2001. "Effects of Violent Video Games on Aggressive Behavior, Aggressive Cognition, Aggressive Affect, Physiological Arousal, and Prosocial Behavior: A Meta-Analytic Review of the Scientific Literature." *Psychological Science* 12, no. 5 (September): 353–359.

Anderson, C. A., and K. E. Dill. 2000. "Video Games and Aggressive Thought, Feelings, and Behaviors in the Laboratory and in Life." *Journal of Personality and Social Psychology* 78, no. 4 (April): 772–790.

Anderson, S. 2000. *Views from the South: The Effects of Globalization and the WTO on Third World Countries*. Chicago: Food First Books.

Armstrong, E. G. 2001. "Gangsta Misogyny: A Content Analysis of the Portrayals of Violence Against Women in Rap Music, 1987–1993." *Journal of Criminal Justice and Popular Culture* 8, no. 2:96–126.

Arteaga, A. 1997. *Chicano Poetics: Heterotexts and Hybridities*. New York: Cambridge University Press.

Avalos, M. 1996. "Economic Restructuring and Young Latino Workers in the 1980s." In *Chicanas and Chicanos in Contemporary Society*, ed. R. M. De Anda. Boston: Allyn and Bacon.

Banes, S. 2004. "Breaking." In *The Hip Hop Studies Reader*, ed. M. Forman and M. A. Neal, 13–20. London: Routledge.

Barongan, C., and G. C. Nagayama Hall. 1995. "The Influence of Misogynous Rap Music on Sexual Aggression Against Women." *Psychology of Women Quarterly* 19:195–207.

Bartlett, A. 1994. "Airshafts, Loudspeakers, and the Hip-Hop Sample: Context and African-American Musical Aesthetics." *African American Review* 28:639–652.

Barvosa-Carter, E. 2000. "Breaking the Silence: Developments in the Publication and Politics of Chicana Creative Writing, 1973–1998." In *Chicano Renaissance: Contemporary Cultural Trends*, ed. D. R. Maciel, I. D. Ortiz, and M. Herrera-Sobek, 261–284. Tucson: University of Arizona Press.

Bello, W. 1994. *Dark Victory*. San Francisco: Food First Books.

Berger, M., B. Wallis, and S. Watson, eds. 1995. *Constructing Masculinity*. New York: Routledge.

Berry, V. T. 1990. "Rap Music, Self-Concept, and Low-Income Black Adolescents." *Popular Music and Society* 14, no. 3:89–107.

Bhabha, H. 1995. "Are You a Man or a Mouse?" In *Constructing Masculinity*, ed. M. Berger, B. Wallis, and S. Watson, 57–65. New York: Routledge.

Boyd, T. 1997. *Am I Black Enough for You: Popular Culture from the 'Hood and Beyond*. Bloomington: Indiana University Press.

Bragg, B. "Lil Kim's Hardcore Subversion of Heterosexual Norms." Unpublished manuscript.

Bragg, B., and L. McFarland. 1998. "Quiet as It's Keep: Rap as a Model for Resisting the Academy." *Black Arts Quarterly* 3, no. 1:15–17.

Brecher, J., T. Costello, and B. Smith. 2000. *Globalization from Below: The Power of Solidarity*. Cambridge, MA: South End Press.

Brittan, A. 1989. *Masculinity and Power*. Oxford: Basil Blackwell.

Broyles-González, Y. 1994. *El Teatro Campesino: Theater in the Chicano Movement*. Austin: University of Texas Press.

———. 2001. *Lydia Mendoza's Life in Music: La historia de Lydia Mendoza*. New York: Oxford University Press.

———. 2002. "Ranchera Music(s) and the Legendary Lydia Mendoza: Performing Social Location and Relations." In *Chicana Traditions: Continuity and Change*, ed. N. Cantú and O. Nájera-Ramirez, 183–206. Urbana: University of Illinois Press.

Brown, M. 2002. *Gang Nation: Delinquent Citizens in Puerto Rican, Chicano, and Chicana Narratives*. Minneapolis: University of Minnesota.

Butler, J. 1990. *Gender Trouble: Feminism and the Subversion of Identity*. New York: Routledge.

Castañeda, A. I. 1993. "Sexual Violence in the Politics and Policies of Conquest: Amerindian Women and the Spanish Conquest of Alta California." In *Building With Our Hands: New Directions in Chicana Studies*, ed. A. de la Torre and B. Pesquera, 15–33. Berkeley: University of California Press.

Castillo, A. 1994a. *Massacre of the Dreamers: Essays on Xicanisma*. New York: Plume Books.

———. 1994b. *So Far From God*. New York: Plume Books.

Center for the Advancement of Women (CAW). 2003. Progress and Perils: New Agenda for Women. New York: CAW. www.advancewomen.org.

Chacon, J. A., and M. Davis. 2006. *No One Is Illegal: Fighting Violence and State Repression on the U.S.-Mexico Border*. Chicago: Haymarket Books.

Chávez, E. 2002. *"Mi Raza Primero!" (My People First!): Nationalism, Identity, and Insurgency in the Chicano Movement in Los Angeles, 1966–1978*. Berkeley: University of California Press.

Chavez, L. R. 1992. *Shadowed Lives: Undocumented Immigrants in American Society*. Forth Worth, TX: Harcourt Brace College Publishers.

Chavez, L. R., and R. G. Martínez. 1996. "Mexican Immigration in the 1980s and Beyond: Implications for Chicanas/os." In *Chicanas/Chicanos at the Crossroads: Social, Economic, and Political Change*, ed. D. Maciel and I. D. Ortiz, 25–51. Tucson: University of Arizona Press.

Chuck D. 1997. *Fight the Power: Rap, Race, and Reality*. New York: Delacorte Press.

Churchill, W. 1996. *From a Native Son: Essays on Indigenism, 1985–1995*. Boston: South End Press.

———. 2003. *On The Justice of Roosting Chickens*. San Francisco: AK Press.

Churchill, W., and J. Van der Wall. 1988. *Agents of Repression*. Boston: South End Press.

Cisneros, S. 1992. *My Wicked, Wicked Ways*. New York: Turtle Bay Books.

Cooper, M. 2004. "Border Justice." *Nation*, February 21, p. 22.

Córdova, T. 1999. "Anti-Colonial Chicana Feminism." In *Latino Social Movements: Historical and Theoretical Perspectives*, ed. R, Torres and G. Katsiaficas, 11–41. London: Routledge.

Cross, B. 1993. *It's Not About a Salary: Rap, Race, and Resistance in Los Angeles*. London: Verso.

Curry, G. D., C. L. Maxson, and J. C. Howell. 2001. "Youth Gang Homicides in the 1990's." OJJDP Fact Sheet No. 3, March. Washington, D.C.: U.S. Department of Justice, Office of Juvenile Justice and Delinquency Prevention. www.ncjrs.org/pdffiles1/ojjdp/fs200103.pdf.

Danaher, K., ed. 1994. *50 Years is Enough: The Case Against the World Bank and the International Monetary Fund*. Boston: South End Press.

Danaher, K., and R. Burbach. 2000. *Globalize This!: The Battle Against the World Trade Organization and Corporate Rule*. Monroe, ME: Common Courage Press.

Davis, A. 1981. *Women, Race and Class*. New York: Random House.

———. 1989. *Women, Culture, and Politics*. New York: Random House.

———. 1997. "The Prison Industrial Complex." Audio recording. San Francisco: AK Press.

———. 2003. *Are Prisons Obsolete?* Seven Stories Press.

Davis, M. 1990. *City of Quartz: Excavating the Future in Los Angeles*. London: Verso.

———. 2000. *Magical Urbanism: Latinos Reinvent the U.S. City*. London: Verso.

De Anda, R. M. 1996. "Falling Back: Mexican-Origin Men and Women in the U.S. Economy." In *Chicanas and Chicanos in Contemporary Society*, ed. R. M. de Anda. Boston: Allyn and Bacon.

de Genova, N. 1995. "Gangsta Rap and Nihilsm in Black America." *Social Text* 43:89–132.

del Barco, M. 1996. "Rap's Latino Sabor." In *Droppin' Science: Critical Essays on Rap Music and Hip Hop Culture*, ed. W. E. Perkins, 63–84. Philadelphia: Temple University Press.

Delgado, F. P. 1998. "Chicano Ideology Revisited: Rap Music and the (Re)articulation of Chicanismo." *Western Journal of Communication* 62, no. 2:95–113.

Democracy Now!. 2003. "Police Beat to Death African American Man." December 2. www.democracynow.org/article.pl?sid = 03/12/02/ 1537209&mode = thread&tid = 25.

Dent, G. 1992. *Black Popular Culture*. Seattle: Bay Press.

Denzin, N. K. 2002. *Reading Race: Hollywood and the Cinema of Racial Violence*. Sage.

Dette, D. 1995. "Of Arms, Men, and Ethnic War in (Former) Yugoslavia." In *Feminism, Nationalism, and Militarism*. Arlington, VA: American Anthropological Association.

Dixon, T. L., and D. Linz. 2000. "Race and Misrepresentation of Victimization on Local Television News." *Communication Research* 27, no. 5 (October): 547–573.

Donnerstein, E. 1980. "Aggressive erotica and violence against women." *Journal of Personality and Social Psychology* 39, no. 2 (August): 269–277.

Donnerstein, E., and L. Berkowitz. 1981. "Victim Reactions in Aggressive Erotic Films as a Factor in Violence Against Women." *Journal of Personality and Social Psychology* 41, no. 4 (October): 710–724.

Donnerstein, E., and D. Linz. 1986. "Mass Media Sexual Violence and Male Viewers." *American Behavioral Scientist* 29, no. 5 (May): 601–618.

Donziger, S. R., ed. 1996. *The Real War on Crime: The Report of the National Criminal Justice Commission*. New York: Harper Perennial.

Dowd Hall, J. 1983. "'The Mind That Burns in Each Body': Women, Rape, and Racial Violence." In *Powers of Desire: The Politics of Sexuality*, ed. A. Snitow, C. Stansell, and S. Thompson, 328–349. New York: Monthly Review Press.

Dunn, T. 1996. *The Militarization of the U.S.-Mexico Border, 1978–1992: Low-Intensity Conflict Doctrine Comes Home*. Austin: Center for Mexican American Studies Books, University of Texas Press.

Eckes, T., and H. M. Trautner. 2000. *The Developmental Social Psychology of Gender*. Mahwah, NJ: Lawrence Erlbaum Associates.

Eitzen, D. S., and M. B. Zinn. 1998. *In Conflict and Order: Understanding Society*. 8th edition. New York: Allyn and Bacon.

Epstein, J. S., D. Pratto, and J. Skipper. 1990. "Teenagers, Behavioral Problems, and Preferences for Heavy Metal and Rap Music: A Case Study of a Southern Middle School." *Deviant Behavior* 11:382.

Escalante, V. 2000. "The Politics of Chicano Representation in the Media." In *Chicano Renaissance: Contemporary Cultural Trends*, ed. D. R. Maciel, I. D. Ortiz, and M. Herrera-Sobek, 131–168. Tucson: University of Arizona Press.

Esteva, G., and M. S. Prakash. 1998. *Grassroots Postmodernism: Remaking the Soil of Cultures*. London: Zed.

Faludi, S. 1992. *Backlash*. New York: Anchor Books.

Faux, J. 2004. "NAFTA at Ten: Where Do We Go from Here?" *Nation* February 2, 11–14.

Ferber, A. 1998. *White Man Falling: Race, Gender, and White Supremacy*. Boulder, CO: Rowan and Littlefield.

Fishman, A., and G. Cavender, eds. 1998. *Entertaining Crime: Television Reality Program*. New York: Aldine de Gruyter.

Flores, J. 1996. "Puerto Rocks: New York Ricans Stake Their Claim." In *Droppin' Science: Critical Essays on Rap Music and Hip Hop Culture*, W. E. Perkins, 85–116. Philadelphia: Temple University Press.

———. 2000. *From Bomba to Hip Hop: Puerto Rican Culture and Latino Identity*. New York: Columbia University Press.

Fox, R. E. 1999. "Diasporacentrism and Black Aural Texts." In *The African Diaspora*, ed. I. Okpewho, C. B. Davies, and A. A. Mazrui, 367–378. Bloomington: Indiana University Press.

Fregoso, R. L. 1993a. *The Bronze Screen: Chicana and Chicano Film Culture*. Minneapolis: University of Minnesota Press.

———. 1993b. "The Mother Motif in *La Bamba* and *Boulevard Nights*." In *Building with Our Hands: New Directions in Chicana Studies*, ed. A. de la Torre and B. Pesquera, 130–145. Berkeley: University of California Press.

Freire, P. 1973. *Pedagogy of the Oppressed*. New York: Seabury Press.

Fried, C. B. 1999. "Who's Afraid of Rap: Differential Reactions to Music Lyrics." *Journal of Applied Social Psychology* 29, no. 4:705–721.

García, A., ed. 1997. *Chicana Feminist Thought: The Basic Historical Writings*. New York: Routledge.

García, G. 2004. "Shysti-Border Music." Brown Pride Online. www.brownpride. com/reviews.

García, I. 1997. *Chicanismo: The Forging of a Militant Ethos Among Mexican Americans*. Tucson: University of Arizona Press.

García, M. 1998. "'Memories of El Monte': Intercultural Dance Halls in Post-World War II Greater Los Angeles." In *Generations of Youth: Youth Cultures and History in Twentieth-Century America*, ed. J. Austin and M. N. Willard, 157–172. New York: NYU Press.

Gaspar de Alba, A. 1998. *Chicano Art Inside/Outside the Master's House: Cultural Politics and the CARA Exhibition*. Austin: University of Texas Press.

———. 1999. *Sor Juana's Second Dream*. Albuquerque: University of New Mexico Press.

———. ed. 2003. *Velvet Barrios: Popular Culture and Chicana/o Sexualities*. New York: Palgrave Macmillan.

George, N. 1998. *Hip Hop America*. New York: Penguin Books.

Gerbner, G. 1993. "Miracles of Communication Technology: Powerful Audiences, Diverse Choices, and Other Fairy Tales." In *Illuminating the Blind Spots*, ed. J. Waski. New York: Albex.

———. 1995. "Television Violence: The Power and the Peril." In *Gender, Race and Class in Media*, ed. G. Dines and J. M. Humez, 552–556. Thousand Oaks, CA: Sage.

Giroux, H. 1996. *Fugitive Cultures: Race, Violence, and Youth*. New York: Routledge.

Glaser, D. 1956. "Criminality Theories and Behavioral Images." *American Journal of Sociology* 61 (March): 440–441.

Gonzales, P. B. 1993. "Historical Poverty, Restructuring Effects, and Integrative Ties: Mexican American Neighborhoods in a Peripheral Sunbelt Economy." In *In the Barrios: Latinos and the Underclass Debate*, ed. J. Moore and R. Pinderhughes, 149–172. New York: Russell Sage Foundation.

González-Baker, S. 1996. "Demographic Trends in the Chicana/o Population: Policy Implications for the Twenty-first Century." In *Chicanas/Chicanos at the Crossroads: Social, Economic, and Political Change*, ed. D. R. Maciel and I. D. Ortiz, 5–24. Tucson: University of Arizona Press.

Gramsci, A. 1971. *Selections from the Prison Notebooks*. New York: International Publishers.

Green, C., ed. 2001. *Globalization and Survival in the Black Diaspora: The New Urban Challenge*. New York: State University of New York Press.

Griswold del Castillo, R., T. McKenna, and Y. Yarbro-Bejarano, eds. 1991. *CARA: Chicano Art Resistance and Affirmation, 1965–1985*. Los Angeles: Wight Art Gallery.

Grossberg, L. 1995. "On Postmodernism and Articulation: An Interview with Stuart Hall." In *Stuart Hall: Critical Dialogues in Cultural Studies*, ed. D. Morley and K. Chen, 131–150. London: Routledge.

Grossman, D. 1995. *On Killing: The Psychological Cost of Learning to Kill in War and Society*. Boston: Little, Brown.

Guant, K. D. 1998. "Dancin' in the Street to a Black Girl's Beat: Music, Gender, and the 'Ins and Outs' of Double-Dutch." In *Generations of Youth: Youth Cultures and History in Twentieth-Century America*, ed. J. Austin and M. N. Willard, 272–292. New York: NYU Press.

Guerra, C. 2001. "The Unofficial Conjunto Primer for the Uninitiated Music Lover." In *Puro Conjunto: An Album in Words and Pictures from the Tejano Conjunto Festival en San Antonio, 1982–1998*, ed. J. Tejeda and A. Valdez, 3–9. Austin, TX: CMAS Books.

Guevara, N. 1996. "Women Writin' Rappin' Breakin'." In *Droppin' Science: Critical Essays on Rap Music and Hip Hop Culture*, ed. W. E. Perkins, 49–62. Philadelphia: Temple University Press.

Hahnel, R. 1999. *Panic Rules: Everything You Need to Know About the Global Economy*. Cambridge, MA: South End Press.

Hansen, C. H. 1995. "Predicting Cognitive and Behavioral Effects of Gangsta Rap." *Basic and Applied Social Psychology* 16, nos. 1/2:43–52.

Harper, P. B. 1996. *Are We Not Men? Masculine Anxiety and the Problem of African-American Identity*. New York: Oxford University Press.

Hatty, S. 2004. *Masculinities, Violence, and Culture*. London: Sage.

Hayden, T. 2003. *Street Wars: Gangs and the Future of Violence*. New York: New Press.

Heath, L., L. B. Bresolin, and R. C. Rinaldi. 1989. "Effects of media violence and aggressive behavior on children." *Archives of General Psychiatry* 46, no. 4 (April): 376–380.

Hebdige, D. 1987. *Cut 'n' Mix: Culture, Identity, and Caribbean Music*. New York: Routledge.

Hernandez-Castillo, R. A., ed. 1998. *La otra palabra: Mujeres y violencia en Chiapas, antes y después de Acteal*. Mexico City: Panagea Editores.

Herrera-Sobek, M. 1990. *The Mexican Corrido: A Feminist Analysis*. Bloomington: Indiana University Press.

———. 2002. "Danger! Children at Play: Patriarchal Ideology and the Construction of Gender in Spanish-Language Hispanic/Chicano Children's Songs and Games." In *Chicana Traditions: Continuity and Change*, ed. N. E. Cantú and O. Nájera-Ramírez, 81–99. Urbana: University of Illinois Press.

Hill Collins, P. 1990. *Black Feminist Thought: Knowledge, Consciousness, and the Politics of Empowerment*. Cambridge, MA: Unwin Hyman.

Holman, M. 2004. "Breaking: The History." In *The Hip Hop Studies Reader*, ed. M. Forman and M. A. Neal, 31–40. London: Routledge.

hooks, bell. 1994. "Gangsta Culture—Sexism, Misogyny: Who Will Take the Rap?" In *Outlaw Culture: Resisting Representations*, 115–123. New York: Routledge.

———. 2003. *We Real Cool: Black Men and Masculinity*. New York: Routledge.

Huaco-Nuzum, C. 1996. "(Re)constructing Chicana, Mestiza Representation: Frances Salomé España's *Spitfire* (1991)." In *The Ethnic Eye: Latino Media Arts*, ed. C. Noriega and A. M. López, 260–274. Minneapolis: University of Minnesota Press.

Huesmann, L. R. 1986. "Psychological Process Promoting the Relation Between Exposure to Media Violence and Aggressive Behavior by the Viewer." *Journal of Social Issues*. 42, no. 3:125–139.

ibarra, a. 2000. *Santa Perversa and Other Erotic Poems*. San Diego: Calaca Press.

Jensen, R. 2004. "A Cruel Edge: The Painful Truth About Today's Pornography —and What Men Can Do About It." *Ms. Magazine*, Spring, 54–58.

Johnson, G. T. M. 2002. "A Sifting of Centuries: Afro-Chicano Interaction and Popular Musical Culture in California, 1960–2000." In *Decolonial Voices:*

Chicana and Chicano Cultural Studies in the 21st Century, ed. A. Aldama and N. Quiñonez. Bloomington: Indiana University Press.

Johnson, J. D., L. A. Jackson, and L. Gatto. 1995. "Violent Attitudes and Deferred Academic Aspirations: Deleterious Effects of Exposure to Rap Music." *Basic and Applied Social Psychology* 16, nos. 1/2:27–41.

Joint, M. "Road Rage." March. Washington, DC: American Automobile Association (AAA) Foundation for Traffic Safety. www.aaafoundation. org/resources/indexcfm?button = agdrtext#Road%20Rage.

Kamalipour, Y. R., ed. 1995. *The U.S. Media and the Middle East*. London: Praeger.

Keller, G. D. 1994. *Hispanics and United States Film: An Overview and Handbook*. Tempe, AZ: Bilingual Review.

Kelley, R. D. G. 1994. *Race Rebels: Culture, Politics, and the Black Working Class*. New York: Free Press.

Kelly, R. 1993. "Hiphop Chicano: A Separate but Parallel Story." In *It's Not About a Salary: Rap, Race, and Resistance in Los Angeles*, ed. B. Cross, 65–75. London: Verso.

Keyes, C. L. 2002. *Rap Music and Street Consciousness*. Urbana: University of Illinois Press.

Kimmel, M. 1987. "The Contemporary Crisis of Masculinity." In *The Making of Masculinities: The New Men's Studies*, ed. H. Brod, 121–151. Boston: Allyn and Bacon.

———. 1994. "Masculinity as Homophobia: Fear, Shame, and Silence in the Construction of Gender Identity." In *Theorizing Masculinities*, ed. H. Brod and Kaufman, 119–141. New York: Sage.

LaFrance, E. 1995. *Men, Media and Masculinity*. Dubuque, IA: Kendall/Hunt.

Leal, L. 1983. "Female Archetypes in Mexican Literature." In *Women in Hispanic Literature: Icons and Fallen Idols*, ed. B. Miller, 227–242. Berkeley: University of California Press.

Levine, L. 1977. *Black Culture and Black Consciousness*. Oxford: Oxford University Press.

Lewis, Andrea. 2005. "Virtual Combat." *Progressive*, July, 32–33.

Limón, J. 1992. *Mexican Ballads, Chicano Poems: History and Influence in Mexican-American Social Poetry*. Berkeley: University of California Press.

Linz, D. G. 1989. "Exposure to Sexually Explicit Materials and Attitudes Toward Rape: A Comparison of Study Results." *Journal of Sex Research* 26:50–84.

Lipsitz, G. 1998. "The Hip Hop Hearings: Censorship, Social Memory, and Intergenerational Tension Among African Americans." In *Generations of Youth: Youth Cultures and History in Twentieth Century America*, ed. J. Austin and M. N. Willard, 395–411. New York: NYU Press.

Loeffler, J. 1999. *La Música de los Viejitos: Hispano Folk Music of the Rio Grande del Norte*. Albuquerque: University of New Mexico Press.

Lomax, J. N. 2003. "Money and Masa." *Houston Chronicle*, September 4.

Lomelí, F. A., T. Márquez, and M. Herrera-Sobek. 2000. "Trends and Themes in Chicana/o Writings in Postmodern Times." In *Chicano Renaissance:*

Contemporary Cultural Trends, ed. D. R. Maciel, I. D. Ortiz, and M. Herrera-Sobek, 285–312. Tucson: University of Arizona Press.

Lorde, A. 1984. In *Sister Outsider: Essays and Speeches*. Trumansburg, NY: Crossing Press.

Lowenthal, L. 1989. "Historical perspectives on Popular Culture." In *Critical Theory and Society*, ed. Bronner and Kellner, 184–198. New York: Routledge.

Loza, S. 1993. *Barrio Rhythm: Mexican American Music in Los Angeles*. Urbana: University of Illinois Press.

Lusane, C. 1997. *Race in the Global Era: African Americans at the Millennium*. Boston: South End Press.

Maciel, D. R., and S. Racho. 2000. "'Yo Soy Chicano': The Turbulent and Heroic Life of Chicanas/os in Cinema and Television." In *Chicano Renaissance: Contemporary Cultural Trends*, ed. D. R. Maciel, I. D. Ortiz, and M. Herrera-Sobek, 93–130. Tucson: University of Arizona Press.

Malamuth, N., and J. V. P. Check. 1981. "The Effects of Mass Media Exposure on the Acceptance of Violence Against Women: A Field Experiment." *Journal of Research in Personality* 15:436–446.

Marcuse, H. 1964. *One-Dimensional Man*. Boston: Beacon Press.

Mazón, M. 1984. *The Zoot-Suit Riots: The Psychology of Symbolic Annihilation*. Austin: University of Texas Press.

McFarland, L. 1999. "A New Democracy: A Genealogy of Zapatista Autonomy." Ph.D. diss., University of Texas.

McFarland, P. 2002. "'Here is Something You Can't Understand . . .': Chicano Rap and the Critique of Globalization." In *Decolonial Voices: Chicana and Chicano Cultural Studies in the 21st Century*, ed. A. Aldama and N. Quiñonez, 297–315. Bloomington: Indiana University Press.

McGregor, T. 1997. "Mothers of the Culture." *Source*, October, 115–122.

Mesa-Bains, A. 1991. "El Mundo Feminino: Chicana Artists of the Movement." In *Chicano Art: Resistance and Affirmation, 1965–1985*, ed. R. Griswold del Castillo, T. McKenna, and Y. Yarbro-Bejarano, 131–140. Los Angeles: Wight Art Gallery.

Miller, R. M., ed. 1980. *The Kaleidoscope Lens: How Hollywood Views Ethnic Groups*. Englewood Cliffs, NJ: J. S. Ozer.

Mirandé, A. 1997. *Hombres y Machos: Masculinity and Latino Culture*. Boulder, CO: Westview Press.

Mizell, L., M. Joint, and D. Connell. 1997. *Aggressive Driving: Three Studies*. March. Washington, DC: AAA Foundation for Traffic Safety. http://www.aaafoundation.org/resources/index.cfm?button=agdrtext.

Montoya, J. 1972. "El Louie." In *Aztlan: An Anthology of Mexican American Literature*, ed. L. Valdez and S. Steiner, 333–337. New York: Vintage.

Moore, J., and R Pinderhughes, eds. 1993. *In the Barrios: Latinos and the Underclass Debate*. New York: Russell Sage Foundation.

Moraga, C. 1983. *Loving in the War Years: Lo que nunca pasó por sus labios*. Boston: South End.

Morales, Gabe. 2006. "Chicano Music: An Influence on Gang Violence and Culture." www.angelfire.com/biz4/stopvarriowar/Latino_Gangster_Rap-Part_1.pdf.

Morley, D., and K. Chen, 1996. *Stuart Hall: Critical Dialogues in Cultural Studies*. London: Routledge Press.

Muñoz, C. 1989. *Youth, Identity, Power: The Chicano Movement*. London: Verso.

Nagel, J. 1996. *American Indian Ethnic Renewal: Red Power and the Resurgence of Identity and Culture*. Oxford, England: Oxford University Press.

National Institute on Drug Abuse (NIDA). 2000. "NIDA Announces Multimedia Public Education Initiative Aimed at Reversing Rise in Use of Anabolic Steroids by Teens." News release, April 14. www.drugabuse.gov/MedAdv/00/NR4-14.html.

Navarro, A. 1995. *Mexican American Youth Organization: Avant-Garde of the Chicano Movement in Texas*. Austin: University of Texas Press.

Ndlovu, D. 2000. "Back with a Boom: Cypress Hill." At www.cypresshill.com.

NietoGomez, A. 1997. "La Chicana—Legacy of Suffering and Self-Denial." In *Chicana Feminist Thought: The Basic Historical Writings*, ed. A. García, 48–50. New York: Routledge.

Nikolic-Ristanovic, V. 1996. "War and Violence Against Women." In *The Gendered New World Order: Militarism, Development and the Environment*, ed. J. Turpin and L. A. Lorentzen, 195–210. New York: Routledge.

Noriega, C., ed. 1992. *Chicanos and Film: Essays on Chicano Representation and Resistance*. New York: Garland.

O'Keefe, G. J., and K. Reid-Nash. 1987. "Crime News and Real World Blues: The Effects of the Media on Social Reality." *Communication Research* 14, no. 2 (April): 147–163.

Paredes, A. 1959. *With His Pistol in His Hand: A Border Ballad and Its Hero*. Austin: University of Texas Press.

———. 1976. *A Texas-Mexican Cancionero: Folksongs of the Lower Border*. Urbana: University of Chicago Press.

Parenti, C. 1999. *Lockdown America: Police and Prisons in the Age of Crisis*. Verso Books.

Parsons, J., and C. Padilla. 1999. *Low 'n Slow: Lowriding in New Mexico*. Santa Fe: Museum of New Mexico Press.

Pease, S. E. 1992. *PSYWAR: Psychological Warfare in Korea, 1950–1953*. Harrisburg, PA: Stackpole Books.

Peña, M. 1985. *The Texas-Mexican Conjunto: History of a Working-Class Music*. Austin: University of Texas Press.

Pérez, S. M., and D. de la Rosa Salazar. 1997. "Economic, Labor Force, and Social Implications of Latino Educational and Population Trends." In *Latinos and Education: A Critical Reader*, ed. A. Darder, R. D. Torres, and H. Gutiérrez, 45–79. New York: Routledge Press.

Perkins, W. E., ed. 1996a. *Droppin' Science: Critical Essays on Rap Music and Hip Hop Culture*. Philadelphia: Temple University Press.

———. 1996b. "The Rap Attack: An Introduction." In *Droppin' Science*, 1–48.

Phillips, S. A. 1999. *Wallbangin': Graffiti and Gangs in L.A.* Chicago: University of Chicago Press.

Pough, G. D. 2004. *Check It While I Wreck It: Black Womanhood, Hip Hop Culture, and the Public Sphere.* Boston: Northeastern University Press.

Pulido, L. 1996. "Development of the 'People of Color' Identity in the Environmental Justice Movement of the Southwestern United States." *Socialist Review* 26, nos. 3/4:145–180.

Ramírez, A. 2000. "Contemporary Chicano Theater." In *Chicano Renaissance: Contemporary Cultural Trends,* ed. D. R. Maciel, I. D. Ortiz, and M. Herrera-Sobek, 233–260. Tucson: University of Arizona Press.

Ramirez, S. 2002. "Borders, Feminism, and Spirituality: Movements in Chicana Aesthetic." In *Decolonial Voices: Chicana and Chicano Cultural Studies in the 21st Century,* ed. A. J. Aldama and N. H. Quiñonez, 223–242. Bloomington: Indiana University Press.

Rathbone, D. B., and J. C. Huckabee. 1999. "Controlling Road Rage: A Literature Review and Pilot Study." Washington, DC: AAA Foundation for Traffic Safety. www.aaafoundation.org/resources/index.cfm?button = roadrage.

Ready, T., and A. Brown-Gort. 2005. *The State of Latino Chicago: This Is Home Now.* South Bend, IN: Institute for Latino Studies, University of Notre Dame.

Reeves, J. L., and R. Campbell. 1994. *Cracked Coverage: Television News, the Anti-Cocaine Crusade, and the Reagan Legacy.* Durham, NC: Duke University Press.

Renzetti, C. M., and D. J. Curran. 1999. *Women, Men, and Society.* Boston: Allyn and Beacon.

Reyna, J. 2001. "Tejano Music as an Expression of Cultural Nationalism." In *Puro Conjunto,* ed. Tejeda and Valdez, 191–198.

——. N.d. *Chicano Joke Tradition in Texas.* San Antonio: Penca Books.

Rincón, B. 1997. "La Chicana: Her Role in the Past and Her Search for a New Role in the Future." *Chicana Feminist Thought: The Basic Historical Writings,* ed. A. García, 24–28. New York: Routledge.

Rivera, Raquel. 2002. "Hip Hop and New York Puerto Ricans." In *Latina/o Popular Culture,* ed. M. Habell-Pallán and M. Romero, 127–143. New York: NYU Press.

——. 2003. *New York Ricans in the Hip Hop Zone.* New York: Palgrave Macmillan.

Robb, J. D. 1980. *Hispanic Folk Music of New Mexico and the Southwest.* Norman: University of Oklahoma Press.

Roberts, R. 1994. "Ladies First": Queen Latifah's Afrocentric Feminist Music Video. *African American Review* 28, no. 2:245–257.

Robinson, C. 1993. "Race, Capitalism, and Antidemocracy." In *Reading Rodney King, Reading Urban Uprising,* ed. R. Gooding-Williams, 73–80. London: Routledge.

Robinson, W. I. 1996. "Globalisation: Nine Theses on Our Epoch." *Race and Class* 38, no. 2 (October–December): 13–32.

———. 1998. "Latin America and Global Capitalism." *Race and Class* 40, nos. 2/3:111–131.

Rochín, R. I., and A. de la Torre. 1996. "Chicanas/os in the Economy: Issues and Challenges Since 1970." In *Chicanas/Chicanos at the Crossroads: Social, Economic, and Political Change*, ed. D. Maciel and I. D. Ortiz, 52–80. Tucson: University of Arizona Press.

Rodriguez, G. 2002. "Boxing and Masculinity: The History and (Her)story of Oscar de la Hoya." In *Latina/o Popular Culture*, ed. M. Habell-Pallán and M. Romero, 252–268. New York: NYU Press.

Rodriguez, L. 1994. *Always Running: La Vida Loca, Gang Days in L.A.* Willimantic, CT: Curbstone Press.

———. 2001. *Hearts and Hands: Creating Community in Violent Times.* New York: Seven Stories Press.

Rodriguez, N. P. 1993. "Economic Restructuring and Latino Growth in Houston." In *In the Barrios: Latinos and the Underclass Debate*, ed. J. Moore and R. Pinderhughes, 101–128. New York: Russell Sage Foundation.

Rodriguez, R. T. 2003. "The Verse of the Godfather: Signifying Family and Nationalism in Chicano Rap and Hip-Hop Culture." In *Velvet Barrios: Popular Culture and Chicana/o Sexualities*, ed. A. Gaspar de Alba, 107–122. New York: Palgrave McMillan.

Rodriguez y Gibson, E. 2000. Foreword to *Santa Perversa and Other Erotic Poems*, by a. ibarra. San Diego, CA: Calaca Press.

Romero, B. 2002. "The Indita Genre of New Mexico: Gender and Cultural Identification." In *Chicana Traditions: Continuity and Change*, ed. N. E. Cantú and O. Nájera-Ramírez, 56–80. Urbana: University of Illinois Press.

Rose, T. 1990. "Never Trust a Big Butt and a Smile." *Camera Obscura* 23:109–131.

———. 1994. *Black Noise: Rap Music and Black Culture in Contemporary America.* London: Wesleyan University Press.

Rosenbaum, R. J. 1981. *Mexicano Resistance in the Southwest.* Austin: University of Texas Press.

Rule, B. G., and T. J. Ferguson. 1986. "The Effects of Media Violence on Attitudes, Emotions, and Cognitions." *Journal of Social Issues* 42, no. 3:29–50.

Saldívar, J. D. 2002. "On the Bad Edge of La Frontera." In *Decolonial Voices: Chicana and Chicano Cultural Studies in the 21st Century*, ed. A. J. Aldama and N. H. Quiñonez, 262–296. Bloomington: Indiana University Press.

Saldívar, R. 1990. *Chicano Narratives: The Dialectics of Difference.* Madison: University of Wisconsin Press.

Salinas, L. O. 1972. "Aztec Angel." In *Aztlan: An Anthology of Mexican American Literature*, ed. L. Valdez and S. Steiner, 324–236. New York: Vintage.

Salinas, R. 1972. "Un Trip through the Mind Jail." In *Aztlan: An Anthology of Mexican American Literature*, ed. L. Valdez and S. Steiner, 339–344. New York: Vintage.

Sanchez, R. 2001. *My Bloody Life: The Making of a Latin King*. Chicago: Chicago Review Press.

Sánchez-González, L. 1999. "Reclaiming Salsa." *Cultural Studies* 13, no. 2:237–250.

Sandoval, C. 2002. "Afterbridge: Technologies of Crossing." In *This Bridge We Call Home*, ed. G. E. Anzaldúa and A. Keating, 21–26. New York: Routledge.

Schneider, S. J., ed. 2004. *New Hollywood Violence*. Manchester, United Kingdom (UK): Manchester University Press.

Schrag, R. L., and M. N. Javidi. 1995. "Through a Glass Darkly: American Media Images of Middle Eastern Cultures and Their Potential Impact on Young Children." In *The U.S. Media and the Middle East*, ed. Y. R. Kamalipour, 212–221. London: Praeger.

Schwartz, M. L. 2002. "Pentagon Poison with MTV Flavor: Army Markets Free 'War Game' to Youths." *Workers World*, July 4. www.workers.org/ww/2002/wargame0704.php.

Scott, J. W. 1987. *Weapons of the Weak: Everyday Forms of Peasant Resistance*. New Haven: Yale University Press.

Scott, P. D., and J. Marshall. 1998. *Cocaine Politics: Drugs, Armies, and the CIA in Central America*. Berkeley: University of California Press.

Sherman, B. L., and J. R. Dominick. 1986. "Violence and Sex in Music Videos: TV and Rock 'n' Roll." *Journal of Communications* 36, no. 1:79–93.

Siegel, Jeff. 2005. "Warfare on the Highway: Road Rage." Swedish Medical Center. www.swedish.org.

Slack, J. D. 1996. "The Theory and Method of Articulation in Cultural Studies." In *Stuart Hall: Critical Dialogues in Cultural Studies*, ed. D. Morley and K. Chen, 112–129. London: Routledge.

Sommers, E. K., and J. V. Check. 1987. "An Empirical Investigation of the Role of Pornography in the Verbal and Physical Abuse of Women." *Violence and Victims* 2, no. 3 (Fall): 189–209.

St. Lawrence, J. S., and D. J. Joyner. 1991. "The Effects of Sexually Violent Rock Music on Males' Acceptance of Violence Against Women." *Psychology of Women Quarterly* 15, no. 1:49–63.

Takaki, R. 1989. *Strangers from a Different Shore: A History of Asian Americans*. New York: Penguin Books.

Toop, D. 2000. *Rap Attack 3: African Rap to Global Hip Hop*. London: Serpent's Tail.

Trujillo, C. 1991a. "Chicana Lesbians: Fear and Loathing in the Chicano Community." In *Chicana Lesbians: The Girls our Mothers Warned Us About*, ed. C. Trujillo, 186–194. Berkeley: Third Woman Press.

———, ed. 1991b. *Chicana Lesbians: The Girls Our Mothers Warned Us About*. Berkeley: Third Woman Press.

U.S. Department of Justice (USDJ), Office of Justice Programs, Bureau of Justice Statistics. 2002. "Rape and Sexual Assaults: Reporting to Police and

Medical Attention, 1992–2000." Washington, DC: USDJ. www.ojp.usdoj. gov/bjs/abstract/rsarp00.htm.

———. 2006. "Prison Statistics: Summary Findings." October. Washington, DC: USDJ. www.ojp.usdoj.gov/bjs/prisons.htm.

USA Today. 2003. "Bush: 'Bring on' Attackers of U.S. Troops." July 2. www. usatoday.com/news/world/iraq/2003-07-02-bush-iraq-troops_x.htm.

Vaca, N. C. 2004. *The Presumed Alliance: The Unspoken Conflict Between Latinos and Blacks and What It Means for America.* New York: Rayo.

Valle, V. M., and R. D. Torres. 2000. *Latino Metropolis.* Minneapolis: University of Minnesota Press.

Vargas, R. 1972. "Jail Flashes." In *Aztlan: An Anthology of Mexican American Literature,* ed. L. Valdez and S. Steiner, 330–331. New York: Vintage.

Vigil, E. 1999. *The Crusade for Justice: Chicano Militancy and the Government's War on Dissent.* Madison: University of Wisconsin Press.

Vigil, J. D. 2002. *A Rainbow of Gangs: Street Cultures in the Mega-City.* Austin: University of Texas Press.

Villa, R. H. 1996. "Of *Corridos* and Convicts: *Gringo* (In)Justice in Early Border Ballads and Contemporary *Pinto* Poetry." In *Chicanas and Chicanos in Contemporary Society,* ed. R. De Anda, 113–125. Boston: Allyn and Bacon.

Wallach, L., and M. Sforza. 1999. *The WTO: Five Years of Reasons to Resist Corporate Globalization.* New York: Seven Stories Press.

Walser, R. 1998. "Clamor and Community in the Music of Public Enemy." In *Generations of Youth: Youth Cultures and History in Twentieth-Century America,* ed. J. Austin and M. N. Willard, 293–110. New York: NYU Press.

Watkins, S. C. 2005. *Hip Hop Matters: Politics, Pop Culture, and the Struggle for the Soul of a Movement.* Boston: Beacon.

West, Cornel. 1994. *Race Matters.* New York: Vintage.

———. 2001. *Sketches of My Culture.* Audio recording. New York: Artemis Records.

Wilson, C. C., and F. Gutierrez. 1995. *Race, Multiculturalism, and the Media.* 2d edition. London: Sage.

Wilson, W. J. 1987. *The Truly Disadvantaged: The Inner City, the Underclass, and Public Policy.* Chicago: University of Chicago Press.

Wool, A. L. 1980. "Bandits and Lovers: Hispanic Images in American Film." In *The Kaleidoscope Lens: How Hollywood Views Ethnic Groups,* ed. R. M. Miller, 54–72. Englewood Cliffs, NJ: J. S. Ozer.

Yarbro-Bejarano, Y. 1996. "Chicana Literature from a Chicana Feminist Perspective." In *Chicana Creativity and Criticism: New Frontiers in American Literature,* ed. M. Herrera-Sobek and H. M. Viramontes, 213–219, 2d edition. Albuquerque: University of New Mexico Press.

Zavella, P. 2003. "'Talkin' Sex: Chicanas and Mexicanas Theorize About Silences and Sexual Pleasures." In *Chicana Feminisms: A Critical Reader,* ed. G. F. Arredondo, 228–253. Durham, NC: Duke University Press.

Zillman, D., and J. Bryant. 1982. "Pornography, Sexual Callousness, and the
    Trivialization of Rape." *Journal of Communication* 32, no. 1 (March): 10–21.
Zinn, H. 2003. *A People's History of the United States*. New York: Harper Collins.